Lecture Notes in Computer Science 595

Edited by G. Goos and J. Hartmanis

Advisory Board: W. Brauer   D. Gries   J. Stoer

M. Levene

The Nested Universal Relation Database Model

Springer-Verlag

Berlin Heidelberg New York
London Paris Tokyo
Hong Kong Barcelona
Budapest

Series Editors

Gerhard Goos
Universität Karlsruhe
Postfach 69 80
Vincenz-Priessnitz-Straße 1
W-7500 Karlsruhe, FRG

Juris Hartmanis
Department of Computer Science
Cornell University
5149 Upson Hall
Ithaca, NY 14853, USA

Author

Mark Levene
Department of Computer Science, University College London
Gower Street, London WC1E 6BT, UK

CR Subject Classification (1991): H.2.1, H.2.3

ISBN 3-540-55493-9 Springer-Verlag Berlin Heidelberg New York
ISBN 0-387-55493-9 Springer-Verlag New York Berlin Heidelberg

© Springer-Verlag Berlin Heidelberg 1992
Printed in Germany

Typesetting: Camera ready by author/editor
Printing and binding: Druckhaus Beltz, Hemsbach/Bergstr.
45/3140-543210 - Printed on acid-free paper

Preface

During the 1980's the *flat relational model* (relational model), which was initiated by Codd in 1970, gained immense popularity and acceptance in the market place. One of the main reasons for this success is that the relational model provides *physical data independence*, i.e. changing the physical organization of the database does not require alteration of the database at the conceptual level. However, the relational model does not provide *logical data independence*, since users must navigate amongst the flat relations in the database when posing queries to the database. Logical data independence would imply that changing the database at the conceptual level does not have an effect on the user's view of the database.

The *universal relation model* (UR model) endeavours to achieve logical data independence in the relational model by allowing the user to view the flat database as if it were composed of a single flat relation. To this end, the user is provided with a UR interface - with all the semantics embedded into the attributes - encapsulating the user's view of the flat database at the external level, on top of the conceptual level. The UR model was firmly established in mainstream relational database theory during the mid 1980's with the introduction of the *weak instance* approach. In the weak instance approach to the UR model, the *representative instance* becomes the underlying data structure of the UR model, which is suitable for storing all the data in the flat database in a single flat relation. Although the application areas of the UR model are slightly restricted by several underlying assumptions it could serve well as the foundation of a natural language interface to a database.

In recent years there has been a growing demand to use databases in non-business applications, such as: office automation, computer aided design (CAD), computer aided software engineering (CASE), image processing, text retrieval, expert systems and geographical and statistical analyses. The flat structure of relations imposed by the first normal form assumption on relational databases poses a severe restriction on the modelling capabilities of the relational model for such non-business applications.

In order to facilitate the modelling of the above non-business applications the *nested relational model* was developed during the 1980's as an extension of the relational model. The nested relational model achieves this wider applicability by allowing hierarchically structured objects, also referred to as *complex objects*, to be modelled directly, whilst maintaining the sound theoretical basis of the relational model.

One of the problems with the nested relational model is that it may prove to be too complex for non-technical users to interact with. This *usability problem* arises because of the fact that queries posed to a nested database involve navigation both amongst and within the structure of nested relations in the nested database. Thus, as in the flat relational model, the nested relational model does not provide logical data independence. Moreover, posing queries to the nested database is much more difficult in the nested relational model than in the flat relational model due to the hierarchical structure of nested relations.

In this monograph we propose to alleviate the usability problem by providing logical data independence to the nested relational model. To this end we extend the UR model to nested relations by defining a new database model, called the *nested Universal Relation model* (nested UR model). Logical data independence is achieved by allowing users to view the nested database as if it were composed of a single nested relation. Moreover, the nested UR model allows users to interact with the nested database without having to know its structure, which may be complex.

In order to formalize the nested UR model we present a comprehensive formalization of the nested relational model, which incorporates null values into the model. We provide semantics to the nested relational model in terms of *null extended data dependencies*. These dependencies are obtained by extending from flat relations to nested relations both functional data dependencies and the classical notion of lossless decomposition. Furthermore, we define the *extended chase* procedure in order to test the satisfaction of the said null extended data dependencies and to infer more information from a given nested relation. The theory of the nested UR model is established by extending the weak instance approach to the classical UR model to the *nested weak instance* approach to the nested UR model. The nested weak instance approach leads naturally to the definition of the underlying data structure for the nested UR model, namely, the *nested representative instance* (NRI) over the *nested universal relation scheme* (NURS).

A major result of the monograph is that the NRI over the NURS is a suitable model for storing the data in a nested database in a single nested relation. Thus, the classical UR model becomes a special case of the nested UR model. An important implication of this result is that a UR interface can be implemented by using the nested UR model, thus gaining the full advantages of nested relations over flat relations. In particular, redundancy is minimized, query processing becomes more efficient, semantics are often explicitly represented within the nested relations, and we gain more expressive power as both flat and hierarchical data may be presented to the user.

We believe that usability of complex object databases is one of the challenges of the 1990's in the area of database management, as the research into database models for complex objects is gaining maturity. Therefore, both database researchers and practitioners can benefit from the approach of the nested UR model, which is to formally show how one can reduce the complexity of the user interface at the external level of a database in order to gain usability.

This monograph is a slightly revised version of my thesis, which was submitted in fulfilment of the requirements for the degree of Doctor of Philosophy in the University of London in November 1989 and was obtained in June 1990. The thesis was written at the Computer Science Department of Birkbeck College, which is part of the University of London.

I would like to thank my supervisor Professor George Loizou for the many hours he devoted to discussing and carefully reading the thesis. It has been a pleasure for me to work with George who has always had the patience to find and painstakingly correct my mistakes and give me the necessary guidance. I am also grateful to my parents and the rest of the family for giving me the moral and financial support I needed during my studies. In particular, I would like to thank my brother Dan for designing the illustration on the cover of the monograph. I also wish to thank the Wingate Foundation for the financial support that was provided during my last year of study. Finally, I would like to dedicate this monograph to Sara.

London   Mark Levene
February 1992

Table of Contents

Chapter 1

Introduction

This monograph describes a method of data modelling whose basic aim is to make databases easier to use. It presents the *nested Universal Relation model* (nested UR model), which extends the classical UR model to nested relations. In Section 1.1 we give some background material and motivation for defining the nested UR model, and in Section 1.2 we briefly outline the results obtained in the remaining chapters of the monograph.

1.1 Background and Motivation of the Monograph

A *database management system* (DBMS) can be viewed via three levels of abstraction: the physical level, the conceptual level (or the logical level) and the external level (or the view level) [ANSI 1975; Ullman 1982a]. The physical level is concerned with the implementation of the database on physical devices. The conceptual level is concerned with the modelling of the database, i.e., how to represent an abstraction of the real world. Finally, the external level is concerned with the user's view of the database, i.e., it is an abstraction of the conceptual database.

The three DBMS levels can provide two levels of *data independence* via a database model. A database model provides *physical data independence* if changing the physical organization of the database does not require alteration of the database at the conceptual level. On the other hand, a database model provides *logical data independence* if changing the database at the conceptual level does not have an effect on the user's view of the database.

One of the main reasons the *flat relational model* (relational model) [Codd 1970, 1979] has recently gained immense popularity and acceptance in the market place is that it provides physical data independence. However, the relational model does not provide logical data independence, since users must navigate amongst the relations in the database when posing queries to the database. It, therefore, follows that changes at the conceptual level of the database will necessitate changes to the queries posed to the database, and thus application programs may be impaired.

The *universal relation model* (UR model) [Ullman 1982b, 1983a; Maier & Ullman 1983; Sagiv 1983; Maier et al. 1984, 1986; Mendelzon 1984; Brosda & Vossen 1988] endeavours to achieve logical data independence in the relational model by allowing the user to view the database as if it were composed of a single relation. To this end, the user is provided with a UR interface [Ullman 1983a] - with all the semantics embedded into the attributes - encapsulating the user's view of the database at the external level, on top of the conceptual level. It is important to point out that a database application using the

UR model must satisfy several assumptions, hereafter called the *UR assumptions* [Maier et al. 1984, 1986]. The most fundamental UR assumption is the *universal relation scheme assumption*, which states that there is a universal set of attributes, U, for the application being modelled, and each attribute in this universal set, U, has a unique meaning. It is also assumed that every set of attributes, $X \subseteq U$, has a *basic relationship* which results in a flat relation over X, denoted as [X], and called the *window* for X [Maier et al. 1986].

The theory of the UR model was firmly established in the mid 1980's with the introduction of the *weak instance* approach [Honeyman 1982; Maier et al. 1984; Mendelzon 1984; Graham et al. 1986; Atzeni & Bernardis 1987]. In the weak instance approach to the UR model, the *representative instance* (RI) [Sagiv 1981, 1983; Maier et al. 1984; Mendelzon 1984] becomes the underlying data structure of the UR model, which is suitable for storing all the data in the database in a single relation.

A database model consists of three main components, which we now enumerate:

(1) The data structures of the model.

(2) The query language of the model.

(3) The integrity constraints of the model.

In the relational model the data structures are relations (also referred to as *flat relations*), the query language is the relational algebra, and the integrity constraints are data dependencies [Codd 1979; Ullman 1982a; Maier 1983].

In recent years there has been a growing demand to use databases in non-business applications, such as: office automation, computer aided design (CAD), image processing, text retrieval, expert systems and geographical and statistical analyses [Scholl & Schek 1987; Abiteboul et al. 1989b]. The *nested relational model* [Makinouchi 1977; Roth et al. 1985, 1988; Abiteboul & Bidioit 1986; Schek & Scholl 1986; Thomas & Fischer 1986; Ozsoyoglu & Yuan 1987a; Van Gucht & Fischer 1988; Levene & Loizou 1989a] was developed as an extension of the relational model in order to facilitate the modelling of the above non-business applications. The nested relational model achieves this wider applicability by allowing hierarchically structured objects, also referred to as *complex objects*, to be modelled directly, whilst maintaining the sound theoretical basis of the relational model.

Some of the advantages of nested relations in comparison to flat relations are now mentioned. Nested relations minimize redundancy of data, and allow efficient query processing since some of the joins are realized within the nested relations themselves. In addition, nested relations allow explicit representation of the semantics of the application within their structures, and provide a more flexible user interface, which allows both flat and hierarchical data to be presented to the user.

One of the problems with the nested relational model is that it may prove too complex for non-technical users to interact with. This *usability problem* arises because of the fact that queries posed to a nested database involve navigation both amongst and within the structure of nested relations in the nested database. Thus, as in the relational model, the nested relational model does not provide logical data independence. Moreover, posing queries to the nested database is much more difficult in the nested relational model than in the flat relational model due to the hierarchical structure of nested relations. The usability problem escalates even further when we take into account the application programs which may be impaired because of changes to the nested database at the conceptual level.

In this monograph we propose to alleviate the usability problem by providing logical data independence to the nested relational model. To this end we extend the UR model to nested relations by defining a new database model, called the *nested Universal Relation model* (nested UR model).

1.2 Outline of the Monograph

We now outline our presentation of the nested UR model as given in the monograph. The preliminary material needed to develop the nested UR model is given in Chapter 2, wherein we present the underlying database models. In Section 2.1 we describe the flat relational model, in Section 2.2 we present the nested relational model, and finally in Section 2.3 we describe the classical UR model.

In order to formalize the nested UR model, we first define the *null extended nested relational model* in Chapters 3 and 4. Nulls [Biskup 1981; Zaniolo 1984; Roth et al. 1985; Codd 1986, 1987; Levene & Loizou 1989a, 1989c] play an important role in the nested UR model, and thus the null extended nested relational model is essentially a comprehensive extension of the nested relational model so as to include nulls.

In Section 3.1 we define null extended nested relations (from now on referred to simply as nested relations) over null extended domains, which are the domains of nested relations that may include null values. We then define the *null extended algebra* in Section 3.2, which is a *complete* extended algebra for manipulating nested relations (cf. [Abiteboul et al. 1989a]). The motivation for defining the null extended algebra is that previously defined extended algebras for nested relations [Jaeschke 1985a, 1985b; Roth et al. 1985, 1988; Abiteboul & Bidoit 1986; Schek & Scholl 1986; Thomas & Fischer 1986; Deshpande & Larson 1987; Gyssens 1987; Houben & Paredaens 1987; Colby 1989; Levene & Loizou 1989a] are not suitable for the nested UR model. This is mainly due to the fact that in order to formulate queries with the aforementioned extended algebras the structure of the nested relations in the nested database needs to be known, whilst the null extended algebra, presented in this monograph, frees the user from navigation within the individual nested relations in the nested database. In addition, the extended (natural) join operators defined in the aforementioned extended algebras have been very limited, which is a major drawback in a UR environment. Finally, the outer join operator [Codd 1979; Date 1987b] and the total projection operator [Maier et al. 1984], which are essential to the UR model, have not so far been extended to nested relations. Thus in order to solve these problems, the null extended algebra provides us with the general *null extended join* operator, the *null extended outer join* operator, and the *null extended total projection* operator.

In Sections 4.1 to 4.4 we define semantics for the null extended nested relational model in terms of *null extended data dependencies*, which are integrity constraints over nested relations.

Although there is a growing body of work on the nested relational model, data dependency theory for nested relations has mainly concentrated on extending the functional dependency (FD) to nested relations [Makinouchi 1977; Jaeschke & Schek 1982; Arisawa et al. 1983; Fischer et al. 1985; Miura et al. 1986, 1987; Van Gucht & Fischer 1986, 1988]. The class of *null extended data dependencies* which we define for the null extended nested relational model includes: *null functional dependencies* (NFDs), *null extended functional dependencies* (NEFDs), and *null extended join dependencies* (NEJDs). NFDs provide a redefinition of FDs so as to include null values in the context of nested relations, NEFDs provide an extension of NFDs to nested relations, thus allowing relation-valued attributes to appear in NFDs, and finally NEJDs provide an extension of *join dependencies* [Beeri & Vardi 1981; Sciore 1982] so as to include null values in the context of nested relations.

The important notion of a *lossless decomposition* [Ullman 1982a; Maier 1983] from relational database theory has, so far, not been extended to nested relations; it has rather been used in nested relational theory whenever nested relations support a flat relational interface [Kambayashi et al. 1983; Ozsoyoglu & Yuan 1987a, 1987b; Kambayashi & Yamamoto 1987; Scholl et al. 1987]. We fill in this gap, via NEJDs, by defining the novel notion of a *null extended lossless decomposition*, thus extending the classical notion of a lossless decomposition to nested relations. Furthermore, we conjecture that null extended data dependencies are sufficient to model most real-world applications (cf. [Fagin 1982; Beeri & Kifer 1986]).

In Section 4.5 we define the *extended chase* procedure (also referred to simply as the extended chase), which extends the classical *chase* procedure [Maier et al. 1979; Beeri & Vardi 1984; Graham et al. 1986] to nested relations. The extended chase allows us to test the satisfaction of a set of null extended data dependencies and to infer more information from a given nested relation. Thus, the extended chase provides both a theorem prover and an inference engine for the null extended nested relational model.

Example 1.1. Schemas of nested relations are represented by *scheme trees* [Ozsoyoglu & Yuan 1987a], as shown in Figure 1.1. The *nested relation scheme* (NRS), for the scheme tree, T, denoted by R(T), is: TUTOR SALARY (CHILD)* (DAY)*, where attributes with relation-valued domains are marked by *, in order to distinguish them from attributes defined over simple domains [Abiteboul & Bidoit 1986; Ozsoyoglu & Yuan 1987a]. A nested relation, r*, over the NRS, R(T) = TUTOR SALARY (CHILD)* (DAY)*, for the scheme tree, T, of Figure 1.1, is shown in Figure 1.2. We note that *null* in r* denotes a null value in the nested relation. The semantics of null values are such that *null* stands for either: an unknown value, a non-existent value, or a no-information value which may be unknown or non-existent.

The semantics of the nested relation, r*, over the NRS, R(T), are captured by the following set of null extended data dependencies, namely, the NFD: TUTOR $\rightarrow$ SALARY, and the NEFDs: TUTOR,SALARY $\rightarrow$ (CHILD)* and TUTOR,SALARY $\rightarrow$ (DAY)*. In other words, a TUTOR, who has a unique SALARY, has a unique set of

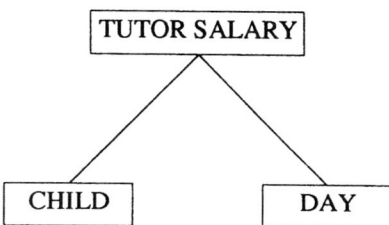

Fig. 1.1. The scheme tree T.

CHILDren and gives tutorials on a unique set of DAYs.

TUTOR	SALARY	(CHILD)*	(DAY)*
		CHILD	DAY
Robert	12000	Hanna Brian	Monday Thursday
Hanna	14000	Annette Ada	null
Martine	null	null	null
null	15000	null	Wednesday
null	null	Ruth	Tuesday Friday

Fig. 1.2. The nested relation, r*, over the nested relation scheme, R(T).

After having defined the null extended nested relational model, we have at our disposal the tools needed to formalize the nested UR model. This formalization is presented in Chapter 5 wherein we define the general case of the nested UR model for a nested database.

The theory of the nested UR model is vigorously established in Sections 5.1 and 5.2 by extending the weak instance approach to the UR model to the *nested weak instance* approach to the nested UR model, under a set of null extended data dependencies for a nested database. This leads us to define the underlying data structure of the nested UR model, namely, the *nested representative instance* (NRI), over the *nested universal relation scheme* (NURS), which allows us to model the semantics of the nested database within a single nested relation. The NRI extends the RI to nested relations, while the NURS provides the necessary NRS over which nested relations in the nested database can be joined automatically by using the null extended join operator, in order to provide the desired logical data independence referred to earlier.

In Section 5.1 we discuss in detail how to obtain the NURS for a given nested database. To this end we provide two restructuring operators on scheme trees and one restructuring operator on the corresponding nested relations in the nested database. We then give an algorithm for obtaining the NURS and we prove its correctness.

In Section 5.2 we define the nested weak instance approach to the nested UR model with its associated NRI under a set of null extended data dependencies for a nested database. Under the nested weak instance approach to the nested UR model, the window, [X], for any $X \subseteq U$, is taken to be the unnesting of the null extended total projection of the NRI onto X. We then proceed to show that the NRI can always be constructed by invoking the extended chase given in Chapter 4.

In Section 5.3 we present one of the major results of the monograph, i.e., showing that the NRI, over the NURS, is a suitable model for the data to be stored in a single nested relation, given a nested database and a set of null extended data dependencies, for any application satisfying the UR assumptions. In other words, the NRI encapsulates all the information in the nested database within a single nested relation satisfying the set of null extended data dependencies. An important implication of this result is that a UR interface providing both flat and hierarchical outputs can be implemented under the nested UR model. Thus, we can gain the advantages of nested relations compared to flat relations via the implementation of a UR interface; therefore, the usability problem can be successfully solved. Furthermore, the classical UR model under the weak instance approach is shown to be a special case of the nested UR model under the nested weak instance approach. We also show that the nested UR model is strictly more expressive than the UR model, since nested relations are strictly more expressive than their flat counterparts [Miura et al. 1986]. This fact implies that the range of applications that can be modelled under the nested UR model is much larger than the corresponding range of applications that can be modelled via the UR model.

The NRI can always be constructed via the extended chase. The extended chase is a very useful theoretical tool; however, constructing the NRI via the extended chase is, in general, computationally inefficient. In addition, the extended chase is unlikely, in the near future, to be supported by a DBMS supporting the null extended nested relational model. Thus, in Section 5.4, we investigate a computational approach to the nested UR model as a special case of the nested weak instance approach to the nested UR model (cf. [Maier et al. 1984]). Our computational approach to the nested UR model is based on the *UMC property*, which we now very briefly discuss.

Results from UR theory have shown a strong connection between γ-acyclic databases and the UR model [Yannakakis 1981; Fagin 1983; Chan & Atzeni 1985; Biskup et al. 1986; Jajodia & Springsteel 1987]. In particular, if a database is γ-acyclic then there is a unique join sequence for computing queries over any subset of the universal set of attributes. In addition, we have in γ-acyclic databases a *unique minimal connection* (UMC) amongst any subset of the universal set of attributes. This property, called the *UMC property*, is defined and extended to nested databases in Chapter 2.

In Section 5.4 we utilize the UMC property in the definition of an algebraic construction of the NRI via the null extended outer join operator of the null extended algebra. In addition, we show that, given the UMC property, query processing over any subset of the universal set of attributes can be done algebraically, by defining a *window function* [Maier et al. 1986] to compute [X] for any $X \subseteq U$.

In order to define the DBMS levels of the nested UR model, we depart from the traditional three-level architecture of a DBMS by adding a fourth level, called the *internal level*, between the physical level and the conceptual level. At the physical level of the nested UR model we have the physical database, which we do not discuss any further in this monograph. At the internal level we have the null extended nested database (which we have simply referred to as the nested database), while at the conceptual level we have the NRI over the NURS. Finally, the nested UR model supports a UR interface at the external level, within which the user may view the data in either a flat or a hierarchical fashion.

In order to summarize the DBMS levels of the nested UR model we show in the diagram of Figure 1.3 the differences between the DBMS levels of the classical UR model and those of the nested UR model.

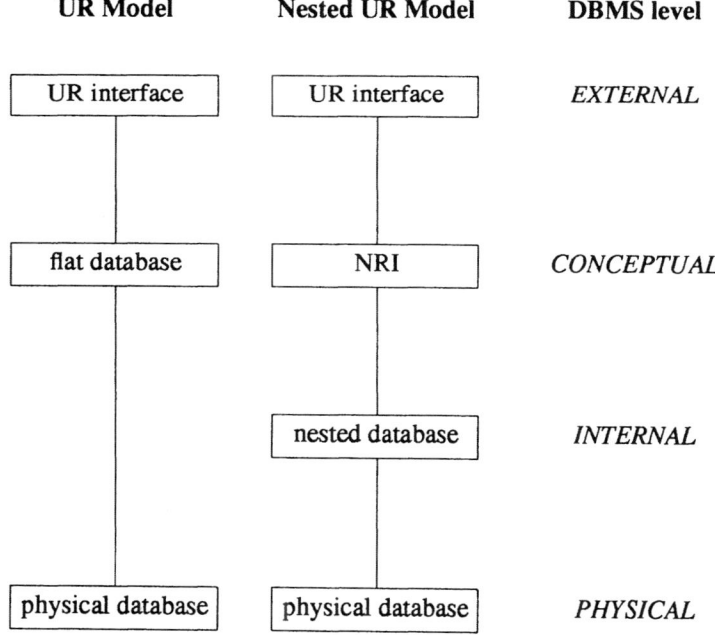

Fig. 1.3. Comparison between the DBMS levels in the classical and the nested UR models.

An important special case of the nested UR model is when we only have a single nested relation in the nested database at the internal level. In this case the internal and conceptual levels of the nested UR model coincide, and we thus obtain the traditional three-level DBMS architecture. The situation of having a nested UR model with a single · nested relation is ideal for query processing, since all the null extended joins are realized within this nested relation.

In Chapter 6 we investigate several ways of viewing the nested UR model comprising a single nested relation and show that these different approaches coincide, when we view the single nested relation as the NRI under a set of null extended data dependencies.

8

Firstly, we show, in Section 6.1, that a nested relation can be viewed in terms of the *association-object database model* [Maier & Warren 1982; Maier et al. 1986, 1987]. Thus, for the scheme tree, T, shown in Figure 1.1, we have the associations: {{TUTOR, SALARY}, {TUTOR, SALARY, CHILD}, {TUTOR, SALARY, DAY}}, and the object: {TUTOR, SALARY, CHILD, DAY}.

Another way of viewing a nested relation is in terms of γ-acyclic databases. Thus, in Section 6.2, we show that nested relations correspond to a subclass of γ-acyclic databases [Levene & Loizou 1989d]; this implies a strong connection between nested relations and the UR model [Biskup et al. 1986]. In fact, for the scheme tree, T, shown in Figure 1.1, we have the induced γ-acyclic database scheme: {{TUTOR, SALARY, CHILD}, {TUTOR, SALARY, DAY}}.

In Section 6.3 we discuss the effects on the NRI, when we assume a nested database composed of a single nested relation satisfying a set of null extended data dependencies. When viewing the single nested relation as the NRI, over the NURS, we obtain all the desirable properties discussed in Chapter 5, and consequently the NRI is fully optimized. In particular, query processing can be effected algebraically, since the window, [X], for any $X \subseteq U$, is now simply the unnesting of the null extended total projection of the single nested relation onto X. Finally, in this special case all of the UR assumptions are automatically satisfied in the nested relation. In order to bring out the advantages of the nested UR model, in this special case of a single nested relation, we give some application examples in Section 6.4.

Example 1.2. Let d* = {r*} be a nested database for the single nested relation, r*, over the NRS, R(T), of Example 1.1, and let D* = {TUTOR $\rightarrow$ SALARY, TUTOR,SALARY $\rightarrow$ (CHILD)*, TUTOR,SALARY $\rightarrow$ (DAY)*} be the set of null extended data dependencies that hold in r*. Then r*, over the NRS, R(T), is the NRI under the set of null extended data dependencies, D*, for the nested database d*.

Finally, in Chapter 7 we conclude the monograph with some final remarks and discuss ongoing research resulting from the formalization of the nested UR model.

1.3 Summary of the Numbering System

This monograph is divided into seven chapters, designated in the text by Chapter 1 to Chapter 7. Each chapter is divided into sections, for example, Section 3.2 is the second section in Chapter 3. Some of the sections are further subdivided into subsections, for example, Subsection 3.2.3 is the third subsection of Section 3.2. All the definitions, figures and examples are globally numbered within each chapter, for example, Definition 4.5 is the fifth definition in Chapter 4. Results in the form of theorems, lemmas, corollaries and propositions are together globally numbered within each chapter, for example, Corollary 4.6 is the sixth result in Chapter 4. At times we also number equations locally within a section, for example, equation (3) may refer to an equation used within the proof of a theorem. References are given in the text by using the name(s) of the authors(s) followed by the year of publication. The full details of the references are given at the end of the monograph in alphabetical order determined by the name(s) of the author(s).

Chapter 2
The Underlying Database Models

In this chapter we give the background and preliminary material needed throughout the monograph. The chapter is divided into three sections each one presenting one of the underlying database models needed to develop the nested UR model.

In Section 2.1 we present the *flat relational model*, in which data is represented in a simple tabular fashion. In fact, since Codd's [1970] seminal paper on the flat relational model (usually referred to as the relational model) and until very recently most researchers into database theory have concerned themselves with some aspect of this model [Ullman 1987].

In Section 2.2 we present the *nested relational model*, which extends the flat relational model in order to allow the representation of hierarchically structured data. Research into the nested relational model began in the late 1970's [Makinouchi 1977] and in recent years a lot of effort has been expended in order to further develop this model [Scholl & Schek 1987; Abiteboul et al. 1989b].

In Section 2.3 we present the *universal relational model* (UR model), which provides the user with an interface through which the database is viewed as if it were composed of a single flat relation. Research into the UR model has proceeded hand in hand with research into the flat relational model and was given a sound theoretical underpinning in the mid 1980's [Sagiv 1983; Maier et al. 1984; Mendelzon 1984].

In the sequel, we employ the following mathematical notation for sets. Let S be a set, then $|S|$ denotes the cardinality of S, and $P(S)$ denotes the finite powerset of S. We also use the standard set operators, $\cup$, $-$, $\cap$ and $\times$ with their usual meaning of: union, difference, intersection and cartesian product, respectively. *On occasion*, in representing a set of attributes we omit the set braces { } and at times we use a space as a separator instead of a comma.

2.1 The Flat Relational Model

In this section we briefly review the flat relational model as defined by Codd [1970,1979]. In Subsection 2.1.1 we define the data structure of the flat relational model, i.e., flat relations over flat relation schemes. In Subsection 2.1.2 we introduce integrity constraints for the flat relational model in the form of data dependencies. Finally, in Subsection 2.1.3 we define a restricted form of acyclic flat database schemes, namely, γ-acyclic flat database schemes that possess some desirable properties which will be useful in our formalism of the nested UR model.

2.1.1 Flat Relations and Flat Relation Schemes

In this subsection we describe the data structure of the flat relational model in which data can be represented in a simple tabular fashion by using the concept of attributes and their underlying domains.

Let $U = \{A_1, A_2, ..., A_p\}$ be the universal set of attributes. Associated with each attribute $A_i \in U$ is a set of atomic values, called the *atomic domain* of A_i, and denoted by $DOM(A_i)$. $DOM(A_i)$ may be finite or countably infinite.

A *flat relation* (or simply a *relation*), r, over U is any finite subset of the set of p-tuples in the Cartesian product of the atomic domains. A flat relation, r, over $X \subseteq U$, will sometimes be denoted by r(X). The restriction of a tuple $t \in r$ to $X \subseteq U$, denoted by t[X], is a tuple constructed from t by keeping all and only those components that belong to attributes in X. In the sequel, t[X] will also be referred to as the X-value of t.

A *flat relation scheme* (FRS), R, is a subset of U; R is also said to be in *first normal form* (1NF) [Maier 1983]. This is sometimes known as the 1NF *assumption*. A *flat database scheme* (FDS) over U is a collection of FRSs over U, the union of this collection being U. Let $\mathbf{R} = \{R_1, R_2, ..., R_m\}$ be a FDS, over U, then $d = \{r_1, r_2, ..., r_m\}$ is a *flat database* (or simply a *database*) over $\mathbf{R}$, where each r_i is a flat relation over R_i, $1 \leq i \leq m$.

Example 2.1. Let U = {STUDENT, DEPT, MAJOR, CLASS, EXAM, PROJECT} be the universal set of attributes. A flat relation, r, over U, is shown in Figure 2.1.

We assume the reader is familiar with the operators of the flat relational algebra [Codd 1970, 1979; Ullman 1982a; Maier 1983]. In particular, we denote the union operator by $\cup$, the difference operator by $-$, the intersection operator by $\cap$, the cartesian product operator by $\times$, the projection operator by Π, the selection operator by σ, the natural join operator (or simply the join operator) by $\bowtie$, and the renaming operator by δ.

STUDENT	DEPT	MAJOR	CLASS	EXAM	PROJECT
Iris	CS	computing	databases	mid	1NF
Iris	CS	computing	databases	final	1NF
Iris	CS	computing	programming	final	C++
Mark	CS	maths	databases	final	NF2
Mark	CS	maths	databases	final	UR
David	philosophy	logic	first-order	mid	prolog

Fig. 2.1. The flat relation r.

2.1.2 Data Dependencies in Flat Relations

Data dependencies are first-order sentences which provide semantics to the relational model and constrain the set of allowable flat relations in a flat database [Ullman 1982a; Maier 1983; Fagin & Vardi 1984]. In this monograph, we are mainly concerned with *functional dependencies* (FDs), *multivalued dependencies* (MVDs) and *join dependencies* (JDs) [Fagin 1977; Beeri & Vardi 1981; Sciore 1982; Ullman 1982a; Maier 1983; Fagin & Vardi 1984], which we now very briefly review.

We first define the notion of implication for a set of data dependencies. Let D be a set of data dependencies, and let SAT(D) denote the set of flat relations, over U, that satisfy D. We say that D implies a single data dependency, d, written in the form of D $|=$ d, if and only if (iff) SAT(D) $\subseteq$ SAT(d). A set D_1 of data dependencies implies a set D_2 of data dependencies, denoted by D_1 $|=$ D_2, iff D_1 $|=$ d for all data dependencies, d $\in$ D_2. Finally, D_1 is equivalent to D_2, denoted by D_1 $\equiv$ D_2, iff D_1 $|=$ D_2 and D_2 $|=$ D_1.

Next we define JDs and MVDs. Let r be a flat relation over U. We say that r *decomposes losslessly* onto a FDS **R**, if r $=$ $\bowtie_{i=1}^{m}\Pi_{R_i}(r)$ [Ullman 1982a; Maier 1983]. Equivalently, we say r satisfies the *join dependency* (JD), $\bowtie[\mathbf{R}]$, over U.

If m $=$ 1, then the JD, $\bowtie[\mathbf{R}]$, is said to be a *trivial* JD, otherwise it is said to be a *non-trivial* JD [Beeri & Vardi 1981; Sciore 1982; Maier 1983].

A *multivalued dependency* (MVD) is a JD with m=2, namely, $\bowtie[\{R_1, R_2\}]$ over U [Fagin 1977]. Let X $=$ $R_1 \cap R_2$, Y $=$ $R_1 - R_2$. We use the standard notation X $\rightarrow\rightarrow$ Y to refer to this MVD. Also, we write X $\rightarrow\rightarrow$ Y (W) to mean X $\rightarrow\rightarrow$ Y in the context of W $\subseteq$ U, and, in general, we omit W whenever the context is understood.

The MVD, X $\rightarrow\rightarrow$ Y (W), is said to be a *trivial* MVD if XY $=$ W or Y $\subseteq$ X, otherwise it is said to be a *non-trivial* MVD.

The last data dependency we define is the *functional dependency* (FD). A FD is a statement of the form X $\rightarrow$ Y, where X,Y $\subseteq$ U. A FD, X $\rightarrow$ Y, holds in a relation r, over U, iff whenever any two tuples of r are equal on X, then they are also equal on Y [Ullman 1982a; Maier 1983; Fagin & Vardi 1984].

A FD, $X \to Y$, is said to be a *trivial* FD if $Y \subseteq X$, otherwise it is said to be a *non-trivial* FD.

We mention the following inference rule for FDs and MVDs: $X \to Y \models X \to\to Y$ (U) [Fagin 1977]; we call the MVD, $X \to\to Y$, the *MVD-counterpart* of $X \to Y$.

In the sequel, we employ the following useful notation for FDSs. Let **R** be a FDS, over U, then MANY(**R**) denotes the set of attributes that appear in at least two FRSs in **R**.

We now give three inference rules for JDs, which are used in proofs in subsequent chapters; these inference rules are taken from the formal system for JDs established by Beeri and Vardi [1981].

Let **R** and **S** be two FDSs, over U. We say that **S** *covers* **R** (or alternatively **S** is a *cover* of **R**), if for every FRS, $R_i \in $ **R**, there exists a FRS, $S_j \in $ **S**, such that $R_i \subseteq S_j$. The set of all FDSs that cover **R** is denoted by COVER(**R**).

RULE 1. The *covering rule* for JDs: $\bowtie[R] \models \bowtie[S]$ if **S** covers **R**, i.e., $S \in$ COVER(**R**).

Now, let **R** be a FDS, over U, and let **S** be a FDS over an $R_i \in$ **R**.

RULE 2. The *substitution rule* for JDs: $\{\bowtie[R], \bowtie[S]\} \models \bowtie[(R - \{R_i\}) \cup S]$.

Finally, let **R** = $\{R_1, R_2, ..., R_m\}$ be a FDS, over U, and let $X \subseteq U$ be a set of attributes such that MANY(**R**) $\subseteq X$.

RULE 3. The *projection rule* for JDs: $\bowtie[R] \models \bowtie[\{R_1 \cap X, R_2 \cap X, ..., R_m \cap X\}]$.

Acyclic FDSs have been widely researched because of the desirable properties such FDSs enjoy [Yannakakis 1981; Lien 1982; Beeri et al. 1983; Fagin 1983]. Furthermore, it has been conjectured [Fagin et al. 1982] that acyclic FDSs are sufficiently general to encompass most *real-world* situations. It has also been established [Fagin 1983] that there are several *degrees* of acyclicity for FDSs, and that strengthening the degree of acyclicity also strengthens the related desirable properties.

We now introduce α-acyclic FDSs which are less restrictive than γ-acyclic FDSs; the latter are reviewed in Subsection 2.1.3.

R is said to be α*-acyclic* iff $\bowtie[R]$ is equivalent to a set of MVDs [Fagin et al. 1982]. Further characterizations of α-acyclic FDSs can be found in Beeri et al. [1983].

Example 2.2. Let r, over U, be the flat relation shown in Figure 2.1. Then it can be verified that the following set of MVDs, denoted as M, hold in r: {STUDENT,DEPT $\to\to$ MAJOR (U), STUDENT,DEPT $\to\to$ CLASS,EXAM,PROJECT (U), STUDENT,DEPT,CLASS $\to\to$ EXAM (U), STUDENT,DEPT,CLASS $\to\to$ PROJECT (U)}.

Let **R** = {{STUDENT, DEPT, MAJOR}, {STUDENT, DEPT, CLASS, EXAM}, {STUDENT, DEPT, CLASS, PROJECT}}. Then **R** is α-acyclic, since it can be verified by the three inference rules for JDs, given above, that $\bowtie[R] \equiv M$.

In conclusion, it can also be verified that the FD, STUDENT $\to$ DEPT, holds in r.

Finally, we define the notions of *key* and *superkey* [Ullman 1982a; Maier 1983; Fagin & Vardi 1984]. Let F be a set of FDs, and X be a set of attributes in U. The *closure* of F, denoted by F^+, is the set of all FDs implied by F. The *closure* of X with respect to (w.r.t.) F, denoted by X^+, is the set of all attributes that are functionally determined by X.

$K \subseteq R_i$ is a *key* of the FRS, $R_i \in \mathbf{R}$, w.r.t. F (or simply K is the key for R_i, whenever F is understood from context) iff

(1) $K^+ = R_i$;

(2) for no $K' \subset K$ is $K'^+ = R_i$.

A *superkey* for R_i w.r.t. F (or simply a superkey for R_i, whenever F is understood from the context) is any superset of a key, K, of R_i w.r.t. F, i.e., $L \supseteq K$ is a superkey for R_i w.r.t. F.

An FD, $X \rightarrow Y$, is *embedded* in a FRS, $R_i \in \mathbf{R}$, if $XY \subseteq R_i$. A set of FDs, F, is *embedded* in a FDS, $\mathbf{R}$, if each FD, $X \rightarrow Y \in F$, is *embedded* in some $R_i \subseteq \mathbf{R}$. A FDS, $\mathbf{R}$, is *cover-embedding* w.r.t. a set of FDs, F, if there exists a set of FDs, G, such that G is embedded in $\mathbf{R}$ and $G^+ = F^+$.

We close this subsection with the definition of *Boyce-Codd Normal Form* [Ullman 1982a; Maier 1983], wherein the semantics of flat relations are fully determined by superkeys.

Definition 2.1. $\mathbf{R}$ is said to be in Boyce-Codd Normal Form (BCNF) w.r.t. F (or simply $\mathbf{R}$ is in BCNF, whenever F is understood from context) if whenever a non-trivial FD, $X \rightarrow Y$, is embedded in some $R_i \in \mathbf{R}$, then X is a superkey for R_i w.r.t. F, i.e., $F \models X \rightarrow R_i$.

$\mathbf{R}$ is said to be a *cover-embedding BCNF* FDS w.r.t. F (or simply a cover-embedding BCNF FDS, whenever F is understood from context) if $\mathbf{R}$ is in BCNF w.r.t. F and $\mathbf{R}$ is also cover-embedding w.r.t. F.

2.1.3 γ-Acyclic Flat Database Schemes

In this subsection we define γ-acyclic FDSs originally introduced by Fagin [1983]. Our interest in γ-acyclic FDSs stems from the strong connection that is known to exist between γ-acyclicity and the UR model [Yannakakis 1981; Fagin 1983; Jajodia & Ng 1984; Biskup et al. 1986; Chan & Atzeni 1986; Jajodia 1987; Jajodia & Springsteel 1987; Levene & Loizou 1989d].

In order to formally introduce γ-acyclicity we view FDSs as *hypergraphs* [Berge 1973]. As usual, a *hypergraph* is a pair (N,E), where N is a finite set of nodes and E is a set of edges (or hyperedges), which are arbitrary subsets of N. Thus, the hypergraph of $\mathbf{R}$, denoted simply by $\mathbf{R}$, is the pair (U,$\mathbf{R}$). In the sequel, $\mathbf{R}$ will refer to both a FDS and the underlying hypergraph. In general, the distinction will be inferred from context, otherwise explicit reference will be made.

A sequence $(e_1, e_2, ..., e_k)$, with $e_i \in E$, $1 \le i \le k$, is called a *path* from e_1 to e_k iff $e_i \cap e_{i+1} \ne \emptyset$, $1 \le i < k$. Two edges of **R** are connected if there is a path from one to the other. A set of edges is connected if *every pair* of the set is connected. The *connected components* of **R** are the maximal connected sets of edges. The *reduction* (N,E′) of a hypergraph (N,E) is obtained by removing from E each edge that is a proper subset of another edge. A hypergraph is reduced if it equals its reduction. For simplicity, we assume for the rest of the monograph that **R** is connected and reduced; if this is not the case, it will, in general, be understood from context. We now proceed to define γ-acyclicity by using *loop-free Bachman diagrams*.

A *Bachman diagram* [Bachman 1969; Yannakakis 1981; Fagin 1983] for **R**, denoted by B(**R**), is constructed as follows: Firstly, we close **R** under intersection, thus obtaining, say **R′**; B(**R**) is then the undirected graph (N,E), where N = **R′**, and an edge e = (u,v) is in E iff

(1)   ATT(u) ⊂ ATT(v), where ATT(n) is the label for a node, n, of B(**R**) and is equal to the set of attributes associated with n;

(2)   there is no node, n, in B(**R**) such that ATT(u) ⊂ ATT(n) ⊂ ATT(v).

A subset, $V = \{v_1, v_2, ..., v_k\}$, of the nodes of B(**R**) is said to be *connected*, if the induced hypergraph, (U′, S), where $U' = \cup_{i=1}^{k} ATT(v_i)$, U′ ⊆ U and S = {ATT($v_1$), ATT($v_2$), ..., ATT($v_k$)}, is a connected hypergraph.

A *loop-free Bachman diagram* (lfbd) [Yannakakis 1981; Lien 1982; Fagin 1983] is a Bachman diagram that is a tree when considered as an undirected graph. The ensuing definition of γ-acyclicity emanates from Theorem 8.1 in Fagin [1983].

Definition 2.2. **R** is *γ-acyclic* iff **R** has a loop-free Bachman diagram.

Next we present an alternative characterization of γ-acyclicity which formally captures the notion of the *Unique Minimal Connection property* (*UMC property*) [Yannakakis 1981; Fagin 1983; Biskup et al. 1986; Chan & Atzeni 1986; Jajodia & Springsteel 1987] among any set of attributes X ⊆ U.

Definition 2.3. Let B(**R**) be the lfbd for a γ-acyclic FDS, **R**. A connected subset, $V = \{v_1, v_2, ..., v_k\}$, of the nodes of B(**R**) is said to possess the *UMC property* among any set of attributes X ⊆ U w.r.t. **R**, if

(1) $X \subseteq \cup_{i=1}^{k} ATT(v_i)$;

(2)   whenever $W = \{w_1, w_2, .., w_p\}$, $k \le p$, is a connected subset of the nodes of B(**R**) such that $X \subseteq \cup_{j=1}^{p} ATT(w_j)$, then there exist k members, $w_{j_1}, w_{j_2} ..., w_{j_k}$, of W such that $ATT(v_m) \subseteq ATT(w_{j_m})$, $1 \le m \le k$.

We say that **R** possesses the UMC property if for each subset, X ⊆ U, there exists a connected subset, $V = \{v_1, v_2, ..., v_k\}$, of the nodes of B(**R**), that possesses the UMC property. We call the set, {ATT(v_1), ATT(v_2), ..., ATT(v_k)}, the UMC among X w.r.t. **R**, and denote this set by $UMC_R(X)$.

The following proposition emanates from Theorem 8.1 in Fagin [1983].

Proposition 2.1. Let **R** be a connected and reduced FDS. Then **R** is γ-acyclic iff **R** possesses the UMC property. □

Example 2.3. Let **R** = {{STUDENT, DEPT, MAJOR}, {STUDENT, DEPT, CLASS, EXAM}, {STUDENT, DEPT, CLASS, PROJECT}} be the connected and reduced FDS from Example 2.2. Then it can easily be verified that **R** is γ-acyclic, since the Bachman diagram for **R**, B(**R**), shown in Figure 2.2, is loop-free, i.e., it is a lfbd.

It can also be verified that **R** possesses the UMC property, which, by Proposition 2.1, is an alternative way of saying that **R** is γ-acyclic.

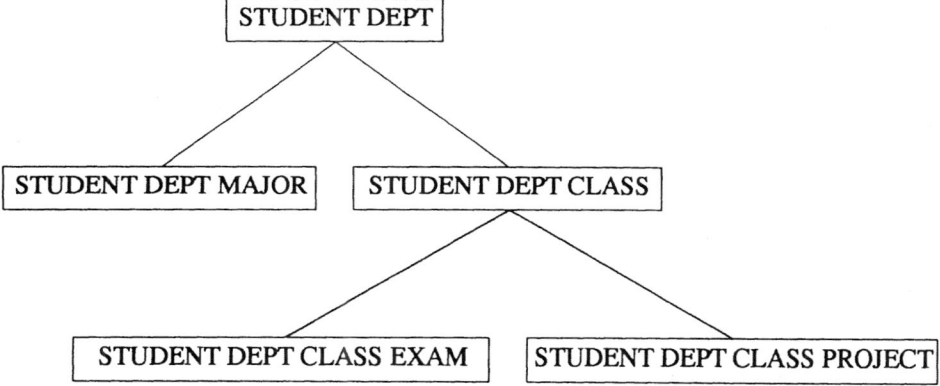

Fig. 2.2. The Bachman diagram of **R**, B(**R**).

We close this subsection with another useful characterization of γ-acyclicity which again emanates from Theorem 8.1 in Fagin [1983].

Proposition 2.2. Let **R** be a connected and reduced FDS. Then **R** is γ-acyclic iff the JD ⋈[**R**] implies that every connected subset **S** of **R** has a lossless join, i.e., ⋈[**S**] holds in the context of $\cup_i S_i$, $S_i \in$ **S**. □

2.2 The Nested Relational Model

The nested relational model [Makinouchi 1977; Bancilhon et al. 1982; Jaeschke & Schek 1982; Schek & Pistor 1982; Kambayashi et al. 1983; Kobayashi 1985; Roth et al. 1988, 1989; Abiteboul & Bidoit 1986; Abiteboul et al. 1986; Dadam et al. 1986; Schek & Scholl 1986; Thomas & Fischer 1986; Deshpande & Larson 1987; Gyssens 1987; Ozsoyoglu & Yuan 1987a; Scholl & Schek 1987; Van Gucht & Fischer 1988; Levene & Loizou 1989a] was developed in order to extend the applicability of the flat relational model to non-business applications. Such applications include office automation, computer aided design (CAD), image processing, spatial data, text retrieval, expert systems, and geographical and statistical analyses [Scholl & Schek 1987; Abiteboul et al. 1989b].

In the nested relational model we drop the 1NF *assumption* obtaining in flat relations, and allow attribute domains to be relation-valued as well as atomic. Thus in the nested relational model attribute domains are defined recursively, i.e., an element of a relation-valued domain may be itself relation-valued. The resulting *non-first normal form relations* are called hereinafter *nested relations* [Scholl & Schek 1987; Abiteboul et al. 1989b] and are also referred to in the literature as *complex objects* [Scholl & Schek 1987; Beeri 1988; Abiteboul et al. 1989b].

In Subsection 2.2.1 we define the data structure of the nested relational model, i.e., nested relations over nested relation schemes (NRSs).

In Subsection 2.2.2 we define the restructuring operators of the nested relational model, namely, the NEST, UNNEST and UNNEST* operators. The NEST operator allows us to transform a flat relation into a nested relation and a nested relation into a "more deeply nested" nested relation. On the other hand, the UNNEST operator allows us to transform a nested relation into a "flatter" nested relation, while the UNNEST* operator allows us to transform a nested relation into a flat relation by repetitively applying the UNNEST operator to the given nested relation. This last operator enables us to naturally define a useful subclass of nested relations, called *nested flat relations*, which are nested relations that can be obtained from flat relations by a sequence of NEST operations [Van Gucht & Fischer 1986, 1988].

In Subsection 2.2.3 we define an important subclass of nested flat relations, called *hierarchical relations*, that embed a set of MVDs within their structure [Roth et al. 1985, 1988; Abiteboul & Bidoit 1986; Van Gucht & Fischer 1986; Ozsoyoglu & Yuan 1987a; Levene & Loizou 1988].

In Subsection 2.2.4 we present the running example used throughout the rest of the monograph. Finally, in Subsection 2.2.5 we give a brief note on the methodology of proofs employed in the monograph.

The main advantages that result from the use of nested relations in comparison to flat relations are the following:

(1) Nested relations minimize redundancy of data.

(2) Query processing is more efficient, since some of the joins are realized within the nested relations themselves.

(3) Nested relations allow a very flexible interface at the external level, since both flat and hierarchical data can be presented to the user.

(4) Nested relations provide for the explicit representation of the semantics of the application, under consideration, within their structure.

The above advantages of the nested relational model will be clarified throughout the monograph by a judicious utilization of the running example. We further note that since the nested relational model is a proper extension of the flat relational model, we can also utilize the above advantages of the nested relational model in order to improve the modelling capability of the flat relational model for standard applications [Kambayashi et al. 1983; Kambayashi & Yamamoto 1987; Levene & Loizou 1987a, 1987b, 1988b; Ozsoyoglu & Yuan 1987a, 1987b; Roth & Korth 1987; Scholl et al. 1987].

2.2.1 Nested Relations

In this subsection we formally define nested relations and nested relation schemes (NRSs), which provide the data structure for the nested relational model. In order to do so, we first define the tree structure over which a NRS is defined, hereafter called a *scheme tree* (cf. [Ozsoyoglu & Yuan 1987a]), and present the notation for scheme trees.

Definition 2.4. Let W be a subset of the universal set of attributes, U. Then, a *scheme tree*, T, defined over the set of attributes, W, is a rooted tree whose vertices are labelled by pairwise disjoint sets of attributes partitioning W.

We now introduce the notation for scheme trees. Let T be a scheme tree over a set of attributes $W \subseteq U$, $e = (u,v)$ be an edge of T, and n be a node of T. Then

(1) ATT(n) is a label for node, n, and is equal to the set of attributes associated with node n;

(2) S(T) is the union of all ATT(n) for all nodes n in T;

(3) A(n) is the union of all ATT(v) for all ancestor nodes v of n, including ATT(n);

(4) D(n) is the union of all ATT(v) for all descendant nodes v of n, including ATT(n).

A *scheme forest*, F, over U, is a collection $\{T_1,T_2,...,T_q\}$ of scheme trees such that $S(T_i) \subseteq U$, $1 \le i \le q$, and $S(F) = \cup_{i=1}^{q} S(T_i) = U$.

The FDS induced by F, denoted as FDS(F), is given by $\{S(T_1),S(T_2),...,S(T_q)\}$. The JD induced by F, denoted as JD(F), is given by $\bowtie[FDS(F)]$.

If $u_1,u_2,...,u_m$ are all the leaf nodes of T, then the *path set* of T, denoted by P(T), is given by $P(T) = \{A(u_1),A(u_2),...,A(u_m)\}$. The path set, P(T), is a FDS over S(T).

The path set of F, denoted by P(F), is given by $\cup_{i=1}^{q} P(T_i)$; for simplicity, we assume that P(F) is connected and reduced; if this is not the case, it will, in general, be understood from context. The path set, P(F), is a FDS over S(F), i.e., over U.

The following functions which operate on a scheme tree, T, are now defined.

(1)   ROOT(T) returns the root node of T;

(2)   CHILDREN(T,n) returns all child nodes of a node n in T;

(3)   PARENT(T,n) returns the parent node of node n in T;

(4)   HEIGHT(T,n) returns the *height* of a node, n, in T and is defined inductively by HEIGHT(T,n) = 0 if n = ROOT(T); otherwise HEIGHT(T,n) = HEIGHT(T,PARENT(T,n)) +1;

(5)   HEIGHT(T) returns max({HEIGHT(T,n)|n is a node in T}), where max(S) returns the maximum value of a set, S, of integers.

Following Abiteboul & Bidoit [1986] and Ozsoyoglu & Yuan [1987a], we now define the NRS represented by a scheme tree, T.

Definition 2.5. The *nested relation scheme* (NRS), represented by a scheme tree, T, denoted as R(T), is defined recursively, as a string or a set, by

(1)   if the scheme tree, T, is empty, i.e., T is defined over the attribute set $\emptyset \subseteq U$, then $R(T) = \Lambda$;

(2)   if the scheme tree, T, consists of a single node, n, and ATT(n) = X, then R(T) = X;

(3)   if X = ATT(ROOT(T)) and T_1, T_2, ..., T_s, s $\geq$ 1, denote the first level subtrees of the scheme tree, T, with corresponding attributes $(R(T_1))$*, $(R(T_2))$*, ..., $(R(T_q))$*, then $R(T) = X(R(T_1))*(R(T_2))*...(R(T_s))*$.

Let $R(T) = X(R(T_1))*(R(T_2))*...(R(T_s))*$ be a NRS. Then the empty string, Λ, over the empty attribute set, $\emptyset$, is retained in the substring, $(R(T_1))*(R(T_2))*...(R(T_s))*$, only when it is associated with the root of a tree (or subtree) which itself has at least one subtree which is not empty. In analogy with the standard notation, by $Y \subseteq R(T)$ we mean a substring of R(T) composed of not necessarily consecutive attributes, for example, Y = $X'(R(T_2))*(R(T_s))*$, with $X' \subseteq X$.

We denote a NRS, R(T), where S(T) = U, by U(T). Furthermore, we let Z(R(T)) = R(T) $\cap$ U be the set of attributes in R(T) associated with atomic domains; such attributes are called the *zero order* attributes of R(T). Correspondingly, we let H(R(T)) = R(T) − Z(R(T)) be the set of attributes in R(T) associated with relation-valued domains; such attributes are called the *higher order* attributes of R(T).

A *nested database scheme* (NDS), **R**(F), over U, is a collection {$R(T_1)$,$R(T_2)$,...,$R(T_q)$} of NRSs such that F = {T_1,T_2,...,T_q} is a scheme forest over U.

We say that the NDS, **R**(F), possesses the UMC property, if FDS(F) possesses the UMC property. We note that by a result in Levene & Loizou [1989d], it follows that if P(F) possesses the UMC property then **R**(F) also possesses the UMC property.

Following Abiteboul & Bidoit [1986] and Ozsoyoglu & Yuan [1987a], we now define the domain of a NRS, R(T).

Definition 2.6. The domain of a NRS, R(T), denoted as DOM(R(T)), is defined recursively by

(1) if the scheme tree, T, is empty, i.e., R(T) = Λ, then
    DOM(R(T)) = $\emptyset$;

(2) if the scheme tree, T, consists of a single node, n, and
    ATT(n) = X = {$A_1, A_2, \ldots, A_k$}, then
    DOM(R(T)) = DOM(A_1) × DOM(A_2) × ... × DOM(A_k);

(3) let X = ATT(ROOT(R(T))), let $T_1, T_2, \ldots, T_s$, s ≥ 1,
    denote the first level subtrees of the scheme tree T and
    let DOM($T_1, T_2, \ldots, T_s$) = P(DOM(R(T_1))) × P(DOM(R(T_2))) ×
    ... × P(DOM(R(T_s))). Then,
    if X ≠ Λ, DOM(R(T)) = DOM(X) × DOM($T_1, T_2, \ldots, T_s$),
    otherwise (X = Λ) DOM(R(T)) = DOM($T_1, T_2, \ldots, T_s$).

Finally, we define a nested relation over a NRS and a nested database over a NDS.

Definition 2.7. A *nested relation*, r*, over a NRS, R(T), is a finite subset of
DOM(R(T)). A *nested database*, d*, over a NDS, R(F), is defined by d* = {$r^*_1, r^*_2, \ldots, r^*_q$},
where each r^*_i is a nested relation over R(T_i), 1 ≤ i ≤ q.

Hereafter, if a tuple, t ∈ r*, is defined over R(T), t[Y] will denote the restriction of t
to Y ⊆ R(T) or as before t[Y] will be referred to as the Y-value of t. Moreover, we interpret the empty set, $\emptyset$, over the NRS, Λ, as being an "undefined nested relation" and
assume that t[Λ] = $\emptyset$. On the other hand, for any Y ≠ Λ we exclude t[Y] = $\emptyset$, unless t =
r* = $\emptyset$. We also extend the definition of t[Y], where Y ⊆ R(T), from tuples to nested
relations by

$$r^*[Y] = \{t[Y] \mid t \in r^*\}.$$

Henceforth nested relations will be marked by * where necessary, in order to avoid
ambiguity.

Example 2.4. Let T be the scheme tree over W = {STUDENT, DEPT, MAJOR,
CLASS, EXAM, PROJECT}, shown in Figure 2.3. Thus, we have S(T) = W and P(T) =
{{STUDENT, DEPT, MAJOR}, {STUDENT, DEPT, CLASS, EXAM}, {STUDENT,
DEPT, CLASS, PROJECT}}. Moreover, we obtain the NRS, R(T) = STUDENT DEPT
(MAJOR)* (CLASS (EXAM)* (PROJECT)*)*. A nested relation, r*, over R(T), is
shown in Figure 2.4.

2.2.2 The NEST and UNNEST Operators

In this subsection we discuss the restructuring operators for nested relations. Restructuring nested relations allows us to view the information in the nested database in different
ways by changing the structure of the nested relations. In particular, restructuring allows
us to restructure nested relations into flat relations and to restructure flat relations into
nested relations.

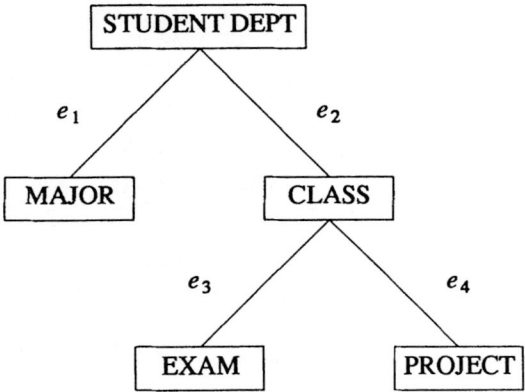

Fig. 2.3. The scheme tree T.

STUDENT	DEPT	(MAJOR)*	(CLASS	(EXAM)*	(PROJECT)*)*
		MAJOR	CLASS	(EXAM)*	(PROJECT)*
				EXAM	PROJECT
Iris	CS	computing	databases	mid final	1NF
			programming	final	C++
Mark	CS	maths	databases	final	NF2 UR
David	philosophy	logic	first-order	mid	prolog

Fig. 2.4. The nested relation r*.

We now define the two well-known operators, NEST and UNNEST [Jaeschke & Schek 1982; Schek & Scholl 1986; Thomas & Fischer 1986; Gyssens 1987; Van Gucht & Fischer 1988], designated by ν and μ, respectively. Intuitively, nesting transforms a nested relation into one which is "more deeply" nested, whilst unnesting transforms a nested relation into a "flatter" one.

Firstly, we define the NEST operator.

Definition 2.8. Let r* be a nested relation over R(T) and let $(Y \neq \Lambda) \subseteq R(T)$. $\nu_Y(r^*)$ is a nested relation over $(R(T) - Y)(Y)^*$ such that a tuple $w \in \nu_Y(r^*)$ iff

(1)   there exists a tuple $t \in r^*$ such that $t[R(T) - Y] = w[R(T) - Y]$;

(2) $w[(Y)^*] = \{t'[Y] \mid t' \in r^* \text{ and } t'[R(T) - Y] = w[R(T) - Y]\}$.

We have excluded the case when $Y = \Lambda$, i.e., $\nu_\Lambda(r^*)$, since as we have already noted we do not retain empty subtrees in scheme trees. Furthermore, when $Y = R(T)$, we take $\nu_{R(T)}(r^*)$ as modifying only the NRS associated with r*, i.e., we define $\nu_{R(T)}(r^*) = r^*$ to be a nested relation over the NRS, $\Lambda(R(T))*$. Thus, at times, we can consider the NRS, $R(T)$, to be equivalent to the NRS, $\Lambda(R(T))*$, since for a nested relation, over $R(T)$, there always exists an equal nested relation over $\Lambda(R(T))*$. ($\nu_{R(T)}(r*) = r*$.)

Secondly, we define the UNNEST operator.

Definition 2.9. Let $r*$ be a nested relation over $R(T)$ and let $(Y)* \in H(R(T))$. $\mu_{(Y)*}(r*)$ is a nested relation over $(R(T) - (Y)*)Y$ such that a tuple $t \in \mu_{(Y)*}(r*)$ iff there exists a tuple $w \in r*$ such that $t[R(T) - (Y)*] = w[R(T) - (Y)*]$ and $t[Y] \in w[(Y)*]$.

Next we define the UNNEST* operator [Thomas & Fischer 1986], denoted by $\mu*$, which transforms any nested relation, $r*$, (or a tuple thereof) into a flat relation. Thomas and Fischer [1986] showed that the order of unnesting does not affect the resulting flat relation, $\mu*(r*)$, whose computation is realized by the following algorithm [Levene & Loizou 1988] (where := stands for assignment):

```
while H(R(T)) ≠ Ø do
    choose (Y)* ∈ H(R(T));
    r* := μ(Y)* (r*);
    R(T) := (R(T) - (Y)*) ∪ Y;
end while;
```

Example 2.5. It can easily be verified that for the flat relation, r, shown in Figure 2.1, and the nested relation, $r*$, shown in Figure 2.4, we have that $r = \mu*(r*)$.

We now define a subclass of nested relations which have the property that they can be obtained from their flat counterparts by using only NEST operations.

Definition 2.10. A *nested flat relation*, $r*$, over a NRS, $R(T)$, is a nested relation that can be obtained from the flat relation, $\mu*(r*)$, over $S(T)$, by using a sequence of NEST operations. In other words, let r be a flat relation over $S(T) \subseteq U$, then, for an integer $n \geq 0$,

$$r* = \nu_{Y_n}(\nu_{Y_{n-1}} \cdots (\nu_{Y_1}(r)) \cdots)$$

is a nested relation over the NRS, $R(T) = R(T_n)$, with $Y_i \in R(T_{i-1})$, $1 \leq i \leq n$, where $R(T_0) = S(T)$ and $R(T_i) = (R(T_{i-1}) - Y_i)(Y_i)*$, $i > 0$, is the NRS over which $\nu_{Y_i}(\nu_{Y_{i-1}} \cdots (\nu_{Y_1}(r)) \cdots)$ is defined.

Example 2.6. Let r over the FRS, {CHILD, PARENT}, be the flat relation shown in Figure 2.5. Then the nested flat relation $r* = \nu_{CHILD}(\nu_{PARENT}(r))$, over the NRS, $R(T) = \Lambda(CHILD)*(PARENT)*$, is shown in Figure 2.6. We note that $P(T)$ is not connected.

The following example shows that not all nested relations are nested flat relations. In particular, we show that nested relations are strictly more expressive than flat relations, since the equality, $r* = \nu_Y(\mu_{(Y)*}(r*))$, where $r*$ is a nested relation over the NRS, $R(T)$, and $(Y)* \in H(R(T))$, is, in general, *false*.

CHILD	PARENT
c_1	p_1
c_1	p_2
c_2	p_1
c_2	p_2
c_3	p_1
c_3	p_3
c_4	p_4
c_4	p_5

Fig. 2.5. The flat relation r.

Λ	(CHILD)*	(PARENT)*
	CHILD	PARENT
	c_1 c_2	p_1 p_2
	c_3	p_1 p_3
	c_4	p_4 p_5

Fig. 2.6. The nested flat relation $r^* = \nu_{CHILD}(\nu_{PARENT}(r))$.

Example 2.7. Let r^* be the nested relation over the NRS, AREA(X-COORD Y-COORD)*, shown in Figure 2.7. Thus, r^* stores the area and the x and y coordinates of two triangles, both of which have the same area, say $1cm^2$. It can easily be verified that $r^* \neq \nu_{(X-COORD\ Y-COORD)}(\mu_{(X-COORD\ Y-COORD)*}(r^*))$. Thus, r^* is not a nested flat relation. Moreover, the semantics of r^* cannot be expressed by the flat relation, $\mu^*(r^*)$, over the FRS, {AREA, X-COORD, Y-COORD}, since it can easily be verified that r^* cannot be obtained from $\mu^*(r^*)$ by any sequence of NEST and UNNEST operations.

The above problem of loss of information in the general class of nested relations, which are not nested flat relations, whereby a nested relation cannot be recovered, after having been transformed by UNNEST operations, via the corresponding NEST operations, is called the *1NF normalizability problem* [Miura et al. 1986]. In order to solve the 1NF normalizability problem, an additional nested relational operator can be defined that preserves the identity of the unnested tuples by maintaining a key value for each unnested tuple. Variations of such an operator have been the *keying* operator [Jaeschke & Schek 1982; Jaeschke 1985a, 1985b], the *index* operator [Van Gucht & Fischer 1988], and the *copying* operator [Gyssens 1987].

AREA	(X-COORD	Y-COORD)*
	X-COORD	Y-COORD
1	0	0
	1	0
	0	2
1	0	0
	2	0
	0	1

Fig. 2.7. A nested relation r*, which is more expressive than $\mu*(r*)$.

In this monograph we do not deal any further with ways of solving the 1NF normalizability problem. On the other hand, we do point out, when necessary, situations when the general class of nested relations is more expressive than the subclass of nested flat relations.

2.2.3 Hierarchical Relations

In this subsection we introduce an important subclass of nested flat relations, called *hierarchical relations* [Delobel 1978; Roth et al. 1985, 1988; Abiteboul & Bidoit 1986; Levene & Loizou 1987a; Ozsoyoglu & Yuan 1987a]. The main characteristic of hierarchical relations is that they explicitly represent a set of data dependencies within their structure.

Following Ozsoyoglu & Yuan [1987a], we now introduce more notation for a scheme tree, T, in order to define the set of MVDs represented by T.

Definition 2.11. Let e = {u,v} be an edge in the scheme tree, T. Then we denote by M(e) the MVD represented by the edge, e, namely, $A(u) \rightarrow\rightarrow D(v)$ (S(T)).

We let MVD(T) denote the set of MVDs represented by all the edges of T. Thus, the set of MVDs represented by F, denoted by MVD(F), is given by MVD(F) = $\cup_{i=1}^{q}$ MVD(T_i).

We note that the set of MVDs, MVD(T), is equivalent to a *generalized hierarchical decomposition* [Delobel 1978].

We are now ready to define hierarchical relations.

Definition 2.12. A *hierarchical relation*, r*, over a NRS, R(T), is a nested flat relation such that its flat counterpart, $\mu*(r*)$, over S(T), satisfies the set of MVDs, MVD(T).

The following lemma gives some of the properties of T. The first part is from Chapter 6, Lemma 6.4, and the second part is from Ozsoyoglu and Yuan [1987a], Proposition 4.1 therein.

Lemma 2.3. Let T be a scheme tree, then

(1)   The FDS, P(T), is a γ-acyclic FDS;

(2)   MVD(T) $\equiv \bowtie[P(T)]$. $\Box$

Example 2.8. For the scheme tree, T, shown in Figure 2.3, we have:

$M(e_1)$ = STUDENT,DEPT $\rightarrow\rightarrow$ MAJOR (S(T))

$M(e_2)$ = STUDENT,DEPT $\rightarrow\rightarrow$ CLASS,EXAM,PROJECT (S(T))

$M(e_3)$ = STUDENT,DEPT,CLASS $\rightarrow\rightarrow$ EXAM (S(T))

$M(e_4)$ = STUDENT,DEPT,CLASS $\rightarrow\rightarrow$ PROJECT (S(T)).

Thus, the set of MVDs represented by the edges of T is given by MVD(T) = $\{M(e_1), M(e_2), M(e_3), M(e_4)\}$.

It can be verified that the nested relation, r*, shown in Figure 2.4, is a hierarchical relation, i.e., r* is a nested flat relation and $\mu^*(r^*)$, shown in Figure 2.1, satisfies MVD(T). It can also be verified that the result of Lemma 2.3 holds, i.e., P(T) is γ-acyclic and MVD(T) $\equiv \bowtie[P(T)]$, and thus $\mu^*(r^*)$ also satisfies $\bowtie[P(T)]$.

Finally, it can be verified that the nested flat relation, r*, shown in Figure 2.6, is not a hierarchical relation, since the flat relation, $\mu^*(r^*)$, shown in Figure 2.5, does not satisfy its set of MVDs, namely, $\{\emptyset \rightarrow\rightarrow$ CHILD, $\emptyset \rightarrow\rightarrow$ PARENT$\}$.

2.2.4 The Running Example

In this subsection we present the running example used throughout the monograph.

Let U = {CHILD, CLASS, DAY, DEPT, EXAM, MAJOR, PROJECT, SALARY, STUDENT, TEXT, TUTOR} be the universal set of attributes. The semantics of U are as follows: a STUDENT is enrolled in a department DEPT and MAJORs in one or more subjects within the department. A STUDENT attends several CLASSes, each CLASS having several EXAMs during the academic year, which the STUDENT has to sit, and one or more PROJECTs, which the STUDENT has to complete. Each CLASS has several TUTORs and several TEXT books. Also, each TUTOR gives the lectures for the CLASSes the TUTOR teaches on one or more prearranged DAYs. Independently, a TUTOR has a SALARY and may have zero or more CHILDren.

Now, let F = $\{T_1, T_2, T_3\}$ be a scheme forest. The scheme tree T_1 is the scheme tree T, shown in Figure 2.3, the scheme tree T_2 is shown in Figure 2.9, and the scheme tree T_3, previously shown in Figure 1.1, is shown in Figure 2.11. The NDS, over U, is $R(F) = \{R(T_1), R(T_2), R(T_3)\}$, where

| STUDENT | DEPT | (MAJOR)* | (CLASS | (EXAM)* | (PROJECT)*)* |
| | | MAJOR | CLASS | (EXAM)* | (PROJECT)* |
				EXAM	PROJECT
Iris	CS	computing	databases	mid final	1NF
			programming	final	null
Mark	CS	maths	databases	final	NF2 UR
David	philosophy	logic	first-order	mid	prolog
null	philosophy	null	null	mid final	null
			first-order	null	functions predicates
Naomi	null	languages	french	mid	null
			null	final	Moscow
			hebrew	null	Genesis

Fig. 2.8. The nested relation r_1^* of the running example.

$R(T_1)$ = STUDENT DEPT (MAJOR)* (CLASS (EXAM)* (PROJECT)*)*,

$R(T_2)$ = CLASS (TUTOR)* (TEXT)*, and

$R(T_3)$ = TUTOR SALARY (CHILD)* (DAY)*.

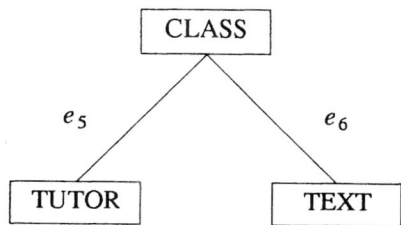

Fig. 2.9. The scheme tree T_2 of the running example.

The notation used in the figures of nested relations is based on the notation found in Roth et al. [1985, 1988] and Thomas & Fischer [1986]. We indicate null values in the figures of nested relations by *null*; their semantics are discussed in Chapter 3, wherein we define the null extended nested relational model. From now on, until Chapter 3, we simply assume that *null* is a placeholder for missing information indicating that only partial information is given for an attribute value.

Let d* = $\{r_1^*, r_2^*, r_3^*\}$ be the nested database, over **R**(F), for the running example. The nested relation r_1^* is shown in Figure 2.8, the nested relation r_2^* is shown in Figure

CLASS	(TUTOR)*	(TEXT)*
	TUTOR	TEXT
databases	Robert	Date Ullman
programming	Hanna Richard	Knuth
first-order	*null*	Mendelson
french	Martine	*null*
hebrew	*null*	Bible
null	*null*	Lenin Dostoyevsky

Fig. 2.10. The nested relation r_2^* of the running example.

2.10, and the nested relation r_3^*, previously shown in Figure 1.2, is shown in Figure 2.12.

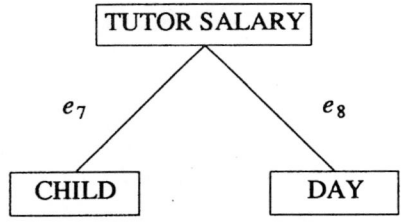

Fig. 2.11. The scheme tree T_3 of the running example.

TUTOR	SALARY	(CHILD)*	(DAY)*
		CHILD	DAY
Robert	12000	Hanna Brian	Monday Thursday
Hanna	14000	Annette Ada	*null*
Martine	*null*	*null*	*null*
null	15000	*null*	Wednesday
null	*null*	Ruth	Tuesday Friday

Fig. 2.12. The nested relation r_3^* of the running example.

2.2.5 A Note on the Methodology of Proofs

In this subsection we briefly comment on the main methodology employed throughout the monograph in order to prove properties, which hold for nested relations over NRSs.

Let r* be a nested relation over the NRS, R(T). Suppose that we want to prove that some desirable property holds for the nested relation, r*. Let **PRED** be a predicate representing this desirable property. In other words, we want to prove that **PRED**(r*) is true. Our main method of proving such a result is by induction on the height of the scheme tree, T. We now illustrate this approach in some detail.

BASIS. If HEIGHT(T) = 0, then r* is a flat relation over the FRS, ATT(ROOT(T)). Thus, in order to prove the base case we need to show that **PRED**(r*) is true for flat relations. This can be viewed as a general desirable property, namely, that the flat relational model is a special case of the nested relational model.

INDUCTION. Assume that **PRED**(r*) is true for HEIGHT(T) = n, we then need to prove that **PRED**(r*) is true for HEIGHT(T) = n+1. Let r'* be the resulting nested relation over, say R(T'), after unnesting r* over all the attributes in H(R(T)). We now have that HEIGHT(T') = n, so, by inductive hypothesis, **PRED**(r'*) is true. We conclude the proof by showing that **PRED**(r*) is also true. □

2.3 The Universal Relation Model

The relational model provides *physical data independence* but not *logical data independence*. Thus, in the relational model navigating amongst the relations in a given database is left to the user. On the other hand, the (classical) Universal Relation model (UR model) provides *logical data independence* by freeing the user from navigating amongst the relations in a given database. This logical data independence is achieved by providing the database with an interface which allows the user to view the database as if it were composed of a single relation.

The UR model has generated heated debate and controversy [Kent 1981, 1983; Atzeni & Parker 1982; Ullman 1982a, 1983b]. This is due, we believe, to the variety of proposals put forward and the argument that the assumptions made may not be reasonable or desirable in practice. In defence of the UR model we recall the spirit of Ullman's reply [Ullman 1983b] (cf. [Ullman 1987]): *The UR as a user view serves as a very convenient user interface and has similarities with a natural language interface to a database.*

On a historical note we mention Carlson and Kaplan [1976], who were among the first to study ways a DBMS can select connections among attributes automatically, and Schenk and Pinkert [1977], who investigated a way whereby a DBMS can automatically find a lossless join with a minimal number of relations to be joined. Another early suggestion of a UR model is that of Babb [1982], who formalized the notion of storing a flat database in one relation, which is in *joined normal form*. In its essence, the flat relation in joined normal form is a UR constructed by a union of joins over the flat database padded with blank (null) values.

From the practitioner's point of view we need only mention that several implementations of UR interfaces have been developed over the past few years [Ullman 1983a]. The most recent approaches adopted in these implementations entail the computation of the union of one or more joins [Osborn 1979; Sagiv 1981, 1983; Kuck & Sagiv 1982; Maier & Ullman 1983; Korth et al. 1984; Biskup et al. 1986; Maier et al. 1986; Vardi 1988; Atzeni & Chan 1989].

2.3.1 The Universal Relation Assumptions

We begin by assuming, at the external level (see Figure 1.3), a UR interface over U. The usual assumptions of the UR model are:

(1)   The *universal relation scheme assumption* (URSA) [Maier & Warren 1982; Maier et al. 1984, 1986]. This assumption means that each attribute $A_i \in U$, $1 \le i \le p$, is assumed to play a unique role. In other words, the URSA requires an attribute to have the same meaning everywhere it appears. Thus, in the running example, SALARY means the salary of a TUTOR and not that of a CHILD.

(2)   The *unique role assumption* (URA) [Maier & Warren 1982; Maier et al. 1984, 1986]. This assumption means that the user has in mind a unique semantic relationship amongst the attributes of any set $X \subseteq U$. This assumption is sometimes called the *relationship uniqueness assumption*. This does not mean that there can be only one relationship on X, but rather that this one relationship is more *basic* and, unless explicitly stated otherwise, it is taken to be that of the user's intention. Thus, in the running example, {STUDENT, DEPT} means the department a STUDENT is MAJORing in and not a department in which the STUDENT is taking some other CLASS.

The *basic relationship* [Maier et al. 1984] on X results in a relation over X denoted by [X] and is called the *window* for X [Maier et al. 1986]. A *window function* [Maier et al. 1986] maps a set of attributes $X \subseteq U$ and a database, d, to a relation, r(X), which results in [X].

For a *window function* to be consistent with the URA it needs to satisfy the *containment condition* [Maier et al. 1986], namely, whenever $X \subseteq Y$, then $\Pi_X([Y]) \subseteq [X]$ holds.

(3)   The *one-flavor assumption* (OFA) [Maier et al. 1984, 1986; Biskup et al. 1986]. Intuitively, the OFA says that the real-world significance of any tuple in the window for X does not depend on the details of its construction that put it there. Thus, for example, if more than one access path is used for answering a query over $X \subseteq U$, then the tuples returned from either path retain the same "flavor" of the basic relationship on X.

There are two basic approaches to the realization of the UR model, namely,

(1)   we consider the UR as a *user view*, u, over U, and [X] is taken to be the projection of u onto X;

(2) we allow the user to query the database over any set of attributes $X \subseteq U$, and the DBMS with its associated UR interface provides a computational procedure, in the form of a relational algebra expression, to calculate [X] w.r.t. a flat database defined over a FDS over U. In this approach no explicit reference is made to a UR, u, over U.

Consequently, in order to answer a query under the UR model, two steps are required [Maier et al. 1984, 1986]:

(1) *Binding*, in which the window, [X], for $X \subseteq U$, involved in the query is constructed.

(2) *Evaluation*, during which further relational algebra operators are applied to [X] to generate the required answer to the query.

Under the UR model the operands of a query are variables over windows rather than variables over FRSs as in the relational model. Thus, a query may require the construction of more than one window in the binding stage of query processing.

2.3.2 Nulls in the Universal Relation Model

In this subsection we briefly discuss nulls in the context of the UR model. If we consider a flat relation, r, over U, as a UR interface providing a user view, then null values are necessary, since, in general, some of the tuples in r may have missing information, i.e., they may be incomplete. We discuss nulls comprehensively in Chapter 3 wherein we define the null extended nested relational model, but for now let us assume that we have one type of null value, denoted as *null*, which provides a placeholder for missing information.

There are two main approaches to nulls in the UR model, which we now very briefly review:

The first approach uses *unmarked nulls* [Biskup & Bruggemann 1983; Jajodia & Ng 1984; Stein & Maier 1985; Atzeni & Bernardis 1987; Jajodia & Springsteel 1987; Levene & Loizou 1988]. In this case, if two tuples in a relation contain the null value, *null*, then we consider $null \neq null$. (This approach is justified in Subsection 3.1.1, where in Definition 3.3 we define the equality rule for nulls.) For example, in the flat relation, $\mu^*(r_2^*)$, where r_2^* is shown in Figure 2.10, we have the two {CLASS, TUTOR}-values: <first-order, *null*>, <hebrew, *null*>. Thus, in this approach, we consider at this point in time, the TUTORs for the CLASSes, first-order and hebrew, to be different, although it may turn out that the same TUTOR teaches these two CLASSes when *null* is replaced in both tuples by a non-null value.

The second approach, which has traditionally been employed in the UR model, uses *marked nulls* [Sagiv 1981, 1983, 1988; Honeyman 1982; Maier et al. 1984; Mendelzon 1984; Graham et al. 1986]. In this case , each null value is marked with a distinguishing subscript (index), i, and is denoted as $null_i$. Thus, two null values, $null_i$ and $null_j$, are equal iff i = j. For example, if our previous {CLASS, TUTOR}-values are: <first-order, $null_1$>, <hebrew, $null_1$>, then we know that the same TUTOR teaches both the

CLASSes, first-order and hebrew, although the information about this TUTOR is only partial. On the other hand, if the two {CLASS, TUTOR}-values are: <first-order, $null_2$>, <hebrew, $null_3$>, then, at this point in time, we consider the TUTORs that teach the CLASSes, first-order and hebrew, to be different as is the case with unmarked nulls.

In the UR model when we query over a window, [X], where $X \subseteq U$, the window contains tuples of the basic relationship over X. If we assume that a relation, r, over U, is a user view, then [X] traditionally contains tuples, over X, which contain only non-null values [Maier et al. 1984]. This naturally leads us to the following two definitions of *X-total* tuples and *total projection* [Sagiv 1981, 1983; Maier 1983; Maier et al. 1984; Stein & Maier 1985], respectively.

Definition 2.13. Let r be a flat relation, over U, and t be a tuple of r; also, let $X = \{A_1, A_2, ..., A_k\}$ be a set of attributes such that $X \subseteq U$. Then, the X-value, t[X], is said to be *X-total* if it contains no null values, i.e., $t[A_i]$, $1 \le i \le k$, are non-null values.

Definition 2.14. Let r be a flat relation, over U, and $Y \subseteq U$ be a set of attributes. Then the *total projection* of r onto Y, denoted as $\Pi\!\downarrow_Y(r)$, is defined by

$$\Pi\!\downarrow_Y (r) = \{t[Y] \mid t \in r \text{ and } t[Y] \text{ is } Y\text{-total}\}.$$

2.3.3 The Weak Instance Approach to the Universal Relation Model

A widely used approach to the UR model is afforded by the concept of *weak instances* [Sagiv 1981, 1983; Yannakakis 1981; Honeyman 1982; Mendelzon 1984; Maier et al. 1984, 1986; Graham et al. 1986; Atzeni & Bernardis 1987]; this provides the UR model with a sound theoretical basis. The weak instance approach to the UR model allows us to model all the data stored in the flat database by a single flat relation. It was originally introduced in order to define the satisfaction of a set of data dependencies in the global context of a flat database [Vassiliou 1980; Honeyman 1982], and as a basis for query answering in user interfaces [Sagiv 1981, 1983; Yannakakis 1981]. Later [Maier et al. 1984; Mendelzon 1984; Atzeni & Bernardis 1987], the weak instance approach was used to relax the restrictive *pure UR assumption* [Kent 1981; Atzeni & Parker 1982; Fagin et al. 1982; Ullman 1982b], whereby the UR is modelled by a flat relation, r, over U, such that $\Pi_{R_i}(r) = r_i$, $1 \le i \le m$, for a flat database $d = \{r_1, r_2, ..., r_m\}$, over **R**.

We are now ready to define the concept of a weak instance.

Definition 2.15. Let $\mathbf{R} = \{R_1, R_2, ..., R_m\}$ be a FDS, over U, and let $d = \{r_1, r_2, ..., r_m\}$ be a flat database, over **R**, together with a set of data dependencies, D. Then, a flat relation, I, over U, is a *weak instance* (also called a *containing instance*) under D for d, if

(1)   I satisfies D; and

(2) $r_i \subseteq \Pi_{R_i}(I)$, $1 \le i \le m$.

Thus in the weak instance approach, the database, d, is, in general, an incomplete description of a weak instance, I, satisfying the semantics of d in the form of the set of data dependencies, D. From the above definition, it follows that there are infinitely many weak instances under D for d (or a very large number, if the atomic domains for the attributes in U are all finite). Thus, we assume that the only facts that can be deduced from the UR model, given the relations in the database d, are those that hold in *all* weak instances. That is, under the weak instance approach to the UR model, the window, [X], for a set of attributes $X \subseteq U$, contains exactly the X-total tuples that appear in every weak instance under D for d. Thus, informally, a *representative instance* (RI), over U, is a weak instance, I, under a set of data dependencies, D, for a given flat database, d, such that [X] is defined, over I, as above.

The following declarative definition of a RI (cf. [Sagiv 1981, 1983; Ullman 1983a; Mendelzon 1984; Maier et al. 1984, 1986; Stein & Maier 1985; Graham et al. 1986; Atzeni & Bernardis 1987]) encapsulates this fact.

Definition 2.16. A flat relation, I (which may contain null values), over U, is a *representative instance* (RI) under a set of data dependencies, D, for a database d, over **R**, if

(1) I is a weak instance under D for d; and

(2) $[X] = \Pi\downarrow_X(I)$, for any set of attributes $X \subseteq U$.

We note that a unique RI, henceforth called the RI, can be obtained via the *chase* procedure [Maier et al. 1979; Beeri & Vardi 1984; Graham et al. 1986] (cf. Sections 4.5 and 5.2).

In the weak instance approach to the UR model we assume that the current information in the database is incomplete. Thus, the RI contains the maximum information that can be deduced at any given moment and it is, therefore, a suitable model of the data as stored in one flat relation.

A result, which is relevant later in the monograph, was shown in Maier et al. [1986], namely, Lemma 3 therein, proving that a *window function* based on the RI satisfies the *containment condition*, i.e., whenever $X \subseteq Y$, then $\Pi_X([Y]) \subseteq [X]$ holds.

Finally, we note than an interesting correspondence between the RI and deductive databases was shown in Sagiv [1988], wherein the RI was shown to be equivalent to a fragment of Horn-clause programs under certain conditions.

Chapter 3
The Null Extended Nested Relational Model

In this chapter we present the null extended nested relational model which extends the nested relational model in order to include null values. The null extended nested relational model provides the underlying database model used to formalize the nested UR model. In Section 3.1 we define the data structure pertaining to the null extended nested relational model, i.e, null extended nested relations, discuss some of their properties and define the null extended NEST and null extended UNNEST operators. In Section 3.2 we present the null extended nested relational algebra which extends the flat relational algebra [Codd 1979; Ullman 1982a; Maier 1983] to null extended nested relations.

We now briefly review some relevant work relating to nulls in flat relations and to nulls in nested relations.

Handling incomplete information in databases is very important since, in general, we do not expect to have a complete model of the real world. Zaniolo [1984] and Codd [1986] observed that missing information generally falls into two categories: applicable information, i.e., "value exists but is unknown at present", denoted as *unk*, and inapplicable information, i.e., "value does not exist", denoted as *dne*. Varied interpretations of null values within these two categories were listed in ANSI [1975].

Nulls of type *unk* were first proposed by Codd [1979] in the framework of a three-valued logic and thereafter Biskup [1983] provided a theoretical basis for Codd's model of nulls. Lipski [1979, 1981] and Grant [1980] extended Codd's theory of null values of type *unk* so that *unk* null values represent only a subset of the attribute domain rather than the whole attribute domain. Codd [1986, 1987] extended his original model further to include nulls of type *dne*, which can be incorporated into a four-valued logic. Additional results on nulls of type *dne* in the context of the relational model can be found in Lerat & Lipski [1986].

A first-order logic approach to the theory of nulls was developed by Biskup [1981], Maier [1983] and Gottlob & Zicari [1988]. On the other hand a denotational semantics approach to nulls was proposed by Vassiliou [1979], where the bottom element of the resulting lattice is a null value of type *unk* and the top element of the lattice is an over-determined null value. Another approach to nulls was adopted by Imielinski & Lipski [1984], where marked nulls are used in contrast to unmarked nulls, an approach frequently adopted in the formalization of the UR model.

Finally, Zaniolo [1984] unified the two categories of null values, i.e., *unk* and *dne*, by considering a third type of null value which may be *unk* or *dne*, that is to say "no information is available for the attribute value"; this type of null value is denoted as *ni*. On the other hand, Keller & Wilkins [1984] consider sets of nulls and conditional tuples which provide additional knowledge in the context of an incomplete database.

It is worth mentioning at this juncture that existing DBMS's, currently on the market, with an SQL interface based on the standard SQL [Date 1987c] allow only one type of null value, i.e., *unk*, which is insufficient for modelling many applications where missing information occurs naturally.

In a nested relation the value of a higher order attribute may be the empty set, $\emptyset$, which can be given an interpretation in terms of missing information. The standard interpretation of the empty set, $\emptyset$, is a null value of type *dne* [Makinouchi 1977; Abiteboul & Bidoit 1986; Lerat & Lipski 1986; Scholl 1986; Gottlob & Zicari 1988]. Other semantics given to the empty set are: a null value of type *ni* [Roth et al. 1985] and a null value of type *unk* [Levene & Loizou 1988]. On the other hand, Gyssens [1987] and Levene & Loizou [1989a] do not fix the semantics of the empty set to be a null value of any given type.

A comprehensive theory of nulls in nested relations was given by Roth et al. [1985]; they basically extended the results of Zaniolo [1984] concerning nulls in flat relations to hierarchical relations. A theory of nulls in nested sequences of tuples rather than nested relations was given by Guting et al. [1987]; this theory takes account of the empty sequence as well as the sequence with no information. Finally, a more general theory of nulls in nested relations, which is independent of the semantics of the incomplete information to be modelled, was given by Levene & Loizou [1989a], where a domain-theoretic approach was adopted.

3.1 Nulls in Nested Relations

Null extended nested relations are subsets of the null extended domains to be defined in the next subsection. We define the semantics of null extended domains via five types of null: *unk*, *dne* and *ni*, which are included in null extended domains over zero order attributes and, *unk** and *ni**, which are included in null extended domains over higher order attributes. Although two nulls of the same type are considered to be *information-wise equivalent* (cf. *symbolic equality* [Codd 1986]), they are not considered to be *equal* (cf. *semantic equality* [Codd 1986]); this provides us with the motivation for the *equality rule for nulls* given in Definition 3.3. We also investigate the relative information content of tuples in null extended nested relations by defining a partial order on null values, which is induced by the *information lattice* defined on null extended domains. By using this concept *less informative* and *more informative* tuples are defined and a canonical representation of a null extended nested relation can be obtained; such a null extended nested relation is called a *reduced nested relation*. Finally, we discuss and justify our approach to the null extended NEST and null extended UNNEST operators, where we employ information-wise equivalence rather than equality as is the case with the standard NEST and standard UNNEST operators given in Definitions 2.8 and 2.9, respectively.

3.1.1 Null Extended Domains

In our null extended nested relational model and consequently in the nested UR model, we choose to use unmarked nulls as in Stein & Maier [1985], Atzeni & Bernardis [1987] and Jajodia & Springsteel [1987] rather than marked nulls as in Sagiv [1981, 1983, 1988], Honeyman [1982], Maier et al. [1984] and Graham et al. [1986] or equivalence classes of nulls as is the case in Vassiliou [1980]. Although marked nulls are very useful for enforcing dependency satisfaction [Maier et al. 1979; Imielinski & Lipski 1983; Grahne 1984; Graham et al. 1986], they are expensive to maintain and do not always provide more information in the database.

The following types of null are included in the null extended domains over zero order attributes:

(1)   *unk* [Codd 1979, 1986, 1987; Lipski 1979, 1981; Vassiliou 1979; Grant 1980; Biskup 1981, 1983; Sagiv 1981, 1983; Maier 1983; Imielinski & Lipski 1984; Maier et al. 1984] - "value exists but is unknown at the present time" or "value is applicable and missing at the present time". For example, with regard to the running example, it may not be known at the present time which PROJECT a STUDENT is doing.

(2)   *dne* [Lien 1979, 1982; Stein & Maier 1985; Codd 1986, 1987; Lerat & Lipski 1986] - "value does not exist" or "value is inapplicable". For example, with regard to the running example, a STUDENT may not have an EXAM to sit in a given academic year if that STUDENT is a research STUDENT. In this case no EXAM exists for that STUDENT.

(3)   *ni* [Zaniolo 1984; Roth et al. 1985] - "no information is available for the value", i.e., it is either *unk* or *dne*. For example, with regard to the running example, we may not have any information available as to whether a STUDENT has to sit an EXAM in a given academic year. In this case either no EXAM exists for that STUDENT or it is unknown which EXAM he is sitting for.

A formal theory that integrates into flat relations the above-mentioned types of null can be found in Zaniolo [1984], and an extension of this theory to hierarchical relations can be found in Roth et al. [1985].

The following types of null are included in null extended domains over higher order attributes:

(4)   *unk** - "a higher order attribute domain value is unknown", i.e., one or more values are unknown for a higher order attribute. For example, with regard to the running example, we may know that a STUDENT is doing one or more PROJECTS but we do not know at present what they are.

(5)   *ni** (cf. [Guting et al. 1987]) - "no information is available for a higher order attribute domain value", i.e., it is either *unk** or {*dne*}. For example, with regard to the running example, we may not have any information available as to whether a STUDENT has to sit one or more EXAMs or none at all in a given academic year.

Prior to defining null extended domains, we first null-extend the definition of a domain for zero order attributes.

Definition 3.1. Let $A \in U$ be a zero order attribute. Then the *null extended domain* of A, denoted as EDOM(A), is defined by EDOM(A) = DOM(A) $\cup$ {*dne, unk, ni*}.

We next generalize the definition of null extended domain to NRSs in order to include all the types of null we have defined over zero order and higher order attributes in nested relations.

Definition 3.2. The *null extended domain* of a NRS, R(T), denoted as EDOM(R(T)), is defined by

(1) if the scheme tree, T, is empty, i.e., R(T) = Λ, then EDOM(R(T)) = $\emptyset$;

(2) if the scheme tree, T, comprises a single node, n, and ATT(n) = $\{A_1, A_2, \ldots, A_k\}$, then EDOM(R(T)) = EDOM(A_1) $\times$ EDOM(A_2) $\times$ ... $\times$ EDOM(A_k);

(3) let X = ATT(ROOT(R(T))), let $T_1, T_2, \ldots, T_s$, s $\geq$ 1, denote the first level subtrees of the scheme tree T and let EDOM($T_1, T_2, \ldots, T_s$) = (P(EDOM(R(T_1))) $\cup$ {unk*, ni*}) $\times$ (P(EDOM(R(T_2))) $\cup$ {unk*, ni*}) $\times$ ... $\times$ (P(EDOM(R(T_s))) $\cup$ {unk*, ni*}). Then, if X $\neq \Lambda$, EDOM(R(T)) = EDOM(X) $\times$ EDOM($T_1, T_2, \ldots, T_s$), otherwise (X = Λ) EDOM(R(T)) = EDOM($T_1, T_2, \ldots, T_s$).

A *null extended nested relation*, or simply a *nested relation*, r*, over a NRS, R(T), is a finite subset of EDOM(R(T)). At times we consider a tuple, t* $\in$ r*, to be the singleton nested relation, {t*}; this will be obvious from context. Correspondingly, we call a *null extended nested database*, d* = $\{r_1^*, r_2^*, \ldots, r_q^*\}$, over a NDS, **R**(F), simply a nested database.

In the special case when R(T) is a FRS, i.e., R(T) = Z(R(T)), we call the nested relation, r*, over R(T), a *null extended flat relation* or simply a *flat relation*. Correspondingly, in the special case when **R**(F) is a FDS, we call the nested database, d*, over **R**(F), a *null extended flat database*, or simply a *flat database*.

We now define the notion of equality between two null values and between a null value and a non-null value and then justify our definition.

Definition 3.3. When testing for equality of two values, v_1, v_2, be they values of zero order or higher order attributes, we consider the following rule, referred to as the *equality rule for nulls*:

(1) if one of v_1, v_2 is null and the other is non-null then $v_1 \neq v_2$;

(2) if both v_1, v_2 are null then $v_1 \neq v_2$.

An immediate consequence of the above equality rule for nulls is that we now have: *dne* ≠ *dne*, *unk* ≠ *unk*, *ni* ≠ *ni*, *unk** ≠ *unk** and *ni** ≠ *ni**. The above choice of equality rule for nulls can be justified as follows: when two null values of the same type appearing in a nested relation are updated they may be replaced by two distinct non-null values. In Roth et al. [1985] two nulls of type *dne* are considered equal, the justification being that *dne* is just another domain value. W.r.t. this type of null we justify our Definition 3.3, whence *dne* ≠ *dne*, by the fact that equality, namely, *dne* = *dne*, can be used to deduce semantic information in the nested database only via the null extended nested relational algebra and the null extended data dependencies defined in Section 3.2 and Chapter 4, respectively; however, we claim that the fact that a tuple contains a *dne* null value is not sufficient for deducing semantic information. We give two simple, yet striking, examples pertaining to this last argument.

Example 3.1. Assume that, STUDENT → DEPT, is a FD, i.e., each student is affiliated with only one department. Then, if we consider *dne* = *dne*, the relation shown in Figure 3.1 would violate this FD; however, since no student yet exists for the two departments, the FD, STUDENT → DEPT, ought not to be semantically violated.

STUDENT	DEPT
dne	CS
dne	philosophy

Fig. 3.1. An example using a FD to show the justification for *dne* ≠ *dne*.

Example 3.2. Let R_1 = {STUDENT, CLASS}, R_2 = {CLASS, TUTOR} and t_1, t_2 be tuples over, R_1 and R_2, respectively, as shown in Figure 3.2. If we join t_1 with t_2, we can deduce that Robert is Mark's tutor, if we were to assume that *dne* = *dne*; however, this deduction is obviously false, in general, since Mark may not enroll in any of the CLASSes for which Robert is a TUTOR.

R_1	STUDENT	CLASS
t_1	Mark	*dne*

R_2	CLASS	TUTOR
t_2	*dne*	Robert

Fig. 3.2. An example using the join to show the justification for *dne* ≠ *dne*.

If all the information in a tuple (subtuple) is missing, i.e., all the components of the tuple (subtuple) contain null values, then we call such a tuple (subtuple) a *null tuple* (*null subtuple*). In the sequel, we shall use the term *null tuple* in a generative sense, i.e., it will mean either a *null tuple* or a *null subtuple*. **We denote such a null tuple by** *null*, and take *null* over the NRS Λ to be equal to ∅. A null tuple containing only nulls of type, *ni*, is called a *ni-null tuple* and is denoted as *ni-null*. Similarly, a null tuple containing only nulls of type, *unk*, is called an *unk-null tuple* and is denoted as *unk-null*; likewise a null tuple containing only nulls of type *dne* is called a *dne-null tuple* and is denoted as *dne-null*. Regarding the higher order types of null we take *unk** to be *unk-null* and *ni** to be *ni-null*.

Incorporating the empty set into nested relations has been a controversial issue, as it was not clear (and still is up to this point!) what the result of unnesting the empty set should be. The problem arises in Schek [1985], where unnesting the empty set produces "undefined values" and in Kobayashi [1985], where unnesting the empty set results in an "unnatural null value". In Abiteboul & Bidoit [1986] the empty set is allowed only for higher order attributes and thus when the empty set is unnested the resulting tuples are removed; however, such an approach is unsatisfactory, since information is lost. Gyssens [1987] integrated the empty set formally into the nested relational model by considering it as an alternative to null values. The extended nested relational algebra of Gyssens [1987] provides operators to guarantee that no loss of information is incurred when manipulating nested relations which may contain the empty set.

In our model for nested relations we interpret the empty set, $\emptyset$, over Λ, as an "undefined nested relation". Thus there is no problem when nesting $\emptyset$, over Λ, which results in $\emptyset$, or when unnesting $\emptyset$, over Λ, which again results in $\emptyset$. For a non-empty NRS, say R(T), our semantic interpretation of the empty set, $\emptyset$, coincides with that of Makinouchi [1977], Abiteboul & Bidoit [1986], Lerat & Lipski [1986], Scholl [1986] and Gottlob & Zicari [1988], namely, we consider the semantics of the empty set to be "value does not exist", i.e., *dne-null*. Thus, we represent $\emptyset$ at the internal level of the nested relational database as *dne-null*, while at the external level of the user interface we maintain the symbol $\emptyset$.

We now further elaborate on our semantic interpretation of the empty set. Let $(A)^*$ $\in$ H(R(T)) be a higher order attribute, and let the empty set, $\emptyset$, be the $(A)^*$-value for a tuple, say t, over R(T), i.e., $t[(A)^*]$ is $\{dne\text{-}null\}$. When we null-extend UNNEST t, over $(A)^*$, we have that t[A] is *dne-null* and, conversely, when we null-extend NEST t, over $(A)^*$, we have that $t[((A)^*)^*]$ is $\{\{dne\text{-}null\}\}$. The justification for our approach is that it provides simple and clear semantics for the empty set, $\emptyset$, i.e., as the null tuple *dne-null*. In addition, the null extended NEST and null extended UNNEST operators, to be defined later in this section (see Definitions 3.6 and 3.7), handle all the types of null in a uniform fashion and in such a way so that no loss of information is incurred during a null extended NEST or null extended UNNEST operation as is the case with the standard NEST and standard UNNEST operators given in Definitions 2.8 and 2.9, respectively [Jaeschke & Schek 1982; Thomas & Fischer 1986; Van Gucht & Fischer 1988].

In order to define the relative information content of tuples, we define the *information lattice* [Zaniolo 1984; Roth et al. 1985; Levene & Loizou 1989a] over a null extended domain EDOM(A), where A is a zero order attribute. The information lattice, denoted as *inf(A)*, induces a partial order among the elements of EDOM(A) as shown in Figure 3.3.

We denote the *greatest lower bound* between two values v_1, $v_2 \in inf(A)$ by $glb(v_1, v_2)$. Since the bottom element of *inf(A)* is always *ni*, it follows that $glb(v_1, v_2)$ always *exists*. For example, let a, b $\in$ DOM(A), then $glb(a, dne) = ni$, $glb(a, unk) = unk$, $glb(unk, ni) = ni$, $glb(dne, unk) = ni$ and $glb(a, b) = unk$. We note that we do not consider the *least upper bound* between two values, since we are interested only in incomplete information and not in overdetermined information [Vassiliou 1979].

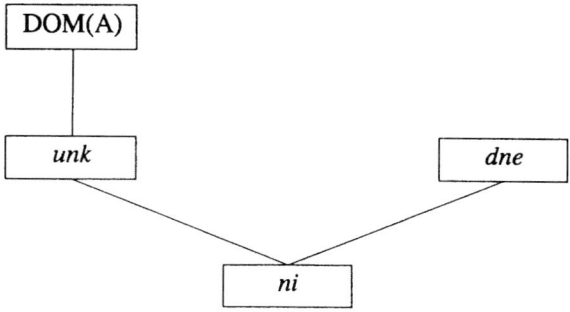

Fig. 3.3. The information lattice on EDOM(A).

We are now ready to introduce the notion of *more informative* tuples [Zaniolo 1984; Roth et al. 1985], which allows us to deduce the most information available from a given nested relation. As a result, we introduce a partial ordering, based upon the relative information content of the tuples in a nested relation. The concept of *more informative* tuples is synonymous with the concept of *subsumption* [Lien 1979, 1982; Maier 1983]. The following definition is from Zaniolo [1984] and is recast in the notation we use herein.

Definition 3.4. An X-value, t[X], of a tuple t is said to be *more informative* than a Y-value, w[Y], of a tuple w, when for each B ∈ Y, if w[B] is not *ni-null*, then B ∈ X and w[B] = glb(t[B], w[B]). If t[X] is *more informative* than w[Y], then w[Y] is said to be *less informative* than t[X].

The tuples t and w in the above definition may belong to the same flat relation or to different flat relations.

The next definition extends the notion of *more informative* tuples to nested relations (cf. [Roth et al. 1985]).

Definition 3.5. Let t_1, t_2 be tuples over the NRSs, $R(T_1)$ and $R(T_2)$, respectively. The tuple t_1 is said to be *more informative* than the tuple t_2, if

(1) for each B ∈ Z(R(T_2)), if t_2[B] is not *ni-null* then B ∈ Z(R(T_1)) and t_2[B] = glb(t_1[B], t_2[B]);

(2) for each C ∈ H(R(T_2)), if u_2 ∈ t_2[C] is a tuple which is not *ni-null*, then C ∈ H(R(T_1)) and there exists a tuple u_1 ∈ t_1[C] which is *more informative* than u_2.

We note that (1) of Definition 3.5 corresponds to the standard definition of a *more informative* tuple given in Definition 3.4. Furthermore, this definition applies also when $R(T_1) = R(T_2)$.

We call a flat relation from which we have removed all tuples which are *less informative* than other distinct tuples in that flat relation a *reduced relation* [Zaniolo 1984]. Correspondingly, a *reduced nested relation* is a nested relation from which we have removed all tuples (subtuples) which are *less informative* than other distinct tuples (subtuples) in that nested relation. If r* is a nested relation over R(T) then the corresponding *reduced nested relation* is denoted by $\{\hat{r^*}\}$ [Roth et al. 1985]. Hereafter, we assume that all nested relations (and thus also all flat relations), whether they be given or generated, are reduced. The *reduction* of r* is advantageous, since redundancy is removed and thus we get a compact representation of the relative information content of a nested relation containing null values. After reduction, each tuple in a nested relation can be identified uniquely. Reduction can also be viewed as a construct similar to that of removing duplicate tuples in nested relations (or flat relations, cf. [Date 1987c]) which contain no null values.

In the sequel, when a nested relation r_1 is *more informative* than, or *subsumes*, a nested relation r_2, i.e., for each tuple $t_2 \in r_2$ there exists a tuple $t_1 \in r_1$, which is *more informative* than t_2, then we shall signify this fact symbolically by $r_1 \geq r_2$ or $r_2 \leq r_1$. Correspondingly, $r_2 \geq r_1$ or $r_1 \leq r_2$ means that r_2 is *more informative* than r_1, or equivalently, that r_1 is *less informative* than r_2. If $r_1 \geq r_2$ and $r_1 \leq r_2$, then we say that r_1 and r_2 are *information-wise equivalent* [Roth et al. 1985] and write $r_1 \cong r_2$.

Example 3.3. Let r* be the nested relation shown in Figure 3.4; r* is not reduced, since $<b_1, null> \leq <b_1, c_1>$ and $<null, \{<b_1, c_1>\}> \leq <a_1, \{<b_1, c_1>\}>$ both hold. The reduction of r*, $\{\hat{r^*}\}$, is shown in Figure 3.5.

A	(B	C)*
	B	C
a_1	b_1	c_1
	b_1	*null*
null	b_1	c_1
null	b_2	c_1

Fig. 3.4. The non-reduced nested relation, r*.

A	(B	C)*
	B	C
a_1	b_1	c_1
null	b_2	c_1

Fig. 3.5. The reduced nested relation, $\{\hat{r^*}\}$.

3.1.2 Null Extended NEST and Null Extended UNNEST

In this subsection we discuss our approach to the null extended NEST and null extended UNNEST operators and give their formal definitions. Our definitions take into account the equality rule for nulls given in Definition 3.3. On the other hand, Roth et al. [1985] do not alter the definitions of standard NEST and standard UNNEST in the presence of nulls. Thus, for example, $v_B(r)$, where r is shown in Figure 3.6, results in r*, shown in Figure 3.7.

A	B
null	b_1
null	b_2

Fig. 3.6. The flat relation, r.

A	(B)*
	B
null	b_1
null	b_2

Fig. 3.7. The nested relation, $r^* \cong v_B(r)$, when nulls are not equated.

Correspondingly, we have $r \cong \mu_{(B)*}(r^*)$, for r* and r of Figures 3.7 and 3.6, respectively.

If we utilize information-wise equivalence, $\cong$, instead of equality, $=$, we can achieve a less redundant representation of $v_B(r)$, for r of Figure 3.6, which is shown in Figure 3.8 and which is denoted by r'*. Correspondingly, we have $r \cong \mu_{(B)*}(r'^*)$, for r'* of Figure 3.8 and r of Figure 3.6. We claim that r'* is a better representation of $v_B(r)$ for r of Figure 3.6, since $r'^* \geq r^*$ but $\neg(r^* \geq r'^*)$. Intuitively, this fact means that r'* contains the maximal information emanating from the corresponding flat relation, r. By using information-wise equivalence, $\cong$, in the definitions of the null extended NEST and the null extended UNNEST operators, we ensure that the standard property of the standard NEST and standard UNNEST operators, namely, $r^* \cong \mu_{(W)*}(v_W(r^*))$, where r* is a nested relation over a NRS, R(T), and $W \subseteq R(T)$, is preserved [Jaeschke & Schek 1982; Thomas & Fischer 1986; Van Gucht & Fischer 1988]. We note that, since we use unmarked nulls in our formalism of nulls, we expect the DBMS's internal representation of each type of null value to be a single unique value.

A	(B)*
	B
null	b_1
	b_2

Fig. 3.8. The nested relation, $r'^* \cong v_B(r)$, when information-wise equivalence is utilized.

Thus, in addition to the compactness referred to earlier, the DBMS can internally consider nulls as normal values when nesting and unnesting takes place, without the need to make special provision for the null extended NEST and the null extended UNNEST operators.

We observe that we do not disallow the representation of r* in Figure 3.7 as a nested relation, but rather that we consider its representation by r′* of Figure 3.8 to be preferable. Given the nested relation, r*, in Figure 3.7, it is possible to convert it to the nested relation, r′*, in Figure 3.8, without unnesting, by using the extended chase, defined in Section 4.5 (see the comments after Definition 4.12).

Roth et al. [1985] raise the question as to how to update a nested relation such as r′*, since it is not known whether the null is to be replaced by one value or more than one value, for each member of the higher attribute value. Our justification for the more compact and flexible representation of null extended nested relations is that for updates to be correct they must be specified precisely. For example, if in r′* the null value for A is to be replaced by the non-null value, say a_1, then the (B)*-values that are affected by this update must be specified. In Figure 3.9, we show the effect of such an update, where (B)* = $\{b_1\}$. We claim that a precise update specification must be given whether the updated value is null or non-null. This is due to the fact that nested relations contain more semantic information than their counterpart flat relations.

A	(B)*
	B
a_1	b_1
null	b_2

Fig. 3.9. r′* after an update of the *null* in Figure 3.8 with a_1, where (B)* = $\{b_1\}$.

We now give the formal definitions of the null extended NEST operator, denoted as ν, and of the null extended UNNEST operator, denoted as μ, by using information-wise equivalence instead of equality.

Definition 3.6. Let r* be a nested relation over R(T) and let $(Y \neq \Lambda) \subset R(T)$. $\nu_Y(r*)$ is a nested relation over (R(T) - Y)(Y)* such that a tuple $w \in \nu_Y(r*)$ iff

(1)   there exists a tuple $t \in r*$ such that $t[R(T) - Y] \cong w[R(T) - Y]$;

(2) $w[(Y)*] \cong \{t'[Y] | t' \in r*$ and $t'[R(T) - Y] \cong w[R(T) - Y]\}$.

We have excluded the case when $Y = \Lambda$, i.e., $\nu_\Lambda(r*)$, since as we have noted in Subsection 2.2.1 we do not retain empty subtrees in scheme trees. Furthermore, when Y = R(T), we take $\nu_{R(T)}(r*)$ as modifying only the NRS associated with r*, i.e., we define $\nu_{R(T)}(r*) \cong r*$ to be a nested relation over the NRS, $\Lambda(R(T))*$. Thus, at times, we can consider the NRS, R(T), to be equivalent to the NRS, $\Lambda(R(T))*$, since for a nested relation, over R(T), there always exists an information-wise equivalent nested relation over $\Lambda(R(T))*$. ($\nu_{R(T)}(r*) \cong r*$.)

Definition 3.7. Let r* be a nested relation over R(T) and let $(Y)* \in H(R(T))$. $\mu_{(Y)*}(r*)$ is a nested relation over (R(T) - (Y)*)Y such that a tuple $t \in \mu_{(Y)*}(r*)$ iff there exists a tuple $w \in r^*$ such that $t[R(T) - (Y)^*] \cong w[R(T) - (Y)^*]$ and $t[Y] \in w[(Y)^*]$.

We note that the definition of the null extended UNNEST* operator remains the same as that of the UNNEST* operator defined in Subsection 2.2.2, and that we modify Definition 2.10 of a nested flat relation to employ information-wise equivalence instead of equality. We stress at this point that the implementation of the null extended NEST and the null extended UNNEST operators is the same as that of the standard NEST and standard UNNEST operators given in Definitions 2.8 and 2.9, respectively, although in the definitions of the former we use information-wise equivalence, $\cong$, instead of equality, $=$. This is due to the fact that unmarked nulls can be represented by a unique value in the DBMS for each type of null value, and thus in the implementation of the null extended NEST and null extended UNNEST operators, the different types of null values can be treated as any other domain value. From now on, for the sake of not overburdening the reader, we shall simply call the null extended NEST, NEST, the null extended UNNEST, UNNEST, and the null extended UNNEST*, UNNEST*.

Example 3.4. Let r be the flat relation over ABC, shown in Figure 3.10. Then, $r^* \cong \nu_C(r)$ is the nested relation, r^*, over AB(C)*, shown in Figure 3.11, and $\mu_{(C)^*}(r^*)$ is the flat relation, shown in Figure 3.10.

A	B	C
a_1	b_1	c_1
a_1	b_1	c_2
null	b_2	c_2
null	b_2	c_3
a_2	null	c_1
null	null	c_4
null	null	c_5

Fig. 3.10. The flat relation, $r \cong \mu_{(C)^*}(r^*)$, of Example 3.4.

For the nested relation r_1^* of the running example, shown in Figure 2.8, we have the flat relation, $\mu^*(r_1^*)$, which is shown in Figure 3.12.

3.2 The Null Extended Nested Relational Algebra

In this section we present the null extended nested relational algebra (or hereinafter simply the null extended algebra) for the null extended nested relational model. We recall that the NEST and UNNEST operators of the null extended algebra were defined in the previous section while the remaining operators of the null extended algebra are defined in this section. The null extended algebra is a *complete algebra* in the sense of Codd [1970, 1979], Ullman [1982a] and Maier [1983], i.e., it includes null extended versions of the

A	B	(C)*
		C
a_1	b_1	c_1
		c_2
null	b_2	c_2
		c_3
a_2	null	c_1
null	null	c_4
		c_5

Fig. 3.11. The nested relation, $r^* \cong v_C(r)$, of Example 3.4.

STUDENT	DEPT	MAJOR	CLASS	EXAM	PROJECT
Iris	CS	computing	databases	mid	1NF
Iris	CS	computing	databases	final	1NF
Iris	CS	computing	programming	final	null
Mark	CS	maths	databases	final	NF2
Mark	CS	maths	databases	final	UR
David	philosophy	logic	first-order	mid	prolog
null	philosophy	null	null	final	null
null	philosophy	null	first-order	null	functions
null	philosophy	null	first-order	null	predicates
Naomi	null	languages	french	mid	null
Naomi	null	languages	null	final	Moscow
Naomi	null	languages	hebrew	null	Genesis

Fig. 3.12. The flat relation $\mu^*(r_1^*)$.

flat relational algebra operators: union, difference, cartesian product, projection, selection and renaming. The inclusion of the NEST and UNNEST operators in the null extended algebra extends the expressive power of the algebra by providing the notion of a *complete extended algebra* in the context of nested relations [Gyssens 1987; Van Gucht 1987] (cf. [Abiteboul et al. 1989a]). Additionally, the null extended algebra includes null extended versions of total projection, (natural) join, intersection and outer join [Codd 1979; Bullers 1987; Date 1987b; Jajodia & Springsteel 1987]. For all the operators of the null extended algebra defined in this section, which have standard counterparts in the flat relational algebra, we investigate how reasonable they are by showing whether or not they are *faithful* and *precise* (cf. [Maier 1983; Roth et al. 1985]) as defined in Subsection 3.2.1.

Recently many extended algebras have been suggested for the nested relational model [Jaeschke & Schek 1982; Jaeschke 1985a, 1985b; Schek 1985; Roth et al. 1985, 1988; Abiteboul & Bidoit 1986; Schek & Scholl 1986; Thomas & Fischer 1986; Bidoit 1987; Deshpande & Larson 1987; Gyssens 1987; Gyssens & Van Gucht 1987, 1988; Houben & Paredaens 1987; Ozsoyoglu et al. 1987; Van Gucht 1987; Van Gucht & Fischer 1988; Colby 1989; Levene & Loizou 1989a]. In order to categorize the various proposed extended algebras, we distinguish between two different characteristics of an extended algebra for the nested relational model.

The first characteristic is whether an extended algebra is *recursive* or *non-recursive*. An extended algebra is *recursive* if expressions of the extended algebra can be constructed recursively, i.e., whenever an attribute appears in an extended algebraic expression, another extended algebraic expression, called a *nested expression*, may appear. Otherwise, an extended algebra is *non-recursive*. Of the above extended algebras, those in [Jaeschke 1985b; Schek 1985; Schek & Scholl 1986; Deshpande & Larson 1987; Colby 1989] are recursive and allow such constructs as nested projection and nested selection, whilst the rest of the said extended algebras are non-recursive.

The second characteristic is whether an extended algebra is *minimal* or *maximal*. An extended algebra is *minimal* if it consists of the flat relational algebra, extended in a natural way to nested relations, i.e., tuples are considered as indivisible units. On the other hand, if some or all of the operators of the flat relational algebra are extended to take advantage of the nested structure of tuples in nested relations then the extended algebra is *maximal*. Of the above extended algebras, those in [Jaeschke 1985a, 1985b; Roth et al. 1985, 1988; Schek 1985; Abiteboul & Bidoit 1986; Schek & Scholl 1986; Bidoit 1987; Deshpande & Larson 1987; Houben & Paredaens 1987; Colby 1989] are maximal whilst the rest of the said extended algebras are minimal.

All the said extended algebras, whether they be minimal or maximal, are augmented with the two restructuring operators NEST and UNNEST. We note that recursive extended algebras are always maximal while minimal extended algebras are always non-recursive. The extended algebra for null extended nested relations defined hereafter, denoted as the *null extended algebra*, is non-recursive and maximal as are the extended algebras of Jaeschke [1985a], Roth et al. [1985, 1988], Abiteboul & Bidoit [1986], Bidoit [1987] and Houben & Paredaens [1987].

The main advantage of recursive extended algebras over non-recursive extended algebras is that they take into account the recursive structure of nested relations in a natural way. On the other hand, non-recursive extended algebras may prove easier to use since their expressions are constructed in the same way as those of the flat relational algebra. Correspondingly, the main advantage of minimal extended algebras over maximal extended algebras is that the semantics of the operators of the former are well known and well understood and the definitions of the operators are relatively simple. On the other hand, maximal extended algebras are much more flexible than minimal extended algebras in that they allow us to interact with the structure of nested relations directly and in a more natural way than is the case with minimal extended algebras.

3.2.1 Faithful and Precise Null Extended Operators

In order to ascertain if our null extended algebra is reasonable, we use the notions of *faithfulness* and *preciseness* (cf. [Maier 1983; Roth et al. 1985]). A null extended operator is *faithful* if it gives the same result, when operating on flat relations, as the corresponding standard operator. A null extended operator is *precise* if unnesting the result, after having applied the null extended operator, gives the same result as first unnesting and then applying the corresponding standard operator to the resulting flat relation(s).

Let op be a standard operator and op^{ne} be the corresponding null extended operator. The formal definitions of faithfulness and preciseness now follow.

Definition 3.8. We say that op^{ne} is *faithful* to op if one of the following two conditions holds:

(1)   when op and op^{ne} are unary operators, $op(r) \cong op^{ne}(r)$, for every flat relation, r, for which $op(r)$ is defined;

(2)   when op and op^{ne} are binary operators, $r \; op \; s \cong r \; op^{ne} \; s$, for all flat relations, r and s, for which $r \; op \; s$ is defined.

Definition 3.9. We say that op^{ne} is a *precise* generalization of op relative to unnesting (or simply op^{ne} is a *precise* generalization of op) if one of the following two conditions holds:

(1)   when op and op^{ne} are unary operators, $\mu^*(op^{ne}(r^*)) \cong op(\mu^*(r^*))$, for every nested relation, r^*, for which $op^{ne}(r^*)$ is defined;

(2)   when op and op^{ne} are binary operators, $\mu^*(r^* \; op^{ne} \; s^*) \cong \mu^*(r^*) \; op \; \mu^*(s^*)$, for all nested relations, r^* and s^*, for which $r^* \; op^{ne} \; s^*$ is defined.

Although the null extended algebra is a maximal extended algebra, we define the null extended union and null extended difference operators in a minimal way. That is, they correspond naturally to the standard union and difference operators whereby tuples in a nested relation are considered as indivisible units. The rest of the operators of the null extended algebra, to be defined in this section, are defined in a maximal way, i.e., they take into account the structure of tuples in a nested relation. That is, their definitions are the same as those of the standard relational algebra operators when applied to flat relations over zero order attributes; however, these definitions are applied recursively to the higher order attribute values of a nested relation until they reduce to their zero order counterparts.

Our motivation for defining the null extended algebra in the above manner is that when querying the nested database the user need not know the details of the structure of the NDS. Thus, using the null extended algebra should not be substantially more difficult than using the standard relational algebra. For this reason the null extended algebra will serve us well in defining the nested UR model.

3.2.2 Null Extended Union and Null Extended Difference

We begin by defining the *null extended union* operator, $\cup^{ne}$, which, intuitively, returns the union of two nested relations when tuples are considered as indivisible units.

Definition 3.10. The *null extended union*, $\cup^{ne}$, of two nested relations, r_1 and r_2, over R(T), is defined by

$$r_1 \cup^{ne} r_2 \cong \hat{\{} \; t \mid t \in r_1 \text{ or } t \in r_2 \; \hat{\}}.$$

(Cf. Zaniolo [1984], Roth et al. [1985, 1988], Thomas & Fischer [1986], Van Gucht [1987], Gyssens [1987], Van Gucht & Fischer [1988] and Levene & Loizou [1989a].)

Example 3.5. Let R(T) = A(B)*(C)*(D(E)*)* be a NRS and let r_1, r_2 be two nested relations over R(T) shown, respectively, in Figures 3.13 and 3.14. The null extended union, r* $\cong r_1 \cup^{ne} r_2$, is shown in Figure 3.15. We note that r* is not a hierarchical relation, since r* is not a nested flat relation; in addition, it can be verified that $\mu^*(r^*)$ does not satisfy MVD(T).

A	(B)*	(C)*	(D	(E)*)*
	B	C	D	(E)*
				E
a_1	b_1	c_1	d_1	*null*
	b_2			
a_1	b_3	*null*	d_2	e_1
a_2	*null*	c_2	*null*	e_1
			d_2	e_2
null	b_2	c_2	*null*	e_2

Fig. 3.13. The nested relation r_1.

A	(B)*	(C)*	(D	(E)*)*
	B	C	D	(E)*
				E
a_1	b_2	c_1	d_1	*null*
a_1	b_3	*null*	d_2	e_1
null	b_2	c_2	d_2	e_1
			d_2	e_2

Fig. 3.14. The nested relation r_2.

Proposition 3.1. The null extended union operator, $\cup^{ne}$, is *faithful* to the standard union operator, $\cup$.

A	(B)*	(C)*	(D	(E)*)*
	B	C	D	(E)*
				E
a_1	b_1	c_1	d_1	null
	b_2			
a_1	b_3	null	d_2	e_1
a_2	null	c_2	null	e_1
			d_2	e_2
null	b_2	c_2	d_2	e_1
			d_2	e_2

Fig. 3.15. The nested relation $r* \cong r_1 \cup^{ne} r_2$.

Proof. It follows directly from Definition 3.10. □

The next theorem shows that the null extended union operator is a precise generalization of the standard union operator.

Theorem 3.2. Let r_1 and r_2 be two nested relations over a NRS R(T). Then the null extended union operator, $\cup^{ne}$, is a *precise* generalization of the standard union operator, $\cup$, in the sense that $\mu*(r_1 \cup^{ne} r_2) \cong \mu*(r_1) \cup \mu*(r_2)$.

Proof. We prove the result by induction on HEIGHT(T).

BASIS. If HEIGHT(T) = 0, then r_1 and r_2 are flat relations and thus $\mu*(r_1) \cong r_1$ and $\mu*(r_2) \cong r_2$. The result now follows, since, by Proposition 3.1, $\cup^{ne}$ is faithful to $\cup$, thus $\mu*(r_1 \cup^{ne} r_2) \cong r_1 \cup^{ne} r_2 \cong r_1 \cup r_2$.

INDUCTION. Assume the result holds for HEIGHT(T) = n, we then need to prove that the result holds for HEIGHT(T) = n+1. Let r'_1 and r'_2 be the resulting nested relations over, say R(T'), after unnesting r_1 and r_2, respectively, over all the attributes in H(R(T)). We now have HEIGHT(T') = n, so, by inductive hypothesis,

$$\mu*(r'_1 \cup^{ne} r'_2) \cong \mu*(r'_1) \cup \mu*(r'_2).$$

Furthermore, since $\mu*(r_1) \cong \mu*(r'_1)$ and $\mu*(r_2) \cong \mu*(r'_2)$, it only remains to show that

$$\mu*(r_1 \cup^{ne} r_2) \cong \mu*(r'_1 \cup^{ne} r'_2).$$

Let $t_1 \in r_1$ and $t_2 \in r_2$. Furthermore, we let t'_1 and t'_2 be the resulting nested relations after unnesting the tuples, t_1 and t_2, respectively, over all the attributes in H(R(T)). We have that $\mu*(t_1) \cong \mu*(t'_1)$ and $\mu*(t_2) \cong \mu*(t'_2)$. In order to conclude the proof we have to show that

$$\mu*(t_1 \cup^{ne} t_2) \cong \mu*(t'_1 \cup^{ne} t'_2).$$

Let $t \in \mu^*(t_1 \cup^{ne} t_2)$. Then, by Definition 3.10, $t \in \mu^*(t_1)$ or $t \in \mu^*(t_2)$. It, therefore, follows that $t \in \mu^*(t'_1)$ or $t \in \mu^*(t'_2)$, proving that

$$\mu^*(t_1 \cup^{ne} t_2) \leq \mu^*(t'_1 \cup^{ne} t'_2).$$

Now, let $t' \in \mu^*(t'_1 \cup^{ne} t'_2)$. Then, by Definition 3.10, $t' \in \mu^*(t'_1)$ or $t' \in \mu^*(t'_2)$. It, therefore, follows that $t' \in \mu^*(t_1)$ or $t' \in \mu^*(t_2)$, proving that

$$\mu^*(t_1 \cup^{ne} t_2) \geq \mu^*(t'_1 \cup^{ne} t'_2),$$

which concludes the proof. $\square$

Example 3.6. It can easily be verified that for the nested relations, r_1, r_2, shown in Figures 3.13 and 3.14, respectively, the result of Theorem 3.2 holds, i.e., $\mu^*(r_1 \cup^{ne} r_2) \cong \mu^*(r_1) \cup \mu^*(r_2)$, where $r_1 \cup^{ne} r_2$ is shown in Figure 3.15.

In formalizing the nested UR model we do not require the *null extended difference operator*, $-^{ne}$, but in order that the null extended algebra be complete, we now give its definition. Intuitively, the null extended difference, $r_1 -^{ne} r_2$, of two nested relations, r_1 and r_2, returns the tuples of r_1, which are not less informative than any of the tuples in r_2.

Definition 3.11. The *null extended difference*, $-^{ne}$, of two nested relations, r_1 and r_2, over R(T), is defined by

$$r_1 -^{ne} r_2 \cong \hat{\{} \; t \mid t \in r_1 \text{ and for all } t' \in r_2 \; \neg(t \leq t') \; \hat{\}}.$$

(Cf. Zaniolo [1984], Roth et al. [1985, 1988], Thomas & Fischer [1986], Van Gucht [1987], Gyssens [1987], Van Gucht & Fischer [1988] and Levene & Loizou [1989a].)

Proposition 3.3. The null extended difference operator, $-^{ne}$, is *faithful* to the standard difference operator, $-$.

Proof. It follows directly from Definition 3.11. $\square$

The next proposition shows that the null extended difference operator is *not* a precise generalization of the standard difference operator.

Proposition 3.4. Let r_1 and r_2 be two nested relations over a NRS, R(T). Then the null extended difference operator, $-^{ne}$, is not a *precise* generalization of the standard difference operator, $-$, namely, $\neg(\mu^*(r_1 -^{ne} r_2) \cong \mu^*(r_1) - \mu^*(r_2))$.

Proof. Let r_1 and r_2 be the nested relations over A(B)*(C)*(D(E)*)*, shown in Figures 3.13 and 3.14, respectively. Also, let $r^* \cong r_1 -^{ne} r_2$ be the nested relation shown in Figure 3.16. Then, it can easily be verified that $\neg(\mu^*(r^*) \cong \mu^*(r_1) - \mu^*(r_2))$, since the tuple $<a_1, b_2, c_1, d_1, null>$ is in $\mu^*(r^*)$ but not in $\mu^*(r_1) - \mu^*(r_2)$. $\square$

We note that the difficulty in obtaining a preciseness result for $-^{ne}$ in the general case is due to the fact that difference is a non-monotone operator [Levene & Loizou 1989a].

A	(B)*	(C)*	(D	(E)*)*
	B	C	D	(E)*
				E
a_1	b_1	c_1	d_1	null
	b_2			
a_2	null	c_2	null	e_1
			d_2	e_2

Fig. 3.16. The nested relation $r^* \cong r_1 -^{ne} r_2$.

3.2.3 Null Extended Projection in Nested Relations

In this subsection we first define the projection of a NRS, R(T), onto a subset of its associated set of attributes, S(T); we call the result a *projected NRS*. We then extend the standard projection operator, defined over flat relations, to the *null extended projection* operator, denoted as Π^{ne}, defined over nested relations. In the nested UR model we are, in general, interested in total tuples over a subset of zero order attributes, $Y \subseteq S(T)$. Thus, we also define the *null extended total projection* operator, $\Pi^{ne}\downarrow$, which filters out from a nested relation those tuples, which are not Y-total.

We begin by defining a projected NRS.

Definition 3.12. A *projected NRS*, R(T′), of R(T) is defined recursively by

(1)   if T′ = $\emptyset$, then R(T′) is a projected NRS of R(T);

(2)   if R(T) = X(R(T_1))*(R(T_2))* ... (R(T_s))*, where X = ATT(ROOT(T)), T_1, T_2, ..., T_s, s ≥ 1, denote the first level subtrees of the scheme tree T and R($T′_1$), R($T′_2$), ..., R($T′_s$) are projected NRSs of R(T_1), R(T_2), ..., R(T_s), respectively, then Y(R($T′_1$))*(R($T′_2$))* ... (R($T′_s$))* is a projected NRS of R(T), with Y ⊆ X.

(Cf. Bidoit [1987].)

We observe that in the above definition we include the case where Y = Λ; we further remark that the empty string, Λ, over the empty set of attributes, $\emptyset$, is retained in the representation of R(T′) only when it is the root of a projected NRS which has at least one non-empty subtree. For this reason *projected NRSs* are more general than the *projected formats* of Bidoit [1987], since no restrictions are placed on the set of attributes Y ⊆ S(T) over which the projection takes place.

Next we define a useful syntax for projected NRSs.

Definition 3.13. Given a NRS, R(T), and a set of attributes X ⊆ S(T), the projection of R(T) onto X, denoted by R(T)[X], is defined by

```
R(T)[X] = R(T'), where R(T') is a projected NRS of R(T)
```
and S(T') = X.

It can easily be seen that R(T)[X] is unique, and also that if $Y \subseteq X$, then (R(T)[X])[Y] is unique, i.e., R(T)[Y] = (R(T)[X])[Y]. The next example illustrates Definitions 3.12 and 3.13.

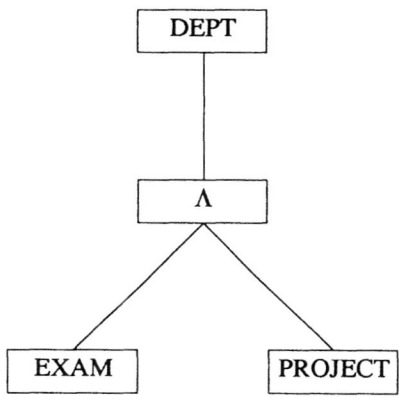

Fig. 3.17. T_1 projected onto {DEPT, EXAM, PROJECT}.

Example 3.7. Let R(T'_1) be the projection of R(T_1), where T_1 is shown in Figure 2.3, onto {DEPT, EXAM, PROJECT}, i.e., R(T'_1) = R(T_1)[{DEPT, EXAM, PROJECT}]. Then, R(T'_1) = DEPT(Λ (EXAM)* (PROJECT)*)*, where T'_1 is shown in Figure 3.17.

We are now ready to define the *null extended projection* operator, Π^{ne}. Given a nested relation r* over a NRS, R(T), Π^{ne}_Y(r*), where $Y \subseteq S(T)$, intuitively returns the largest subset of r*, over a projected NRS of R(T), R(T'), with S(T') = Y, such that it contains only tuples of the form t[Y], where $t \in$ r*.

Definition 3.14. Let R(T') be a projected NRS of R(T) over $Y \subseteq S(T)$, and let r* be a nested relation over R(T). Then the *null extended projection* of r* onto Y, Π^{ne}_Y(r*), is a nested relation, over R(T'), defined recursively by

(1) if T consists of a single node and ATT(ROOT(T)) = X,
```
    then
    Π^ne_Y (r*) ≅ ⌃{ t[Y] | t ∈ r* }, where Y ⊆ X;
```

(2) if R(T) = X(R(T_1))*(R(T_2))* ... (R(T_s))*, where X = ATT(ROOT(T)) and T_1, T_2, ..., T_s, s ≥ 1, denote the first level subtrees of T, let R(T') = X'(R(T'_1))*(R(T'_2))* ... (R(T'_w))*, where X' = ATT(ROOT(T')) and w ≤ s, be a projected NRS of R(T). Then,
```
    Π^ne_Y (r*) ≅ ⌃{ t | there exists t' ∈ r* and t[X'] ≅ t'[X'] and
```

for all j ∈ {1,2,...,w}, if R(T'_j) is the
projected NRS of R(T_i), i ∈ {1,2,...,s}, then
t[(R(T'_j))*] ≅ $\Pi^{ne}_{S(T'_j)}$(t'[(R(T_i))*]) }.

(Cf. Abiteboul & Bidoit [1987] and Bidoit [1987].)

We note that (1) of Definition 3.14 corresponds to the definition of the standard projection operator for flat relations found in Zaniolo [1984].

Let r* be a nested relation over a NRS, R(T), and let t be a tuple of r*. We extend the definition of the Y-value of t, t[Y], where Y ⊆ S(T), by

t[Y] ≅ Π^{ne}_Y(t).

Thus, t[Y] is a nested relation over a projected NRS, say R(T'), of R(T), with Y ⊆ S(T). On the other hand, if Y ⊆ R(T), then t[Y] is the restriction of t to Y.

Λ	(CLASS	(EXAM)*	(PROJECT)*)*
	CLASS	(EXAM)*	(PROJECT)*
		EXAM	PROJECT
	databases	mid final	1NF
	programming	final	*null*
	databases	final	NF2 UR
	first-order	mid	prolog
	null	mid final	*null*
	first-order	*null*	functions predicates
	french	mid	*null*
	null	final	Moscow
	hebrew	*null*	Genesis

Fig. 3.18. The nested relation r'* ≅ $\Pi^{ne}_{CLASS\ EXAM\ PROJECT}$($r_1^*$).

Example 3.8. Let Y = {CLASS, EXAM, PROJECT}. For r_1^* of Figure 2.8, we obtain the nested relation, r'* ≅ $\Pi^{ne}_{(CLASS\ EXAM\ PROJECT)}$($r_1^*$), over the projected NRS, R(T') = R(T_1)[{CLASS, EXAM, PROJECT}], as shown in Figure 3.18. We note that $\Pi^{ne}_{(CLASS\ EXAM\ PROJECT)}$($r_1^*$) is not a hierarchical relation, since r'* is not a nested flat relation; in addition, it can be verified that μ*(r'*) does not satisfy MVD(T').

Proposition 3.5. The null extended projection operator, Π^{ne}, is *faithful* to the standard projection operator, Π.

Proof. It follows from (1) of Definition 3.14. □

We now show that the null extended projection operator is a precise generalization of the standard projection operator.

Theorem 3.6. Let r^* be a nested relation over a NRS, $R(T)$, and let $R(T')$ be the projected NRS of $R(T)$ over $Y \subseteq S(T)$. The null extended projection operator, Π^{ne}, is a *precise* generalization of the standard projection operator, Π, in the sense that $\mu^*(\Pi^{ne}{}_Y(r^*)) \cong \Pi_Y(\mu^*(r^*))$.

Proof. We prove the result by induction on HEIGHT(T).

BASIS. If HEIGHT(T) = 0, then r^* is a flat relation and thus $\mu^*(r^*) \cong r^*$. The result now follows, since, by Proposition 3.5, Π^{ne} is faithful to Π and thus we have $\mu^*(\Pi^{ne}{}_Y(r^*)) \cong \Pi^{ne}{}_Y(r^*) \cong \Pi_Y(r^*)$ as required.

INDUCTION. Assume the result holds for HEIGHT(T) = n, we then need to prove that the result holds for HEIGHT(T) = n+1. Let r'^* be the resulting nested relation over, say $R(T^*)$, after the unnesting of r^* over all the attributes in $H(R(T))$, and let $R(T'^*)$ be the projected NRS of $R(T^*)$ over $Y \subseteq S(T^*)$. We now have HEIGHT(T*) = n, so, by inductive hypothesis,

$$\mu^*(\Pi^{ne}{}_Y(r'^*)) \cong \Pi_Y(\mu^*(r'^*)).$$

Furthermore, since $\mu^*(r^*) \cong \mu^*(r'^*)$, it only remains to show that

$$\mu^*(\Pi^{ne}{}_Y(r^*)) \cong \mu^*(\Pi^{ne}{}_Y(r'^*)).$$

Let $Z(R(T)) = X$ and $H(R(T)) = \{(R(T_1))^*, (R(T_2))^*, ..., (R(T_s))^*\}$, where T_1, T_2, ..., T_s, $s \geq 1$, denote the first level subtrees of the scheme tree T. Also, for $R(T')$, the projected NRS of $R(T)$ over $Y \subseteq S(T)$, we let $Z(R(T')) = X'$ and $H(R(T')) = \{(R(T'_1))^*, (R(T'_2))^*, ..., (R(T'_w))^*\}$, with $w \leq s$, where T'_1, T'_2, ..., T'_w denote the first level subtrees of the scheme tree T'. Now, let $t \in r^*$ and let z' be the resulting nested relation after unnesting the tuple, t, over all the attributes in $H(R(T))$. Thus, we have that $t[X] \cong z'[X]$ and $t[(R(T_i))^*] \cong z'[R(T_i)]$, $1 \leq i \leq s$. In order to conclude the proof we need to show that

$$\mu^*(\Pi^{ne}{}_Y(t)) \cong \mu^*(\Pi^{ne}{}_Y(z')).$$

We establish this by tracing the recursion step in the computation of $\Pi^{ne}{}_Y(t)$, i.e., (2) of Definition 3.14. The result now follows, since it is true that

$$\Pi^{ne}{}_{X'}(t) \cong \Pi^{ne}{}_{X'}(z'),$$

and for all $j \in \{1,2,...,w\}$, if $R(T'_j)$ is the projected NRS of $R(T_i)$, $i \in \{1,2,...,s\}$, then it is also true that

$$\Pi^{ne}{}_{S(T'_j)}(t[(R(T_i))^*]) \cong \Pi^{ne}{}_{S(T'_j)}(z'[R(T_i)]). \;\square$$

Example 3.9. It can easily be verified that the result of Theorem 3.6 holds for $r'^* \cong \Pi^{ne}{}_{(CLASS\ EXAM\ PROJECT)}(r_1^*)$, shown in Figure 3.18; that is, $\mu^*(r'^*) \cong \Pi_{(CLASS\ EXAM\ PROJECT)}(\mu^*(r_1^*))$, holds.

The next definition extends the concept of X-total tuples (for flat relations), given in Definition 2.13, to nested relations. Let r* be a nested relation over R(T) and t ∈ r*. Informally, the *definite portion* of t, DEF(t), returns a set of attributes in S(T) for which the tuple, t, has no null values in its corresponding attributes in R(T). Let X ⊆ S(T), then we say that the tuple, t, is X-total iff X ⊆ DEF(t).

Definition 3.15. Let r* be a nested relation over a NRS, R(T). Then, for t ∈ r*, DEF(t) is defined recursively by

(1) if the scheme tree T consists of a single node, n, and ATT(n) = X, then
DEF(t) = {A | A ∈ X **and** ¬(t[A] ≅ *null*)};

(2) if X = ATT(ROOT(T)) and $T_1, T_2, \ldots, T_s$, s ≥ 1, denote the first level subtrees of the scheme tree, T, then
DEF(t) = DEF(t[X]) ∪ (∪ $_{i=1}^{s}$ {∩ DEF(t') | t' ∈ t[(R(T_i))*]}).

(Cf. Levene & Loizou [1988].)

We note that (1) of this definition corresponds to the standard definition of X-total tuples for flat relations (see Definition 2.13).

Example 3.10. Consider the nested relation $r_1^* ≅ \{t_1, t_2, t_3, t_4, t_5\}$, over R($T_1$), of the running example. For the first tuple, t_1, we have DEF(t_1) = {STUDENT, DEPT, MAJOR, CLASS, EXAM}, since t_1[(PROJECT)*] contains a null value. Thus t_1 is {STUDENT, DEPT, MAJOR, CLASS, EXAM}-total. For the second and third tuples, we have DEF(t_2) = DEF(t_3) = S(T_1), since there are no null values in either t_2 or t_3. Thus t_2 and t_3 are both S(T_1)-total. For the tuple, t_4, we have DEF(t_4) = {DEPT}, since DEPT is the only attribute over which t_4 has no null values. Thus t_4 is DEPT-total. Finally, for the tuple, t_5, we have DEF(t_5) = {STUDENT, MAJOR}, since STUDENT and MAJOR are the only attributes over which t_5 has no null values. Thus t_5 is {STUDENT, MAJOR}-total.

We now define the *null extended total projection*, denoted as $\Pi^{ne}\downarrow$. Given a nested relation r* over a NRS, R(T), $\Pi^{ne}\downarrow_Y(r^*)$, where Y ⊆ S(T), intuitively returns the largest subset of r*, over a projected NRS, of R(T), R(T'), with S(T') = Y, such that it contains only Y-total tuples.

Definition 3.16. Let R(T') be a projected NRS of R(T) over Y ⊆ S(T) and let r* be a nested relation over R(T). Then the *null extended total projection* of r* onto Y, $\Pi^{ne}\downarrow_Y(r^*)$, is a nested relation, over R(T'), defined recursively by

(1) if T consists of a single node and ATT(ROOT(T)) = X (≠ Λ), then
$\Pi^{ne}\downarrow_Y(r^*)$ = { t[Y] | t ∈ r* **and** DEF(t) = Y = S(T') };

(2) if R(T) = X(R(T_1))*(R(T_2))* ... (R(T_s))*, where X = ATT(ROOT(T)) and $T_1, T_2, \ldots, T_s$, s ≥ 1, denote the first

```
level  subtrees  of  T,  let  R(T′)  =  X′(R(T′₁))*(R(T′₂))*  ...
(R(T′w))*,  where  X′  =  ATT(ROOT(T′))  and  w ≤ s,  be a pro-
jected  NRS  of  R(T).  Then,
Πⁿᵉ↓Y(r*) = { t | there exists t′ ∈ r* and t[X′] = t′[X′] and
    for all j ∈ {1,2,...,w}, if R(T′ⱼ) is the
    projected NRS of R(Tᵢ), i ∈ {1,2,...,s}, then
    t[(R(T′ⱼ))*] = Πⁿᵉ↓S(T′ⱼ)(t′[(R(Tᵢ))*]) and
    DEF(t) = Y = S(T′) }.
```

(Cf. Levene & Loizou [1988].)

An immediate consequence of the above definition is that for all t ∈ $\Pi^{ne}\downarrow_Y(r^*)$, DEF(t) = Y = S(T′). We further note that (1) of Definition 3.16 corresponds to the definition of the standard total projection for flat relations (see Definition 2.14).

The following proposition shows that when a nested relation contains no null values then the null extended total projection reduces to the null extended projection. This result follows immediately from Definition 3.16.

Proposition 3.7. Let r*, a nested relation over a NRS, R(T), be such that all the tuples, t ∈ r*, are S(T)-total. Then, for any set of attributes, Y ⊆ S(T), $\Pi^{ne}_Y(r^*) = \Pi^{ne}\downarrow_Y(r^*)$. □

Proposition 3.8. The null extended total projection operator, $\Pi^{ne}\downarrow$, is *faithful* to the standard total projection operator, $\Pi\downarrow$.

Proof. It follows from (1) of Definition 3.16. □

The next theorem shows that the null extended total projection is a precise generalization of the standard total projection operator. We note that its proof follows an argument very similar to that of the proof of Theorem 3.6.

Theorem 3.9. Let r* be a nested relation over a NRS, R(T), and let R(T′) be the projected NRS of R(T) over Y ⊆ S(T). The null extended total projection operator, $\Pi^{ne}\downarrow$, is a *precise* generalization of the standard total projection operator, $\Pi\downarrow$, in the sense that $\mu^*(\Pi^{ne}\downarrow_Y(r^*)) \cong \Pi\downarrow_Y(\mu^*(r^*))$.

Proof. We prove the result by induction on HEIGHT(T).

BASIS. If HEIGHT(T) = 0, then r* is a flat relation and thus $\mu^*(r^*) \cong r^*$. The result now follows, since, by Proposition 3.8, $\Pi^{ne}\downarrow$ is faithful to $\Pi\downarrow$ and thus we have $\mu^*(\Pi^{ne}\downarrow_Y(r^*)) \cong \Pi^{ne}\downarrow_Y(r^*) \cong \Pi\downarrow_Y(r^*)$ as required.

INDUCTION. Assume the result holds for HEIGHT(T) = n, we then need to prove that the result holds for HEIGHT(T) = n+1. Let r′* be the resulting nested relation over, say R(T*), after the unnesting of r* over all the attributes in H(R(T)), and let R(T′*) be the projected NRS of R(T*) over Y ⊆ S(T*). We now have HEIGHT(T*) = n, so, by inductive hypothesis,

$$\mu^*(\Pi^{ne}\downarrow_Y(r′^*)) \cong \Pi\downarrow_Y(\mu^*(r′^*)).$$

Furthermore, since $\mu^*(r^*) \cong \mu^*(r'^*)$, it only remains to show that

$$\mu^* (\Pi^{ne}\downarrow_Y(r^*)) \cong \mu^* (\Pi^{ne}\downarrow_Y(r'^*)).$$

Let $Z(R(T)) = X$ and $H(R(T)) = \{(R(T_1))^*, (R(T_2))^*, ..., (R(T_s))^*\}$, where T_1, T_2, ..., T_s, $s \geq 1$, denote the first level subtrees of the scheme tree T. Also, for $R(T')$, the projected NRS of $R(T)$ over $Y \subseteq S(T)$, we let $Z(R(T')) = X'$ and $H(R(T')) = \{(R(T'_1))^*, (R(T'_2))^*, ..., (R(T'_w))^*\}$, with $w \leq s$, where T'_1, T'_2, ..., T'_w denote the first level subtrees of the scheme tree T'. Now, let $t \in r^*$ and let z' be the resulting nested relation after unnesting the tuple, t, over all the attributes in $H(R(T))$. Thus, we have that $t[X] \cong z'[X]$ and that $t[(R(T_i))^*] \cong z'[R(T_i)]$, $1 \leq i \leq s$. In order to conclude the proof we need to show that

$$\mu^* (\Pi^{ne}\downarrow_Y(t)) \cong \mu^* (\Pi^{ne}\downarrow_Y(z')).$$

We establish this by tracing the recursion step in the computation of $\Pi^{ne}\downarrow_Y(t)$, i.e., (2) of Definition 3.16. Now, since

$$\Pi^{ne}\downarrow_{X'}(t) = \Pi^{ne}\downarrow_{X'}(z'),$$

it follows that

$$\Pi^{ne}\downarrow_{X'}(t) \cong \Pi^{ne}\downarrow_{X'}(z').$$

Finally, for all $j \in \{1,2,...,w\}$, if $R(T'_j)$ is the projected NRS of $R(T_i)$, $i \in \{1,2,...,s\}$, then it is also true that

$$\Pi^{ne}\downarrow_{S(T'_j)}(t[(R(T_i))^*]) = \Pi^{ne}\downarrow_{S(T'_j)}(z'[R(T_i)]),$$

thus

$$\Pi^{ne}\downarrow_{S(T'_j)}(t[(R(T_i))^*]) \cong \Pi^{ne}\downarrow_{S(T'_j)}(z'[R(T_i)]). \quad \square$$

Example 3.11. For r_1^* of Figure 2.8, we obtain the nested relation, $r'^* = \Pi^{ne}\downarrow_{(CLASS\ EXAM\ PROJECT)}(r_1^*)$ over the projected NRS, $R(T') = R(T)[\{CLASS, EXAM, PROJECT\}]$, as shown in Figure 3.19. We note that all tuples $t \in \Pi^{ne}_{(CLASS\ EXAM\ PROJECT)}(r_1^*)$, shown in Figure 3.18, such that $DEF(t) \neq \{CLASS, EXAM, PROJECT\}$, do not appear in r'^*.

It can easily be verified that the result of Theorem 3.9 holds for r'^*, shown in Figure 3.19, i.e., $\mu^*(r'^*) \cong \Pi\downarrow_{(CLASS\ EXAM\ PROJECT)}(\mu^*(r_1^*))$ (see Figure 3.12).

3.2.4 Null Extended Join in Nested Relations

In this subsection we first define the concept of a *joinable NDS*, $\mathbf{R}(F)$, over the universal set of attributes, $U = S(F)$. Intuitively, $\mathbf{R}(F)$ is joinable if all the NRSs $R(T_i) \in \mathbf{R}(F)$, $i=1,2,...,q$, can be combined into a single NRS over U, denoted as $U(T)$, and called the *joined NRS* of $\mathbf{R}(F)$, without violating the definition of a scheme tree. We then generalize the (natural) join operator [Codd 1979; Ullman 1982a; Maier 1983] to the *null extended*

Λ	(CLASS	(EXAM)*	(PROJECT)*)*
	CLASS	(EXAM)*	(PROJECT)*
		EXAM	PROJECT
	databases	mid final	1NF
	databases	final	NF2 UR
	first-order	mid	prolog

Fig. 3.19. $\Pi^{ne} \downarrow_{CLASS\ EXAM\ PROJECT}(r_1^*)$.

join operator, denoted as $\bowtie^{ne}$, and the *outer join* operator [Codd 1979; Bullers 1987; Date 1987a; Jajodia & Springsteel 1987] to the *null extended outer join* operator, denoted as $\overline{\bowtie}^{ne}$. Both $\bowtie^{ne}$ and $\overline{\bowtie}^{ne}$ can only be applied to joinable NDSs.

We note that our null extended join is more general than other extended joins defined for nested relations [Jaeschke & Schek 1982; Roth et al. 1985, 1988; Abiteboul & Bidoit 1986; Thomas & Fischer 1986; Deshpande & Larson 1987], because in our null extended join attributes are joined at all heights of nodes in the scheme trees of a joinable NDS. A similar result to that of the null extended join is achieved by the unnest-join [Korth 1988], the difference being that the null extended join is defined directly on the nested relations while the unnest-join is defined on the corresponding unnested flat relations.

We now formally define a joinable NDS.

Definition 3.17. Let $R(T_1)$ and $R(T_2)$ be NRSs, then $R(T_1)$ and $R(T_2)$ are *joinable NRSs* iff there exists a NRS, $R(T)$, over $S(T_1) \cup S(T_2)$, such that $R(T)[S(T_1)] = R(T_1)$ and $R(T)[S(T_2)] = R(T_2)$. $R(F)$ is said to be a *joinable NDS* iff for each pair $i,j \in \{1,2,...,q\}$ $R(T_i)$ and $R(T_j)$ are *joinable NRSs*.

We observe that *joinable NDSs* are a generalization of *compatible formats* [Abiteboul & Bidoit 1986], since we do not restrict the NRSs in the joinable NDS to have the same attributes in their root nodes.

The next definition builds on the preceding one in order to characterize the resulting NRS of a joinable NDS.

Definition 3.18. Let $R(F)$ be a joinable NDS. Then $U(T)$ is the *joined NRS* of $R(F)$ if

(1) $S(T) = S(F)$;

(2) $U(T)[S(T_i)] = R(T_i)$, $1 \le i \le q$.

The following theorem shows that if a NDS, $R(F)$, is joinable, then this fact implies the existence of a joined NRS, $U(T)$, of $R(F)$. Additionally, the theorem also shows that if $U(T)$ is the joined NRS of a NDS, $R(F)$, then $R(F)$ must be joinable.

Theorem 3.10. A NDS, $R(F)$, is joinable iff there exists a joined NRS, $U(T)$, of $R(F)$.

Proof. *IF*. Let $R(T_i)$ and $R(T_j)$ be two NRSs in $R(F)$, and let $R(T') = U(T)[S(T_i) \cup S(T_j)]$ be a NRS. We now show that $R(T_i)$ and $R(T_j)$ are joinable NRSs.

The result follows by Definition 3.17 and the following facts:

(1) $S(T') = S(T_i) \cup S(T_j)$;

(2) $R(T')[S(T_i)] = (U(T)[S(T_i) \cup S(T_j)])[S(T_i)] = U(T)[S(T_i)] = R(T_i)$; and

(3) $R(T')[S(T_j)] = (U(T)[S(T_i) \cup S(T_j)])[S(T_j)] = U(T)[S(T_j)] = R(T_j)$.

ONLY IF. We prove the result by induction on the number, q, of NRSs in $R(F)$.

BASIS. If $q = 1$ then the result holds trivially, since we have $R(F) = \{R(T_1)\}$, and thus $U(T) = R(T_1)$ is the joined NRS of $R(F)$.

INDUCTION. Assume the result holds for $q = n$. Then, we need to prove the result for $q = n+1$. Let $R(F') = \{R(T_1), R(T_2), ..., R(T_{q-1})\}$ be a joinable NDS over $S(F')$. Then, by the induction hypothesis, there exists a joined NRS, say $U(T')$, of $R(F')$. It now remains to show that $U(T')$ and $R(T_q) \in R(F)$ are joinable NRSs, thus implying the existence of a joined NRS, $U(T)$, of $R(F)$.

We conclude the result by creating T from T' and T_q as follows:

(1) $ATT(ROOT(T)) = ATT(ROOT(T')) \cup ATT(ROOT(T_q))$.

(2) If, for any two nodes $n_i \in T'$ and $n_j \in T_q$, $(ATT(n_i) \cap ATT(n_j)) \neq \emptyset$, then create a node n in T such that $HEIGHT(T,n) = HEIGHT(T',n_i) = HEIGHT(T_q,n_j)$ and $ATT(n) = ATT(n_i) \cup ATT(n_j)$.

(3) If $n_i \neq ROOT(T')$, with $ATT(n_i) \neq \Lambda$, is a node in T' and $ATT(n_i) \cap S(T_q) = \emptyset$, then create a node n in T such that $HEIGHT(T,n) = HEIGHT(T',n_i)$ and $ATT(n) = ATT(n_i)$.

(4) If $n_j \neq ROOT(T_q)$, with $ATT(n_j) \neq \Lambda$, is a node in T_q and $ATT(n_j) \cap S(T') = \emptyset$, then create a node n in T such that $HEIGHT(T,n) = HEIGHT(T_q,n_j)$ and $ATT(n) = ATT(n_j)$.

(5) If there exist nodes, $n_i \in T'$ and $n_j \in T_q$, with $ATT(n_i) = ATT(n_j) = \Lambda$ and $HEIGHT(T',n_i) = HEIGHT(T_q,n_j)$, then create a node n in T such that $HEIGHT(T,n) = HEIGHT(T',n_i) = HEIGHT(T_q,n_j)$ and $ATT(n) = \Lambda$. $\square$

In the *ONLY IF* part of the above proof, the assumption that $R(F)$ is a joinable NDS guarantees that whenever $ATT(n_i) \cap ATT(n_j) \neq \emptyset$, this can only happen for a single pair of nodes and for such a pair of nodes

$$HEIGHT(T',n_i) = HEIGHT(T_q,n_j).$$

Furthermore, a node n in T, with $ATT(n) = \Lambda$, will only exist iff there exist nodes in T' and T_q, respectively, with the same label Λ and equal heights.

The above, besides many other features, will become clear when, in Section 5.1, we consider the restructuring of an arbitrary NDS into a joinable NDS.

Example 3.12. Let T_2 denote the scheme tree shown in Figure 2.9 and let T'_3 be the scheme tree shown in Figure 3.20.

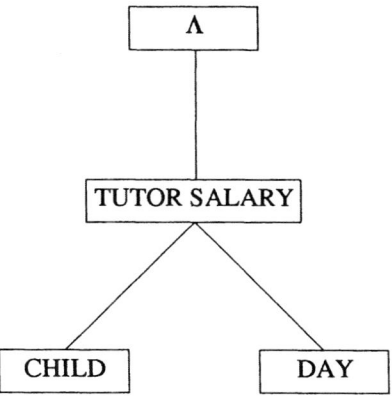

Fig. 3.20. The scheme tree T'_3.

Let $F' = \{T_2, T'_3\}$; then $R(F') = \{R(T_2), R(T'_3)\}$ is a joinable NDS and U(T), where T is shown in Figure 3.21, is the joined NRS of $R(F')$. (See Section 5.1 for the restructuring operations needed to obtain a joinable NDS.)

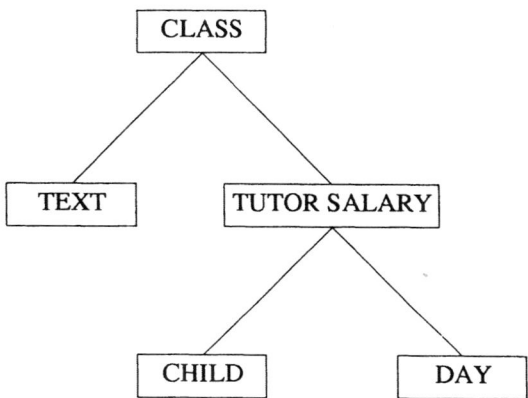

Fig. 3.21. The scheme tree T for U(T) of Example 3.12.

We are now in a position to define the null extended join operator. Informally, the *null extended join* of two nested relations, r_1 and r_2, over a pair of joinable NRSs, $R(T_1)$ and $R(T_2)$, performs a join operation between the tuples of r_1 and r_2 in such a way that the join takes place recursively, at each height of nodes in the corresponding scheme trees, T_1 and T_2, whilst taking into account common attributes labelling the nodes of the two scheme trees.

Definition 3.19. Let $R(T_1)$, $R(T_2)$, with corresponding nested relations, r_1 and r_2, be joinable NRSs such that $R(T)[S(T_1)] = R(T_1)$ and $R(T)[S(T_2)] = R(T_2)$. The *null extended join* of r_1 and r_2, $r_1 \bowtie^{ne} r_2$, yielding r* over $R(T)$, is defined recursively by

(1) if the T_i, $i = 1, 2$, consist of single nodes and
ATT(ROOT(T_i)) $= X_i$, then
$r^* \cong \hat{\{}$ t | there exist $t_1 \in r_1$, $t_2 \in r_2$: $t_1[X_1 \cap X_2] = t_2[X_1 \cap X_2]$ and t$[X_1] \cong t_1[X_1]$ and t$[X_2] \cong t_2[X_2]$ $\}$;

(2) if R(T_i) $= X_i (R(T_1^i))^* (R(T_2^i))^* \ldots (R(T_{s_i}^i))^*$, $i = 1, 2$,
where $X_i = $ ATT(ROOT(T_i)) and $T_1^i, T_2^i, \ldots, T_{s_i}^i$, $s_i \geq 1$, denote
the first level the subtrees of T_i, then
$r^* \cong \hat{\{}$ t | there exist $t_1 \in r_1$, $t_2 \in r_2$:
(2.1) (t$[X_1 X_2] \cong t_1[X_1] \bowtie^{ne} t_2[X_2]$ and
t$[X_1 X_2] \neq \emptyset$ if $(X_1 \neq \Lambda$ or $X_2 \neq \Lambda))$; and
(2.2) (let $j \in \{1, 2, \ldots, s_1\}$, $k \in \{1, 2, \ldots, s_2\}$, then
(2.2.1) for all j, k such that $S(T_j^1) \cap S(T_k^2) \neq \emptyset$:
(t$[(R(T)[S(T_j^1) \cup S(T_k^2)])^*] \cong$
$t_1[(R(T_j^1))^*] \bowtie^{ne} t_2[(R(T_k^2))^*]) \neq \emptyset$; or
(2.2.2) for all j such that for all k
$S(T_j^1) \cap S(T_k^2) = \emptyset$: t$[(R(T_j^1))^*] \cong t_1[(R(T_j^1))^*]$; or
(2.2.3) for all k such that for all j
$S(T_j^1) \cap S(T_k^2) = \emptyset$: t$[(R(T_k^2))^*] \cong t_2[(R(T_k^2))^*]) \hat{\}}$.

(Cf. join in Abiteboul & Bidoit [1986] and Colby [1989], extended natural join in Roth et al. [1985, 1988], intersection join in Jaeschke & Schek [1982] and Thomas & Fischer [1986], natural join in Deshpande & Larson [1987] and unnest-join in Korth [1988].)

We note that (1) of Definition 3.19 corresponds to the standard definition of the join operator found in [Codd 1979; Ullman 1982a; Maier 1983]. Furthermore, the following two technical facts concerning part (2.2.1) of the above definition follow from Definition 2.4 of a scheme tree and Definition 3.17 of joinable NRSs.

(1) If $S(T_j^1) \cap S(T_k^2) \neq \emptyset$, then for all h $(\neq j) \in \{1, 2, \ldots, s_1\}$, $S(T_h^1) \cap S(T_k^2) = \emptyset$, and for all h $(\neq k) \in \{1, 2, \ldots, s_2\}$, $S(T_j^1) \cap S(T_h^2) = \emptyset$.

(2) Let $S(T_j^1) \cap S(T_k^2) = X (\neq \Lambda)$. For all $A \in X$, if $A \in$ ATT(n_1), where $n_1 \in T_j^1$, and $A \in$ ATT(n_2), where $n_2 \in T_k^2$, then HEIGHT(T_j^1, n_1) = HEIGHT(T_k^2, n_2).

Example 3.13. Let R(T_1) = A(B)*(C)*(D(E)*)* and R(T_2) = Λ(BF)*(G)*(Λ(E)*)* be joinable NRSs such that R(T)[S(T_1)] = R(T_1) and R(T)[S(T_2)] = R(T_2), where R(T) = A(BF)*(C)*(G)*(D(E)*)*. Also, let r_1 be the nested relation, over R(T_1), shown in Figure 3.22, and let r_2 be the nested relation, over R(T_2), shown in Figure 3.23. The result of the null extended join, $r^* \cong r_1 \bowtie^{ne} r_2$, is shown in Figure 3.24.

Proposition 3.11. The null extended join operator, $\bowtie^{ne}$, is *faithful* to the standard join operator, $\bowtie$.

Proof. It follows from (1) of Definition 3.19. $\square$

In the next theorem we prove that the null extended join operator is a precise generalization of the standard join operator.

A	(B)*	(C)*	(D	(E)*)*
	B	C	D	(E)*
				E
a_1	b_1 b_2 b_3	c_1 c_2	d_1	e_1 e_2
a_2	b_1	null	d_2	e_1
a_3	b_1 b_2	c_1	null	null
null	b_2	c_2 c_3	null d_3	e_2 null

Fig. 3.22. The nested relation r_1.

Λ	(BF)*	(G)*	(Λ	(E)*)*
	BF	G	Λ	(E)*
				E
	$b_1 f_1$ $b_2 f_1$	g_1 g_2		e_1 e_2

Fig. 3.23. The nested relation r_2.

A	(BF)*	(C)*	(G)*	(D	(E)*)*
	BF	C	G	D	(E)*
					E
a_1	$b_1 f_1$ $b_2 f_1$	c_1 c_2	g_1 g_2	d_1	e_1 e_2
a_2	$b_1 f_1$	null	g_1 g_2	d_2	e_1
null	$b_2 f_1$	c_2 c_3	g_1 g_2	null	e_2

Fig. 3.24. The null extended join, $r^* \cong r_1 \bowtie^{ne} r_2$.

Theorem 3.12. Let $R(T_1)$ and $R(T_2)$ be joinable NRSs such that $R(T)[S(T_1)] = R(T_1)$ and $R(T)[S(T_2)] = R(T_2)$, and with corresponding nested relations, r_1 and r_2. Then the null extended join operator, $\bowtie^{ne}$, is a *precise* generalization of the standard join operator, $\bowtie$, in the sense that $\mu^*(r_1 \bowtie^{ne} r_2) \cong \mu^*(r_1) \bowtie \mu^*(r_2)$.

Proof. We prove the result by induction on HEIGHT(T).

BASIS. If HEIGHT(T) = 0, then r_1 and r_2 are flat relations and thus $\mu^*(r_1) \cong r_1$ and $\mu^*(r_2) \cong r_2$. The result follows, since, by Proposition 3.11, $\bowtie^{ne}$ is faithful to $\bowtie$ and thus

$\mu^*(r_1 \bowtie^{ne} r_2) \cong r_1 \bowtie r_2$, as required.

INDUCTION. Assume the result holds for HEIGHT(T) = n, we then need to prove that the result holds for HEIGHT(T) = n+1. Let r'_1 and r'_2 be the resulting nested relations over, say $R(T'_1)$ and $R(T'_2)$, respectively, after unnesting r_1 and r_2, over all the attributes in $H(R(T_1))$ and $H(R(T_2))$, respectively. We now have that $R(T'_1)$ and $R(T'_2)$ are joinable NRSs such that $R(T')[S(T'_1)] = R(T'_1)$ and $R(T')[S(T'_2)] = R(T'_2)$, and HEIGHT(T') = n. So, by the inductive hypothesis,

$$\mu^*(r'_1 \bowtie^{ne} r'_2) \cong \mu^*(r'_1) \bowtie \mu^*(r'_2).$$

It now remains to show that

$$\mu^*(r_1 \bowtie^{ne} r_2) \cong \mu^*(r'_1 \bowtie^{ne} r'_2),$$

since $\mu^*(r_1) \cong \mu^*(r'_1)$ and $\mu^*(r_2) \cong \mu^*(r'_2)$.

Let $t_1 \in r_1$ and $t_2 \in r_2$. Furthermore, we let $w'_1 \leq r'_1$ and $w'_2 \leq r'_2$ be the resulting nested relations after unnesting t_1 and t_2, over all the attributes in $H(R(T_1))$ and $H(R(T_2))$, respectively. Thus, $\mu^*(t_1) \cong \mu^*(w'_1)$ and $\mu^*(t_2) \cong \mu^*(w'_2)$. In order to conclude the proof we need show that

$$\mu^*(t_1 \bowtie^{ne} t_2) \cong \mu^*(w'_1 \bowtie^{ne} w'_2). \tag{1}$$

We prove equation (1) by tracing its computation in part (2) of Definition 3.19, namely,

(2.1) $t_1[Z(R(T_1))] \bowtie^{ne} t_2[Z(R(T_2))] \cong w'_1[Z(R(T_1))] \bowtie^{ne} w'_2[Z(R(T_2))]$,

   since $t_1[Z(R(T_1))] \cong w'_1[Z(R(T_1))]$ and $t_2[Z(R(T_2))] \cong w'_2[Z(R(T_2))]$.

(2.2.1) $t_1[(R(T_j^1))^*] \bowtie^{ne} t_2[(R(T_k^2))^*] \cong w'_1[R(T_j^1)] \bowtie^{ne} w'_2[R(T_k^2)]$,

   since $t_1[(R(T_j^1))^*] \cong w'_1[R(T_j^1)]$ and $t_2[(R(T_k^2))^*] \cong w'_2[R(T_k^2)]$.

(2.2.2) $t_1[(R(T_j^1))^*] \cong w'_1[R(T_j^1)]$ by the construction of w'_1.

(2.2.3) $t_2[(R(T_k^2))^*] \cong w'_2[R(T_k^2)]$ by the construction of w'_2.

The result now follows, since, by the two technical facts stated after Definition 3.19, we guarantee that there are no more cases to consider. $\square$

Example 3.14. It can easily be verified that the result of Theorem 3.12 holds for $r^* \cong r_1 \bowtie^{ne} r_2$, shown in Figure 3.24, namely, $\mu^*(r^*) \cong \mu^*(r_1) \bowtie \mu^*(r_2)$.

By utilizing our null extended join we can define the *null extended Cartesian product*, denoted as $\times^{ne}$, and the *null extended intersection*, denoted as $\cap^{ne}$. (Cf. [Roth et al. 1985, 1988; Abiteboul & Bidoit 1986].) The null extended join reduces to the null extended Cartesian product when $S(T_1) \cap S(T_2) = \emptyset$, and it reduces to the null extended intersection when $R(T_1) = R(T_2)$.

Example 3.15. Let $r'^*_3 \cong \nu_{R(T_3)}(r^*_3)$ be the nested relation of Figure 2.12, over $R(T'_3)$, where T'_3 is shown in Figure 3.20. Now, let $d'^* = \{r^*_2, r'^*_3\}$ be a nested database over the NDS, $R(F')$, of Example 3.12, where r^*_2 is shown in Figure 2.10. Then, the null extended

CLASS	(TEXT)*	(TUTOR	SALARY	(CHILD)*	(DAY)*)*
	TEXT	TUTOR	SALARY	(CHILD)*	(DAY)*
				CHILD	DAY
databases	Date Ullman	Robert	12000	Hanna Brian	Monday Thursday
programming	Knuth	Hanna	14000	Annette Ada	*null*
french	*null*	Martine	*null*	*null*	*null*

Fig. 3.25. The null extended join $r_2^* \bowtie^{ne} r'^*_3$.

join, $r_2^* \bowtie^{ne} r'^*_3$, over U(T), where T is shown in Figure 3.21, is given in Figure 3.25.

In the joined nested relation shown in Figure 3.25 the third, fifth and sixth tuples from r_2^*, and the fourth and fifth tuples from r_3^* do not appear in the result, since there were no matching tuples in the corresponding nested relations over TUTOR.

The following definition allows us to pad tuples over a projected NRS, R(T'), of a NRS, say R(T), with null values; the definition is needed in Definition 3.21 of the null extended outer join and is also useful subsequently when we consider tuples over a NRI containing null values.

Definition 3.20. Let r'^* be a nested relation over a projected NRS, R(T'), of a NRS, R(T), where S(T') = Y. Then, where t is a tuple in r'^*,

PAD(t) is a tuple over the NRS, R(T), such that PAD(t)[Y] $\cong$ t **and** PAD(t)[S(T) - Y] $\cong$ *null*.

We can now naturally generalize PAD(t) to PAD(r'^*), where r'^* is a nested relation over a projected NRS, R(T'), of R(T), namely,

PAD(r'^*) is a nested relation over the NRS, R(T), such that PAD(r'^*) $\cong \hat{\{}$ PAD(t) | t $\in$ r'^* $\hat{\}}$.

Finally, we can apply PAD to a nested database, $d'^* = \{r'_1, r'_2, ..., r'_q\}$, over a joinable NDS, **R**(F'), over the joined NRS, U(T), namely,

PAD(d'^*) is a nested relation over the joined NRS, U(T), such that PAD(d'^*) $\cong \cup^{ne} {}^q_{i=1}$ (PAD(r'_i)).

We note that, from Definition 3.20, Π^{ne}_Y(PAD(r'^*)) $\cong r'^*$, where Y = S(T'). Thus, by the preciseness of Π^{ne}, shown in Theorem 3.6, we can show that the UNNEST* operator, i.e., μ^*, commutes with the PAD operator, i.e., μ^*(PAD(r'^*)) $\cong$ PAD(μ^*(r'^*)); In fact,

μ^*(PAD(r'^*)) $\cong$ PAD(Π_Y(μ^*(PAD(r'^*)))) $\cong$ PAD(μ^*(Π^{ne}_Y(PAD(r'^*)))) $\cong$ PAD(μ^*(r'^*)).

The *null extended outer join* operator, whose definition follows, guarantees that all the tuples participating in the null extended join will appear in the result, i.e., all the information of the joined relations is preserved. Informally, the null extended outer join of two nested relations consists of the joined tuples, resulting from the null extended join, unioned with the unmatched tuples, resulting from the null extended join, padded with null values.

Definition 3.21. Let r and s be two flat relations over the FRSs, R and S, respectively. The *outer join*, $r \overline{\bowtie} s$, is defined by

$$r \overline{\bowtie} s \cong \hat{\{} (r \bowtie s) \cup \text{PAD}(r) \cup \text{PAD}(s) \hat{\}}.$$

Let r_1 and r_2 be two nested relations over the joinable NRSs, $R(T_1)$ and $R(T_2)$, respectively. Correspondingly, the *null extended outer join* of r_1 and r_2, $r_1 \overline{\bowtie}^{ne} r_2$, is defined by

$$r_1 \overline{\bowtie}^{ne} r_2 \cong (r_1 \bowtie^{ne} r_2) \cup^{ne} \text{PAD}(r_1) \cup^{ne} \text{PAD}(r_2).$$

Proposition 3.13. The null extended outer join operator, $\overline{\bowtie}^{ne}$, is *faithful* to the standard outer join operator $\overline{\bowtie}$.

Proof. Since $\cup^{ne}$ and $\bowtie^{ne}$ are *faithful* by Propositions 3.1 and 3.11, respectively, the result follows from Definition 3.21. □

The next theorem shows that the null extended outer join operator is a precise generalization of the standard outer join operator.

Theorem 3.14. Let $R(T_1)$ and $R(T_2)$ be joinable NRSs such that $R(T)[S(T_1)] = R(T_1)$ and $R(T)[S(T_2)] = R(T_2)$, with corresponding nested relations, r_1 and r_2. Then the null extended outer join operator, $\overline{\bowtie}^{ne}$, is a *precise* generalization of the standard outer join operator, $\overline{\bowtie}$, in the sense that $\mu^*(r_1 \overline{\bowtie}^{ne} r_2) \cong \mu^*(r_1) \overline{\bowtie} \mu^*(r_2)$.

Proof. By Definition 3.21, we have that

$$\mu^*(r_1 \overline{\bowtie}^{ne} r_2) \cong \mu^*(((r_1 \bowtie^{ne} r_2) \cup^{ne} PAD(r_1)) \cup^{ne} PAD(r_2)).$$

On applying to the above Theorem 3.2 twice and then Theorem 3.12, we obtain

$$\mu^*(r_1 \overline{\bowtie}^{ne} r_2) \cong (\mu^*(r_1) \bowtie \mu^*(r_2)) \cup \mu^*(PAD(r_1)) \cup \mu^*(PAD(r_2)).$$

Now, since $\mu^*(\text{PAD}(r_1)) \cong \text{PAD}(\mu^*(r_1))$ and $\mu^*(\text{PAD}(r_2)) \cong \text{PAD}(\mu^*(r_2))$, it follows that

$$\mu^*(r_1 \overline{\bowtie}^{ne} r_2) \cong (\mu^*(r_1) \bowtie \mu^*(r_2)) \cup PAD(\mu^*(r_1)) \cup PAD(\mu^*(r_2)).$$

The result now follows by Definition 3.21. □

Example 3.16. For d'^* of Example 3.15 the result of the null extended outer join, $r'^* \cong r_2'^* \overline{\bowtie}^{ne} r_3'^*$, over the joined NRS, $U(T)$, consists of the three matched tuples shown in Figure 3.25 resulting from the null extended join, unioned with the six unmatched padded tuples shown in Figure 3.26.

CLASS	(TEXT)*	(TUTOR	SALARY	(CHILD)*	(DAY)*)*
	TEXT	TUTOR	SALARY	(CHILD)*	(DAY)*
				CHILD	DAY
databases	Date Ullman	Robert	12000	Hanna Brian	Monday Thursday
programming	Knuth	Hanna	14000	Annette Ada	null
french	null	Martine	null	null	null
programming	Knuth	Hanna	null	null	null
		Richard	null	null	null
first-order	Mendelson	null	null	null	null
hebrew	Bible	null	null	null	null
null	Lenin Dostoyevsky	null	null	null	null
null	null	null	15000	null	Wednesday
null	null	null	null	Ruth	Tuesday Friday

Fig. 3.26. The null extended outer join, $r'^* \cong r_2^* \overline{\bowtie}^{ne} r'^*_3$.

It can easily be verified that the result of Theorem 3.14 holds for r'^*, shown in Figure 3.26, namely, $\mu^*(r'^*) \cong \mu^*(r_2^*) \overline{\bowtie} \mu^*(r'^*_3)$.

3.2.5 Null Extended Selection and Null Extended Renaming

In formalizing the nested UR model we do not require the *null extended selection* operator, σ^{ne}, or the *null extended renaming operator*, δ^{ne}. On the other hand, for processing queries under the nested UR model (and of course under the null extended nested relational model) the null extended selection operator and the null extended renaming operator are of major importance. Firstly, we discuss the null extended selection operator, which is employed in querying a nested database, and then we formally define the null extended renaming operator, which may be necessary to enforce the UR assumptions of Subsection 2.3.1.

The selection operator, denoted as σ [Codd 1979; Ullman 1982a; Maier 1983], returns a set of tuples satisfying a predicate on a given flat relation. The selection operator does not change the FRS of the flat relation on which σ operates, and correspondingly the null extended selection operator, σ^{ne}, for nested relations, defined hereafter, also does not change the NRS of the nested relation on which σ^{ne} operates.

In the recursive extended algebras of Jaeschke [1985b], Schek [1985] and Schek & Scholl [1986] selection is extended to nested relations in such a way so that it can be applied to any attribute in the scheme tree by "navigating" to the said attribute via *nested projections* and *nested selections* [Jaeschke 1985a; Schek 1985, Schek & Scholl 1986]. On the other hand, in the extended algebra of Abiteboul & Bidoit [1986], selection, called *Verso selection*, includes the specification of all the attributes in the scheme tree, thus no "navigation" is needed in a selection expression over a nested relation.

The expressive power of the above extensions to selection, relative to the standard selection operator σ, has also been investigated. In Scholl [1986] a class of queries, called *single pass expressions* (spes), was defined which can be computed within one scan of the tuples in the nested relation over which the query is formulated. A class of expressions, similar to spes, which would normally require a join in the flat relational model, is the *Verso super selection* [Abiteboul & Bidoit 1986]. Bidoit [1987] showed that the Verso super selection is equivalent to a subclass of *select project join* queries in the flat relational model augmented by the *Verso projection* [Bidoit 1987].

The following two definitions give the syntax of selection formulae (cf. [Schek & Scholl 1986]).

Definition 3.22. Let R(T') be a projected NRS of a NRS, R(T), and let *comp-op* $\in$ {=, >, <, $\in$, $\subset$, $\subseteq$, $\supset$, $\supseteq$, $\stackrel{\sim}{=}$, $\geq$, $\leq$}. Then a *simple selection formula* (simple SF), F, over R(T), is defined by

(type1) *attr comp-op constant*, where *attr* $\in$ R(T') and *constant* is a tuple (subtuple) over *attr*;

(type2) *attr1 comp-op attr2*, where *attr1*, *attr2* $\in$ R(T') and EDOM(*attr1*) $\stackrel{\sim}{=}$ EDOM(*attr2*).

If F is a simple SF of type1 and *attr* $\in$ S(T') or if F is a simple SF of type2 and *attr1*, *attr2* $\in$ Z(R(T')), then we call F a *zero order simple SF*. (See the comments pertaining to the boundary case with regards to Definition 3.6 of the nest operator, v.)

We note that the *comp-op*, $\stackrel{\sim}{=}$, is used to compare tuples with null values when we consider information-wise equivalence between two null values in the tuples. We cannot use the equality *comp-op*, =, for this purpose, since by the equality rule for nulls, given in Definition 3.3, nulls are not equal to each other and thus the equality *comp-op*, =, always returns false when two null values are compared. The comparison operators, >, <, have their usual meaning, i.e. greater than and less than, respectively. On the other hand, the operators $\geq$, $\leq$, are used to compare the information content of tuples and mean, more informative than and less informative than, respectively.

We now define a selection formula, F, which, informally, is an arbitrary boolean expression whose operands are simple SFs.

Definition 3.23. A *selection formula* (SF), F, over a NRS, R(T), is defined by

(1) F is a SF if F is a simple SF;

(2) if F is a SF then (F) is a SF, and ¬(F) is a SF;

(3) if F_1 and F_2 are SFs then F_1 and F_2 is a SF, and F_1 or F_2 is a SF.

If all the simple SFs that appear in a SF, F, are zero order simple SFs, then F is called a *zero order* SF. If no negation (¬) appears in a SF, F, then F is called a *positive SF*. Finally, if a SF, F, is both a positive SF and a zero order SF, then F is called a *positive zero order SF*.

We are now in a position to define the *null extended selection* operator, denoted as $\sigma^{ne}{}_F$, where F is a selection formula.

Definition 3.24. Let r* be a nested relation over a NRS, R(T), where R(T) = $X(R(T_1))*(R(T_2))* ... (R(T_s))*$, X = ATT(ROOT(R(T))), and $T_1, T_2, ..., T_s$, s ≥ 1, denote the first level subtrees of T. Then the result of the *null extended selection* operator w.r.t. a simple SF, F, over R(T), applied to r*, i.e., $\sigma^{ne}{}_F(r*)$, yielding a nested relation, over R(T), is defined recursively by

(1) if F is of type1 then $\sigma^{ne}{}_F(r*) \cong \hat{\{}\ t\ |$ there exists t′ ∈ r* **and**

(1.1) t [X] ≅ t′[X] **and** if attr ∈ R(T) then t′[attr] comp-op constant is satisfied, i.e., evaluates to true; **and**

(1.2) t [(R(T_i))*] ≅ $\sigma^{ne}{}_F$(t′[(R(T_i))*]), 1 ≤ i ≤ s $\hat{\}}$;

(2) if F is of type2 then $\sigma^{ne}{}_F(r*) \cong \hat{\{}\ t\ |$ there exists t′ ∈ r* **and**

(2.1) t [X] ≅ t′[X] **and** if attr1, attr2 ∈ R(T) then t′[attr1] comp-op t′[attr2] is satisfied, i.e., evaluates to true; **and**

(2.2) t [(R(T_i))*] ≅ $\sigma^{ne}{}_F$(t′[(R(T_i))*]), 1 ≤ i ≤ s $\hat{\}}$.

(Cf. [Abiteboul & Bidoit 1986; Bidoit 1987].)

We note that (1.1) and (2.1) correspond to the definition of the standard selection operator applied to flat relations w.r.t. zero order simple SFs, and can be found in [Roth et al. 1985] (cf. [Zaniolo 1984]).

We now extend the definition of $\sigma^{ne}{}_F(r*)$ to SFs which comprise parentheses and the (fundamental) boolean operators.

Definition 3.25. Let r* be a nested relation over a NRS, R(T), and let F, F_1, F_2 be SFs over R(T). Then

(1) $\sigma^{ne}{}_{(F)}(r*) \cong (\sigma^{ne}{}_F(r*))$;

(2) $\sigma^{ne}{}_{\neg F}(r*) \cong r* -^{ne} \sigma^{ne}{}_F(r*)$;

(3) $\sigma^{ne}{}_{F_1 \text{ and } F_2}(r*) \cong \sigma^{ne}{}_{F_1}(r*) \cap^{ne} \sigma^{ne}{}_{F_2}(r*)$;

(4) $\sigma^{ne}{}_{F_1 \text{ or } F_2}(r^{\star}) \cong \sigma^{ne}{}_{F_1}(r^{\star}) \cup^{ne} \sigma^{ne}{}_{F_2}(r^{\star})$.

The above definition allows us to consider a SF as being composed of simple SFs, which can be viewed as building blocks, together with boolean operators and parentheses. In (3) above there may arise loss of information because of the equality rule for nulls. This problem can be dealt with by modifying the definition of our null extended join operator, in this case, to compare common attributes using information-wise equivalence rather than equality, or alternatively by using marked nulls.

We could use the following optimization strategy in order to process $\sigma^{ne}{}_F(r^*)$ in a single pass over the nested relation r*.

Let F be a SF containing only simple SFs of type1, which form the set, say $F = \{F_1, F_2, ..., F_n\}$. We show that F can be evaluated in a single pass over r* as follows: Create a partition of $F = \cup_i F'_i$, such that, where $F_i^k \in F'_i$, $1 \le k \le m$, $F'_i = \{F_i^1, F_i^2, ..., F_i^m\}$ is an element of the said partition if the attributes involved in each F_i^k are identical. Now, since, by the definition of $\sigma^{ne}{}_F(r^*)$, we navigate automatically through all of the attributes of projected NRSs of R(T), it is possible to evaluate all the partitions of F in one pass through the nested relation, r*. From this single pass we obtain n intermediate results, so we evaluate a logical **and**, with the null extended intersection, $\cap^{ne}$, a logical **or**, with the null extended union, $\cup^{ne}$, and a logical ¬ with the null extended difference, $-^{ne}$.

For a SF containing also simple SFs of type2, we can use the same evaluation strategy as described above, since, by the definition of type2 SFs, *attr1*, *attr2* are both in a projected NRS, R(T'), of R(T) and they share the same null extended domain.

It now follows that in order to evaluate $\sigma^{ne}{}_F(r^*)$, where F is a SF, only one pass is needed over the nested relation, r*. We do not discuss any further optimization regarding the computation of $\sigma^{ne}{}_F(r^*)$, but we mention that it would be desirable to reduce the number of intermediate results when we are using the above evaluation strategy. It is also worth mentioning that the strategy we have outlined is amenable to parallel processing as the intermediate results are, in general, independent of each other.

The expressive power of the null extended selection is thus analogous to that of the spe queries and the Verso super selection. This is because the null extended selection operator can be processed in a single pass over a nested relation, r*, and because of the fact that a SF, F, allows the participation of all the boolean operators.

The next proposition shows that the null extended selection is faithful to its standard counterpart.

Proposition 3.15. The null extended selection operator, σ^{ne}, is *faithful* to the standard selection operator, σ.

Proof. Let r be a flat relation over S(T), F be a SF and $\sigma^{ne}{}_F(r)$ be the result of applying the null extended selection operator σ^{ne} w.r.t. F to r. The null extended operators $\cup^{ne}$, $-^{ne}$ and $\cap^{ne}$ are faithful to their standard counterparts $\cup$, $-$ and $\cap$, by Propositions 3.1, 3.3 and 3.11, respectively. It therefore, follows, by Definition 3.25, that the evaluation of $\sigma^{ne}{}_F(r)$ reduces to the evaluation of all the simple SFs, over r, contained in F, and then applying one of $\cup$, $-$ or $\cap$, corresponding to the boolean operators **or**, $\neg$ or **and**. Now, since r is a flat relation, it follows that all the simple SFs that appear in F are zero order simple SFs. Thus, the result follows, since, for simple SFs of type1 and type2, only (1.1) and (2.1) of Definition 3.24 are invoked in the computation of $\sigma^{ne}{}_F(r)$. $\square$

The next theorem shows that if we consider only zero order simple SFs, then σ^{ne} is a precise generalization of σ. In the more general case, when we consider zero order SFs instead of just zero order simple SFs, then σ^{ne} is not a precise generalization of σ. This impreciseness is due to $-^{ne}$ not being a precise generalization of $-$ (see Proposition 3.4). However, if we consider only positive zero order SFs, then σ^{ne} is a precise generalization of σ because of the preciseness of $\cup^{ne}$ and $\cap^{ne}$, the latter being a special case of $\bowtie^{ne}$.

Now, if we consider simple SFs instead of zero order simple SFs, then any one of the comparison operators, $\in$, $\subset$, $\subseteq$, $\supset$ and $\supseteq$, can appear in a simple SF, F, which contains a higher order attribute. This causes σ^{ne} to be strictly more expressive than σ. This additional expressive power is due to the fact that applying the set comparison operators when selecting tuples over higher order attributes does not directly translate to the selection of tuples over the corresponding zero order attributes. For example, if the simple SF, F, is, say (TEXT)* $\supseteq$ {Date, Ullman}, then it is not possible to express F by using only a zero order simple SF. Thus, the largest class of SFs for which σ^{ne} is precise is the class of positive zero order SFs.

Theorem 3.16. Let r* be a nested relation over a NRS, R(T), and let F be a zero order simple SF over R(T). Then, w.r.t. F, σ^{ne} is a precise generalization of the standard selection operator, σ, in the sense that $\mu^*(\sigma^{ne}{}_F(r^*)) \cong \sigma_F(\mu^*(r^*))$.

Proof. We prove the result by induction on HEIGHT(T).

BASIS. If HEIGHT(T) = 0, then r* is a flat relation and $\mu^*(r^*) \cong r^*$. The result follows, since, by Proposition 3.15, σ^{ne} is faithful to σ and thus we have $\mu^*(\sigma^{ne}{}_F(r^*)) \cong \sigma^{ne}{}_F(r^*)$ $\cong \sigma_F(r^*)$ as required.

INDUCTION. Assume the result holds for HEIGHT(T) = n, we then need to prove that the result holds for HEIGHT(T) = n+1. Let r'* be the resulting nested relation over, say R(T*), after the unnesting of r* over all the attributes in H(R(T)). We now have HEIGHT(T*) = n, so, by inductive hypothesis,

$$\mu^*(\sigma^{ne}{}_F(r'^*)) \cong \sigma_F(\mu^*(r'^*)).$$

Furthermore, since $\mu^*(r'^*) \cong \mu^*(r^*)$, it only remains to show that

$$\mu^*(\sigma^{ne}{}_F(r^*)) \cong \mu^*(\sigma^{ne}{}_F(r'^*)).$$

Let Z(R(T)) = X and H(R(T)) = {(R(T_1))*, (R(T_2))*, ..., (R(T_s))*}, where T_1, T_2, ..., T_s, s $\geq$1, denote the first level subtrees of the scheme tree T. Now, let t $\in$ r* and let z' be the resulting nested relation after unnesting the tuple, t, over all the attributes in H(R(T)). Thus, we have that t[X] $\cong$ z'[X] and that t[(R(T_i))*] $\cong$ z'[R(T_i)], 1 $\leq$ i $\leq$ s. In order to conclude the proof we need to show that

$$\mu^*(\sigma^{ne}{}_F(t)) \cong \mu^*(\sigma^{ne}{}_F(z')).$$

We establish this by tracing the computation of $\sigma^{ne}{}_F(t)$ in Definition 3.24. Firstly, by tracing (1.1) and (2.1) of Definition 3.24, it is true that

$$\sigma^{ne}{}_F(t[X]) \cong \sigma^{ne}{}_F(z'[X]).$$

Furthermore, by tracing (1.2) and (2.2) of Definition 3.24, it is also true that

$$\sigma^{ne}{}_F(t[(R(T_i))^*]) \cong \sigma^{ne}{}_F(z'[R(T_i)]), \ 1 \le i \le s. \ \square$$

We note that if F were a simple SF rather than a zero order simple SF, then we could not prove the above theorem, since $H(R(T)) \ne H(R(T^*))$.

Example 3.17. Let r_1^* be the nested relation, over $R(T_1)$, of the running example, shown in Figure 2.8. We now give several examples of σ^{ne} applied to r_1^*.

(1) Let F_1 be STUDENT = "Mark", then $\sigma^{ne}{}_{F_1}(r_1^*)$ is the second tuple in r_1^*, which we denote as t_2^*. It can easily be verified that the result of Theorem 3.16 holds, namely, $\mu^*(\sigma^{ne}{}_{F_1}(r_1^*)) \cong \mu^*(t_2^*) \cong \sigma_{F_1}(\mu^*(r_1^*))$.

(2) Let F_2 be (CLASS = "databases") **and** (EXAM = "final"), then $\sigma^{ne}{}_{F_2}(r_1^*)$ is shown in Figure 3.27.

(3) Let F_3 be (CLASS = "databases") **or** (MAJOR= "logic"), then $\sigma^{ne}{}_{F_3}(r_1^*)$ is shown in Figure 3.28.

(4) Let F_4 be PROJECT $\cong$ *null*, then $\sigma^{ne}{}_{F_4}(r_1^*)$ is shown in Figure 3.29.

(5) Let F_5 be $\neg$(CLASS $\in$ {"databases", "programming"}), then $\sigma^{ne}{}_{F_5}(r_1^*)$ is the third, fourth and fifth tuples in r_1^*.

(6) Let F_6 be (EXAM)* $\supseteq$ {"mid", "final"}, then $\sigma^{ne}{}_{F_6}(r_1^*)$ is shown in Figure 3.30.

(7) Let F_7 be (CLASS(EXAM)*(PROJECT)*)* $\ge$ {<*null*, {*null*}, {"Moscow"}>}, then $\sigma^{ne}{}_{F_7}(r_1^*)$ is shown in Figure 3.31.

Iris	CS	computing	databases	final	1NF
Mark	CS	maths	databases	final	NF2 UR

Fig. 3.27. $\sigma^{ne}{}_{F_2}(r_1^*)$.

In order to complete the null extended algebra, we next define the null extended renaming operator (cf. [Maier 1983]), denoted as δ^{ne}, which allows us to rename attributes in the scheme trees of NRSs.

Definition 3.26. Let R(T) be a NRS and r* be a nested relation over R(T). Let A $\in$ S(T) and let n be the node of T such that A $\in$ ATT(n). We say that the NRS, R(T*), is the result of *renaming* the attribute, A $\in$ S(T), to the attribute, B $\in$ (U − S(T)), if the scheme tree, T*, is identical to the scheme tree, T, up to modification of ATT(n) to (ATT(n) − A) $\cup$ B. The *null extended renaming* of A to B in r*, denoted as $\delta^{ne}{}_{A \leftarrow B}(r^*)$, is a nested relation, over R(T*), defined by

Iris	CS	computing	databases	mid final	1NF
Mark	CS	maths	databases	final	NF2 UR
David	Philosophy	logic	first-order	mid	prolog

Fig. 3.28. $\sigma^{ne}_{F_3}(r_1^*)$.

Iris	CS	computing	programming	final	*null*
null	philosophy	*null*	*null*	mid final	*null*
Naomi	*null*	languages	french	mid	*null*

Fig. 3.29. $\sigma^{ne}_{F_4}(r_1^*)$.

Iris	CS	computing	databases	mid final	1NF
null	philosophy	*null*	*null*	mid final	*null*

Fig. 3.30. $\sigma^{ne}_{F_6}(r_1^*)$.

Naomi	*null*	languages	*null*	final	Moscow

Fig. 3.31. $\sigma^{ne}_{F_7}(r_1^*)$.

$\delta^{ne}_{A \leftarrow B}(r*) \cong \widehat{\{}\ t\ |\ t' \in r*\ \textbf{and}\ t[S(T) - B] \cong t'[S(T) - A]$
$\textbf{and}\ t[B] \cong t'[A]\ \widehat{\}}$.

We have now completed the definition of the null extended algebra and close this section by defining a *null extended algebra expression* w.r.t. a NDS, **R**(F), over U, and a nested database, d*, over **R**(F). Informally, a null extended algebra expression is any allowable expression formed by using the operators of the null extended algebra and nested relations in d* (cf. [Maier 1983]).

Definition 3.27. We define a *null extended algebra expression*, recursively, by

(1) $E = r_i^*$, where $r_i^* \in$ d* is a nested relation over $R(T_i) \in$ **R**(F), is a null extended algebra expression.

(2) If E is a null extended algebra expression, then (E) is also a null extended algebra expression.

(3) If E is a null extended algebra expression, then *un-op*(E) is a null extended algebra expression, where *un-op* is an allowable application of a unary operator of the null

extended algebra to E.

(4)   If E_1 and E_2 are null extended algebra expressions, then E_1 *bin-op* E_2 is a null extended algebra expression, where *bin-op* is an allowable application of a binary operator of the null extended algebra to E_1 and E_2.

3.3 Discussion

We now briefly compare the null extended algebra to other extended algebras, mentioned at the beginning of Section 3.2, some of which are defined over the class of hierarchical nested relations, a subclass of nested relations.

The null extended algebra presented herein is more general than other extended algebras, since it is defined over the general class of nested relations whose domains include null values. Due to the general nature of the null extended algebra, we were able to show that all of the null extended operators are faithful and, apart from $-^{ne}$, they are all precise. For the above-mentioned extended algebras however, all their extended operators are faithful but they all lack the near-full preciseness of the null extended algebra. For example, in the maximal algebras of Abiteboul & Bidoit [1986] and Roth et al. [1985, 1988] the extended union, the extended difference and the extended projection are imprecise. A similar situation exists with regards to the minimal algebras of Thomas & Fischer [1986] and Van Gucht & Fischer [1988], wherein both the extended intersection and the extended difference are imprecise.

Another important feature of the null extended algebra is that no user navigation through the NRSs in the NDS is required, when the user queries the nested database. On the other hand, recursive algebras, for example that of Schek & Scholl [1986], rely on navigation in order to query the nested database. By using the null extended algebra, queries to the nested database can be formulated directly via the underlying zero order attributes of the NDS, without the user having to know the details of the structure of the NDS. This feature of the null extended algebra is necessary in the formalization of the nested UR model, as we shall see in Chapter 5. Correspondingly, minimal algebras, for example, that of Thomas & Fischer [1986], rely on the NEST and UNNEST operators in order that queries be formulated over higher attributes; this renders query formulation cumbersome and, moreover, query processing can become potentially inefficient.

Finally, the null extended join operator of the null extended algebra is more general and more powerful than all previously defined extended join operators, since attributes are joined at all the heights of the scheme trees involved in the null extended join. In addition, the null extended outer join is a new operator, previously defined only for flat relations, which is useful when unmatched tuples, resulting from the null extended join, need to be added to the resulting nested relation.

In our presentation of the null extended algebra, we do not define the *powerset* operator [Gyssens & Van Gucht 1987, 1988; Beeri 1988] or the *fixpoint* operator [Gyssens & Van Gucht 1987; Korth & Roth 1989; Linnemann 1987; Rowe & Stonebraker 1987; Beeri 1988], the latter being a generalization of the *transitive closure* operator [Maier 1983; Agrawal 1987]. The reason for excluding these two operators from the null extended algebra is that they are not necessary in the formalization of the nested UR model. We will consider such an extension in the future in order to enhance the expressive power of the null extended algebra with recursion and iteration.

Chapter 4
Null Extended Data Dependencies
and
The Extended Chase

In this chapter we define semantics of the null extended nested relational model in terms of the class of *null extended data dependencies*, which are integrity constraints that hold in nested relations. We also consider the counterparts of the class of null extended data dependencies, called hereafter the class of *null data dependencies*, which hold in the flat relations corresponding to the said nested relations.

In Section 4.1 we generalize FDs so that they hold in flat relations containing null values; we call these generalized FDs *null functional dependencies* (NFDs) [Lien 1982; Atzeni & Morfuni 1986]. Then we redefine NFDs in the context of nested relations. In Section 4.2 we generalize MVDs so that they hold in flat relations containing null values; these generalized MVDs are called *null multivalued dependencies* (NMVDs) [Lien 1979, 1982]. We then redefine hierarchical relations, whose formal definition is given in Definition 2.12, in terms of the NMVDs which hold in the corresponding flat relations.

JDs, as integrity constraints, are of major importance, since they capture the notion of *lossless decomposition* [Beeri & Vardi 1981; Sciore 1982; Ullman 1982a; Maier 1983], the MVD being a special case of the JD when the cardinality of the decomposition is just two [Fagin 1977; Ullman 1982a; Maier 1983]. Furthermore, it has been conjectured that a single acyclic JD over the universal set of attributes, U, and a set of FDs, are sufficient to model most real-world applications [Fagin et al. 1982; Beeri & Kifer 1986]. Thus, in Section 4.2 we generalize NMVDs that hold in flat relations to *null join dependencies* (NJDs). In addition, in Section 4.3 we extend NJDs, which hold in flat relations, to nested relations; we call such extended JDs *null extended join dependencies* (NEJDs). The extension of NJDs to NEJDs is achieved by utilizing the null extended join operator given in Definition 3.19. As a consequence of this approach we are now able to capture the novel notion of losslessness in nested relations, which we call *null extended lossless decomposition*.

FDs are by far the most common data dependency in the real world [Ullman 1982a; Maier 1983] and the notion of keys (which are derived from a given set of FDs) [Codd 1979; Ullman 1982a; Maier 1983] is fundamental to the relational model. Thus, in Section 4.4 we extend the notion of NFDs and keys from flat relations to nested relations in a natural way, namely, instead of zero order attributes appearing on the right-hand side of a NFD we now have a higher order attribute, for example, $X \rightarrow (Y)^*$. Thus, instead of requiring information-wise equivalence over the zero order attribute on the right-hand side of a NFD, we now require information-wise equivalence over $(Y)^*$. These extended NFDs, in the context of nested relations, are called *null extended functional dependencies*

(NEFDs), and correspondingly the induced extended keys are called *extended keys*. (Cf. [Makinouchi 1977; Jaeschke & Schek 1982; Arisawa et al. 1983; Fischer et al. 1985; Fischer & Thomas 1986; Levene & Loizou 1988].) We then proceed to show that hierarchical relations can equivalently be explained in terms of a set of NEFDs that hold in a nested flat relation (see Definition 2.12). It follows, therefore, that in order to test whether a nested flat relation is indeed a hierarchical relation we need not unnest it to a flat relation in order to test satisfaction of its set of NMVDs but rather we can test satisfaction of its set of NEFDs directly on itself, i.e., the nested flat relation.

Previous research on the effect of null values on data dependency satisfaction in flat databases has been carried out by Lien [1979, 1982], Vassiliou [1980], Goldstein [1981], Imielinski & Lipski [1983], Grahne [1984], Atzeni & Morfuni [1986] and Graham et al. [1986], with the emphasis to date being primarily on FDs with nulls.

The representation of data dependencies within the structure of nested relations has been studied mainly in the area of database design for nested relations. To this end normal forms for nested relations have been defined [Makinouchi 1977; Levene & Loizou 1987a, 1987b; Ozsoyoglu & Yuan 1987a, 1987b; Roth & Korth 1987], which have the additional goals of reducing redundancy and providing a lossless join decomposition over the universal set of attributes, U. Another motivation for the study of the representation of data dependencies within the structure of nested relations is the desire to render nested relations as a user interface to a flat database. The benefits of this approach are: redundancy is removed from the database outputs and the outputs are expressed in a more natural and user-friendly fashion. To this end Kambayashi et al. [1983] and Kambayashi & Yamamoto [1987] utilize a set of data dependencies in order to restructure the output, resulting from a query to a flat database, into a set of nested relations.

Different subclasses of nested relations were defined by Fischer & Van Gucht [1984, 1985] and Van Gucht & Fischer [1986, 1988] with the objective of characterizing the desirable properties of such subclasses. These subclasses of nested relations are classified according to the extended FDs (cf. Definition 4.6) that hold in the nested relations and the data dependencies that hold in their corresponding flat relations.

The *chase* procedure [Maier et al. 1979; Graham et al. 1986] allows us to test the satisfaction of a given set of data dependencies, say D, in a flat relation and to infer more information from this flat relation by using the FDs in D to replace some of the null values by non-null values (constants), and also by using the JDs in D to generate extra tuples to be appended to the flat relation. In Section 4.5 we extend the chase procedure to nested relations, and call it the *extended chase* procedure; this procedure is used in order to test satisfaction of a set of null extended data dependencies, say D^*, and to infer more information from a given nested relation by using the null extended data dependencies in D^*.

Herein (apart from the general class of nested relations), the subclasses of nested relations we are interested in, are nested flat relations and hierarchical relations, which we have defined in Definitions 2.10 and 2.12, respectively. The extended chase, presented in Section 4.5, provides us with a novel method of directly testing whether a given nested relation belongs to a subclass of nested relations, the subclass being characterized by a set of null extended data dependencies. The extended chase can then be applied directly on the given nested relation, without unnesting it, since as we show throughout this chapter the null extended data dependencies that hold in nested relations have counterpart null data dependencies that hold in the corresponding flat relations.

Finally, we conclude by defining the notion of implication (cf. Subsection 2.1.2) for a set of null extended data dependencies and the counterpart set of null data dependencies. Let D be a set of null data dependencies, and let SAT(D) denote the set of flat relations, over U, that satisfy D. We say that D implies a single null data dependency, d_i, written in the form of D $\models d_i$ iff SAT(D) $\subseteq$ SAT(d_i). Correspondingly, let D* be a set of null extended data dependencies, and let SAT(D*) denote the set of nested relations, over U(T), that satisfy D* (see D(U) of Section 4.5). We say that D* implies a single null extended data dependency, d_i^*, written in the form of D* $\models d_i^*$ iff SAT(D*) $\subseteq$ SAT(d_i^*). Similarly, we define D* $\models d_i$ iff $\{\mu^*(r^*) \mid r^* \in$ SAT(D*)$\} \subseteq$ SAT(d_i) and D $\models d_i^*$ iff SAT(D) $\subseteq \{\mu^*(r^*) \mid r^* \in$ SAT(d_i^*)$\}$, where D is the counterpart set of null data dependencies corresponding to D* and $d_i \in$ D.

A set D_1 of null extended data dependencies (or null data dependencies) implies a set D_2 of null extended data dependencies (or null data dependencies), denoted by $D_1 \models D_2$ iff $D_1 \models$ d for all null extended data dependencies (or null data dependencies), d $\in D_2$. Finally, D_1 is equivalent to D_2, denoted by $D_1 \equiv D_2$, iff $D_1 \models D_2$ and $D_2 \models D_1$.

4.1 Null Functional Dependencies

In this section we generalize the standard FD that holds in flat relations to the *null functional dependency* (NFD), a member of the class of null data dependencies. We then redefine the NFD, over a set of attributes labelling a node in the scheme tree, T, in order that it holds in a nested relation over the NRS, R(T). Such a NFD is a member of the class of null extended data dependencies. Finally, we discuss some important characteristics of NFDs.

Definition 4.1. Let r be a flat relation over a set of attributes W $\subseteq$ U and let X, A $\subseteq$ U, where A is a single attribute. Then the NFD, X $\rightarrow$ A, holds in r iff whenever there exist tuples $t_1, t_2 \in$ r such that $t_1[X] = t_2[X]$, i.e., t_1 and t_2 are X-total, then $t_1[A] \cong t_2[A]$, i.e., t_1 and t_2 are both A-total or $t_1[A]$ and $t_2[A]$ both contain the same type of null value.

(Cf. [Lien 1982; Atzeni & Morfuni 1986].)

We note that the definition of key, given in Subsection 2.1.2, is easily generalized so that it is w.r.t. a set of NFDs rather than a set of FDs, i.e., the closure of a set of attributes, X $\subseteq$ U, X^+, is taken to be w.r.t. a given set of NFDs [Atzeni & Morfuni 1986]. We now redefine NFDs in the context of nested relations.

Definition 4.2. Let r* be a nested relation over a NRS, R(T), and let X, A $\subseteq$ ATT(n), where n is a node in T and A is a single attribute. Then the NFD, $X \to A$, holds in r* iff $X \to A$ holds in $\mu^*(\Pi^{ne}_{XA}(r^*))$ prior to it being reduced during the computation of Π^{ne} and μ^*.

If $A \in X$ then the NFD, $X \to A$, is said to be a *trivial* NFD, otherwise it is said to be a *non-trivial* NFD.

We denote the set of non-trivial NFDs, which are represented in the nodes of a scheme tree, T, by FF(T), and the set of non-trivial NFDs, which are represented in the nodes of a scheme forest, $F = \{T_1, T_2, ..., T_q\}$, by FF(F), where $FF(F) = \cup^q_{i=1} FF(T_i)$.

We note that Ozsoyoglu & Yuan [1987b] have incorporated FDs directly into scheme trees by distinguishing between MVD-edges and FD-edges in the description of a scheme tree. Ozsoyoglu & Yuan [1987b] allow only hierarchical relations in their model, so the induced nested relations, when incorporating FDs into their scheme trees, are a proper subclass of hierarchical relations. In the null extended nested relational model, we consider the general class of nested relations, which properly contains the class of hierarchical relations, and thus the set of NFDs, FF(T), for a scheme tree, T, does not imply that nested relations over the NRS, R(T), are hierarchical relations. Thus, in the null extended nested relational model the subclass of nested relations that satisfy FF(T) is independent of the subclass of hierarchical relations.

Example 4.1. For the scheme tree, T_1, shown in Figure 2.3, we have ATT(n) = {STUDENT, DEPT}, where n is the root node of T_1. The NFD, STUDENT $\to$ DEPT, holds in the nested relation, r^*_1, shown in Figure 2.8, over the NRS, R(T_1), and thus FF(T_1) = {STUDENT $\to$ DEPT}. Similarly, for the scheme tree, T_3, shown in Figure 2.11, we have ATT(n) = {TUTOR, SALARY}, where n is the root node of T_3. The NFD, TUTOR $\to$ SALARY, holds in the nested relation, r^*_3, shown in Figure 2.12, over the NRS, R(T_3), and thus FF(T_3) = {TUTOR $\to$ SALARY}. Thus, for the running example, FF(F) = FF(T_1) $\cup$ FF(T_3).

We note that the attributes of a NFD may reside in a non-root node. For example, for the scheme tree, T, shown in Figure 3.21, we have ATT(n) = {TUTOR, SALARY}, where n is a non-root node in the scheme tree, T, and the NFD is: TUTOR $\to$ SALARY. This NFD holds in the nested relation, which is shown in Figure 3.25.

An important side-effect emanating from Definition 4.2 is that a nested relation which *may appear* to satisfy a given NFD, due to the fact that we have assumed that all nested relations are reduced, does *not* actually satisfy the said NFD. For example, the nested relation, r*, over the NRS, A(BC)*, shown in Figure 4.1, does not satisfy the NFD, $B \to C$, although $\mu^*(\Pi^{ne}_{BC}(r^*)) \cong \{<b_1, c_1>\}$. This is due to the fact that the violating tuple, $<b_1, null>$, is taken into account in Definition 4.2, since it appears in $\mu^*(\Pi^{ne}_{BC}(r^*))$ prior to it being reduced during the computation of Π^{ne} and μ^*. When we define the extended chase rule for the NFD, $X \to A$, in Definition 4.11 of Section 4.5, we also consider $\mu^*(\Pi^{ne}_{XA}(r^*))$ prior to it being reduced during the computation of Π^{ne} and μ^*, so as to make the maximum possible number of inferences in r* w.r.t. to the NFD, $X \to A$.

A	(B	C)*
	B	C
a_1	b_1	c_1
a_2	b_1	null

Fig. 4.1. A nested relation in which the NFD, B → C, does not hold.

For flat relations without nulls, Definition 4.2 reduces to the standard definition of FD given in Subsection 2.1.2. A sound and complete set of inference rules for NFDs is provided by Lien [1982]; this set does not include transitivity [Ullman 1982a; Maier 1983], which may not hold in the presence of nulls [Lien 1982; Atzeni & Morfuni 1986]. For example, the well-known flat relation [Atzeni & Morfuni 1986], shown in Figure 4.2, satisfies the NFDs, {A → B, B → C}, but violates the NFD, A → C.

A	B	C
a_1	null	c_1
a_1	null	c_2

Fig. 4.2. A relation which violates transitivity for NFDs.

We note that the definitions of key and superkey given in Subsection 2.1.2 remain valid for NFDs. Therefore, Definition 2.1 of BCNF also obtains for NFDs.

Although we consider nulls not to be equal, in deciding whether a NFD holds we have taken into account the possibility that when nulls are replaced by non-null values the said values may become equal. For this reason, when either one of the tuples, t_1, t_2, is not X-total or when both tuples are not A-total and $t_1[A] \cong t_2[A]$, then we consider the NFD, X → A, to be satisfied. This implies that our definition of NFDs is weaker than the standard definition of FDs, in the sense that although a NFD may be satisfied we may not know if the corresponding FD is also satisfied until certain null values are updated with non-null values.

4.2 Null Multivalued Dependencies

In this section we generalize the standard MVD that holds in flat relations to the *null multivalued dependency* (NMVD), which holds in null extended domains. We then redefine the data dependencies that are explicitly represented in hierarchical relations in terms of NMVDs rather than MVDs. Lastly, we generalize NMVDs to *null join dependencies* (NJDs). The NJD is a member of the class of null data dependencies.

Definition 4.3. Let r be a flat relation over a set of attributes $W \subseteq U$ and let X, Y, Z be pairwise disjoint sets of attributes whose union is W. The NMVD, X →→ Y (W), (or X →→ Y when W is understood from context) holds in r iff whenever there exists tuples

$<x, y_1, z_1>$ and $<x, y_2, z_2>$ in r such that the X-value, x, for both of these tuples is X-total, then the tuples $<x, y_1, z_2>$ and $<x, y_2, z_1>$ are also in r.
(Cf. [Lien 1979, 1982].)

We note that in the above definition any of: y_1, y_2, z_1 or z_2 may be information-wise equivalent to *null*.

As with MVDs, the NMVD, $X \rightarrow\rightarrow Y$ (W), is a *trivial* NMVD if XY = W or Y ⊆ X, otherwise it is said to be a *non-trivial* NMVD.

For flat relations without nulls Definition 4.3 reduces to the standard definition of MVD given in Subsection 2.1.2. A sound and complete set of inference rules for NMVDs is provided by Lien [1979, 1982] and a sound and complete set of inference rules for NFDs and NMVDs is also provided by Lien [1982]. These sets do not include transitivity [Ullman 1982a; Maier 1983], which may not hold in the presence of nulls [Lien 1979, 1982].

We observe that it can easily be verified that the *NMVD-counterpart*, $X \rightarrow\rightarrow A$, of a NFD, $X \rightarrow A$, (cf. MVD-counterpart in Subsection 2.1.2) is implied by $X \rightarrow A$, i.e., $X \rightarrow A \models X \rightarrow\rightarrow A$.

We now redefine the set of data dependencies embedded within the structure of a hierarchical relation to be a set of NMVDs instead of MVDs as given in Definition 2.12. That is, MVD(T), for a scheme tree, T, is **hereafter defined** to be a set of NMVDs (rather than MVDs) and a hierarchical relation, r*, over a NRS, R(T), is **hereafter defined** to be a nested flat relation such that its flat counterpart, μ*(r*), over S(T), satisfies the set of NMVDs, MVD(T).

We end this section by generalizing NMVDs to NJDs. Prior to giving the formal definition of NJDs, we first present some necessary background material.

Let r be a flat relation over U and let $\mathbf{R} = \{R_1, R_2, ..., R_m\}$ be a FDS over U. We recall from Subsection 2.1.2 that COVER(**R**) is the set of FDSs that cover **R**, and that MANY(**R**) is the set of attributes which appear in at least two FRSs in **R**.

We say that the FDS, S, over U, is a *covering subset* of the FDS, **R**, if each FRS, S_i ∈ S, is a set of attributes over a connected subset, say S_i, of **R** and such that $\mathbf{R} = \cup_i S_i$. We denote the set of all *covering subset FDSs* of **R** by SUBSET(**R**). We note that if S ∈ SUBSET(**R**), then S ∈ COVER(**R**), but the converse is, in general, false.

We say that n not necessarily distinct tuples, $t_1, t_2, ..., t_n$ ∈ r, are *combinable* on a covering subset FDS, S ∈ SUBSET(**R**), where n = |S| ≤ m, with the resulting tuple, t, over U, if $t[S_i] \cong t_i[S_i]$, S_i ∈ S, $1 \le i \le n$, and t[MANY(S)] is MANY(S)-total. (Cf. [Maier et al. 1979; Stein & Maier 1985].)

In the sequel, whenever the parameters are fully understood from context, we abbreviate the above to: *the tuples, $t_1, t_2, ..., t_n$ ∈ r, are combinable with the resulting tuple, t, over U.*

Definition 4.4. The NJD, ⋈[**R**], holds in r iff whenever there exist n not necessarily distinct tuples, t_1, t_2, ..., $t_n \in$ r, that are combinable with the resulting tuple, t, over the universe, U, then t is a tuple in r, i.e., t $\in$ r.

As with JDs, the NJD, $\bowtie[R]$, is said to be a *trivial* NJD if m = 1, otherwise it is said to be a *non-trivial* NJD.

It can easily be seen that the NMVD is a special case of the NJD, i.e., when m = 2. Also, it can easily be verified that for flat relations without nulls, Definition 4.4 reduces to the standard definition of the JD given in Subsection 2.1.2. Furthermore, it can be verified that the covering and projection rules for JDs (given in Subsection 2.1.2) also hold for NJDs over flat relations with nulls due to Definition 4.4. We note that we can formally show that the said covering rule holds by using a result from Beeri & Vardi [1981], wherein it was shown that a FDS, S, covers a FDS, **R**, iff S can be obtained from **R** by repetitively, either adding a FRS to **R**, or by adding an attribute to a FRS already in **R**.

On the other hand, the substitution rule for JDs (also given in Subsection 2.1.2) does not, in general, hold for NJDs, since, as is the case with NMVDs, transitivity of NJDs may not hold in the presence of nulls. A simple example illustrates this: let D = {AB $\rightarrow\rightarrow$ C | D, A $\rightarrow\rightarrow$ B | CD} and r = {$<a_1$, *null*, c_1, $d_1>$, $<a_1$, *null*, c_2, $d_2>$}. It can easily be verified that r $\in$ SAT(D) but r does not satisfy A $\rightarrow\rightarrow$ C, which would be inferred by using the substitution rule.

We now present a special case of the substitution rule, called the *non-split substitution rule*, which is sufficient for our purposes in this monograph. Let **R** be a FDS, over U, and let S = {S_1, S_2} be a FDS over the attributes of an $R_i \in$ **R** such that either (MANY(**R**) $\cap$ R_i) $\subseteq$ ($S_1 \cap S_2$) or MANY(**R**) $\cap$ S_1 = $\emptyset$. Then, the *non-split substitution rule* for NJDs is given by

$$\{\bowtie[R], \bowtie[S]\} \models \bowtie[(R - \{R_i\}) \cup S].$$

Let r be a flat relation, over U, that satisfies $\bowtie[R]$; assume that $\Pi_{R_i}(r)$ satisfies $\bowtie[S]$. Also, let **Q** $\in$ (SUBSET((**R** - {R_i}) $\cup$ S) – SUBSET(**R**)) be a FDS with |**Q**| = n. We claim that if the tuples, t_1, t_2, ..., $t_n \in$ r, are combinable on **Q** with the resulting tuple, t, over U, then t $\in$ r.

We next outline a proof of the above claim, thereby showing that the non-split substitution rule holds for NJDs over flat relations with nulls.

Assume that $\neg$(t $\in$ r). Now, since $\bowtie[S]$ holds in $\Pi_{R_i}(r)$, it follows that there exists a tuple, t' $\in$ r, such that t'[R_i] $\cong$ t[R_i] and $\neg$(t'[U – R_i] $\cong$ t[U – R_i]). In addition, we have that t'[MANY(**R**) $\cap$ R_i] = t[MANY(**R**) $\cap$ R_i], since either (MANY(**R**) $\cap$ R_i) $\subseteq$ ($S_1 \cap S_2$) or MANY(**R**) $\cap$ S_1 = $\emptyset$.

There must now exist a subset of {t_1, t_2, ..., t_n} whose tuples are combinable on a covering subset **Q'** $\in$ SUBSET(**R**) with the resulting tuple $t'_i \in$ r such that t'_i[U – R_i] $\cong$ t[U – R_i] and t'_i[MANY(**R**) $\cap$ R_i] = t[MANY(**R**) $\cap$ R_i]. It, therefore, follows that t' and t'_i are combinable on {((U – R_i) $\cup$ (MANY(**R**) $\cap$ R_i)), R_i} with the resulting tuple, t $\in$ r, which leads to a contradiction.

We observe that a nested relation, r*, over R(T), is a hierarchical relation iff r* is a nested flat relation and its associated flat relation, i.e., μ*(r*), satisfies the NJD, $\bowtie[P(T)]$, since it can easily be verified that the result of Lemma 2.3 (2), namely, MVD(T) $\equiv$ $\bowtie[P(T)]$, still holds for NMVDs and NJDs, due to Definition 4.4 and Lemma 2.3 (1), and the non-split substitution rule which is used to prove MVD(T) $\models \bowtie[P(T)]$. This implication can also be proved by induction on the cardinality of P(T), or alternatively, by induction on HEIGHT(T).

4.3 Null Extended Join Dependencies

In this section we extend NJDs to nested relations, hereafter called *null extended join dependencies* (NEJDs), by incorporating the null extended join operator, given in Definition 3.19, into the definition of a NJD, namely, Definition 4.4. The NEJD, a member of the class of null extended data dependencies, is a new null extended data dependency, which enables us to capture the novel notion of lossless decomposition in nested relations, which we hereafter call *null extended lossless decomposition*. We then investigate the properties of NEJDs w.r.t. NJDs. In particular, we proceed to show that the NEJD is faithful to the NJD in the sense that a NEJD reduces to a NJD when only flat relations are considered. Finally, we show that the NEJD is a precise generalization of the NJD in the sense that the NEJD holds in a nested relation iff its counterpart NJD holds in the corresponding flat relation.

We begin by extending the notions of a covering subset FDS and combinable tuples to NDSs and tuples of nested relations, respectively. We recall from Subsection 2.2.1 that if F is a scheme forest, over U, then FDS(F) = $\{S(T_1), S(T_2), ..., S(T_q)\}$.

Let **R**(F) be a joinable NDS, over the joined NRS, U(T), and let r* be a nested relation over U(T). Then, the NDS **R**(F'), where F' = $\{T'_1, T'_2, ..., T'_n\}$ is a scheme forest over the joined NRS, U(T), is a *covering subset* of the NDS, **R**(F), if FDS(F') $\in$ SUBSET(FDS(F)). We denote the set of all covering subset NDSs of **R**(F) by SUBSET(**R**(F)).

As before, we say that n not necessarily distinct tuples, $t_1, t_2, ..., t_n \in$ r*, are *combinable* on a covering subset NDS, **R**(F') $\in$ SUBSET(**R**(F)), where n = $|$**R**(F')$| \leq q$, with the resulting tuple, t*, over U(T), if

$$t* \cong \bowtie^{ne} {}_{i=1}^{n} (\Pi^{ne}{}_{S(T'_i)} (t_i)) \neq \emptyset, \tag{1}$$

where $S(T'_i) \in$ FDS(F'), $1 \leq i \leq n$. Consequently, t*[MANY(FDS(F'))] is MANY(FDS(F'))-total, due to Definition 3.19 of $\bowtie^{ne}$.

In the sequel, whenever the parameters are fully understood from context, we abbreviate the above to: *the tuples, $t_1, t_2, ..., t_n \in$ r*, are combinable with the resulting tuple, t*, over U(T)*.

We are now in a position to extend the NJD, defined over flat relations, to the NEJD, defined over nested relations, by utilizing the above concepts.

Definition 4.5. Let $R(F)$ be a joinable NDS, over the joined NRS, $U(T)$, and let r^* be a nested relation over $U(T)$. Then, the NEJD, $\bowtie^{ne}[R(F)]$, holds in r^* iff whenever there exist n not necessarily distinct tuples, $t_1, t_2, ..., t_n \in r^*$, that are combinable with the resulting tuple, t^*, over $U(T)$, then t^* is a tuple in r^*, i.e., $t^* \in r^*$.

We say that a nested relation r^*, over $U(T)$, possesses a *null extended lossless decomposition* onto $R(F)$ iff r^* satisfies the NEJD, $\bowtie^{ne}[R(F)]$.

We further note that a null extended lossless decomposition of r^* onto a joinable NDS, $R(F)$, does *not*, in general, imply that

$$r^* \cong \bowtie^{ne} {}_{i=1}^{q} (\Pi^{ne}{}_{S(T_i)} (r^*))$$

holds as is the case in flat relational database theory without nulls (see Subsection 2.1.2). This is due to the equality rule for nulls (see Definition 3.3), whereby nulls over projected attribute values are not equal. In Theorem 5.8 of Section 5.4, we show that if d^* is a nested database, over a NDS, $R(F)$, possessing the UMC property, then the null extended outer join can be utilized to join all the nested relations in d^* without loss of information.

If $q = 1$, then $\bowtie^{ne}[R(F)]$ is said to be a *trivial* NEJD, otherwise it is said to be a *non-trivial* NEJD. If $q = 2$, i.e., $R(F) = \{R(T_1), R(T_2)\}$, then $\bowtie^{ne}[R(F)]$ is a *null extended multivalued dependency* (NEMVD). In this case we employ, at times, the standard notation used for MVDs and NMVDs, namely,

$$U(T)[S(T_1) \cap S(T_2)] \to\to U(T)[S(T_1) - S(T_2)] (U(T))$$
$$(\text{or simply } U(T)[S(T_1) \cap S(T_2)] \to\to U(T)[S(T_1) - S(T_2)]).$$

The next proposition shows that the NEJD is faithful to the NJD.

Proposition 4.1. Let $R = \{R_1, R_2, ..., R_m\}$ be a FDS, over U, and let r be a flat relation over U. Then, the NEJD, $\bowtie^{ne}[R]$, is *faithful* to the NJD, $\bowtie[R]$, in the sense that $\bowtie^{ne}[R]$ holds in r iff $\bowtie[R]$ holds in r.

Proof. The result follows, since in this case Definition 4.5 of the NEJD reduces to Definition 4.4 of the NJD by the following argument.

Let $t_1, t_2, ..., t_n \in r$ be *combinable* on a covering subset FDS, S, of R, i.e., $S \in$ SUBSET(R), where $n = |S| \leq m$, with the resulting tuple, t, over U. Thus, by Definition 4.4, $t[S_i] \cong t_i[S_i], S_i \in S, 1 \leq i \leq n$, and $t[MANY(S)]$ is MANY(S)-total.

Equivalently, we have that

$$t \cong \bowtie {}_{i=1}^{n} (\Pi_{S_i} (t_i)) \neq \emptyset,$$

where $S_i \in S, 1 \leq i \leq n$, and $t[MANY(S)]$ is MANY(S)-total.

Now, by Proposition 3.5, Π^{ne} is faithful to Π, and, by Proposition 3.11, $\bowtie^{ne}$ is faithful to $\bowtie$. The result thus follows, since, by Definition 4.5, there exists a tuple, t, over U, such that

$$t \cong \bowtie^{ne} {}_{i=1}^{n} (\Pi^{ne}{}_{S_i} (t_i)) \neq \emptyset,$$

where $S_i \in S$, $1 \leq i \leq n$, and $t[\text{MANY}(S)]$ is MANY(S)-total. $\square$

Proposition 4.1 states that the effect of nulls on NJDs (or on NMVDs when m = 2) is the same as the effect of nulls on NEJDs (or on NEMVDs when q = 2), when we consider only flat relations over FDSs.

Example 4.2. Let r be the flat relation, shown in Figure 4.3. Then, it can easily be verified that r satisfies the NMVD, A $\rightarrow\rightarrow$ B | C (or equivalently $\bowtie[\{AB, BC\}]$), and correspondingly r satisfies the NEMVD, A $\rightarrow\rightarrow$ B | C (or equivalently $\bowtie^{ne}[\{AB, AC\}]$).

A	B	C
null	b_1	c_1
null	b_2	c_2

Fig. 4.3. The flat relation with nulls, r, satisfying the NEMVD $\bowtie^{ne}[\{AB, AC\}]$.

The next theorem shows that the NEJD is a precise generalization of the NJD.

Theorem 4.2. Let $R(F) = \{R(T_1), R(T_2), ..., R(T_q)\}$ be the joinable NDS over the joined NRS, U(T), and let r* be a nested relation over U(T). Then, the NEJD, $\bowtie^{ne}[R(F)]$, is a *precise* generalization of the NJD, $\bowtie[FDS(F)]$, in the sense that the NEJD, $\bowtie^{ne}[R(F)]$, holds in r* iff the NJD, $\bowtie[FDS(F)]$, or equivalently the NJD, JD(F), holds in $\mu^*(r^*)$.

Proof. By Proposition 4.1, the NJD, $\bowtie[FDS(F)]$, holds in $\mu^*(r^*)$ iff the NEJD, $\bowtie^{ne}[FDS(F)]$, holds in $\mu^*(r^*)$. It, therefore, suffices to show that $\bowtie^{ne}[R(F)]$ holds in r* iff $\bowtie^{ne}[FDS(F)]$ holds in $\mu^*(r^*)$.

IF. The NEJD, $\bowtie^{ne}[FDS(F)]$, holds in $\mu^*(r^*)$ iff whenever there exist n not necessarily distinct tuples, $t_1, t_2, ..., t_n \in \mu^*(r^*)$, with $n \leq q$, that are combinable on a covering subset FDS, FDS(F') $\in$ SUBSET(FDS(F)), where n = |FDS(F')|, with the resulting tuple, t, over U, then $t \in \mu^*(r^*)$.

Let FDS(F') = $\{S(T'_1), S(T'_2), ..., S(T'_n)\}$. Now, by (1) and the faithfulness of Π^{ne} and $\bowtie^{ne}$, shown in Propositions 3.5 and 3.11, respectively, it follows that

$$t \cong \bowtie {}_{i=1}^{n} (\Pi_{S(T'_i)} (t_i)) \neq \emptyset. \tag{2}$$

It is also true that there exist n not necessarily distinct tuples, $t_i^* \in r^*$, where $t_i \in \mu^*(t_i^*)$, $1 \leq i \leq n$. (In fact there may be more distinct t_i's than t_i^*'s.) It, therefore, follows from (2) that

$$t \in \bowtie {}_{i=1}^{n} (\Pi_{S(T'_i)} (\mu^* (t_i^*))) \neq \emptyset. \tag{3}$$

Thus, from (3) and the preciseness of Π^{ne} and $\bowtie^{ne}$, shown in Theorems 3.6 and 3.12, respectively, we have that

$$t^* \cong \bowtie^{ne} {}_{i=1}^{n} (\Pi^{ne} {}_{S(T'_i)} (t_i^*)) \neq \emptyset, \tag{4}$$

with $t \in \mu^*(t^*)$.

We now conclude the *if* part of the proof; $t^* \in r^*$ must obtain, otherwise the NEJD, $\bowtie^{ne}[FDS(F)]$, would be violated in $\mu^*(r^*)$. Thus, by (4) and Definition 4.5, $\bowtie^{ne}[R(F)]$ holds in r^* as required.

ONLY IF. The NEJD, $\bowtie^{ne}[R(F)]$, holds in r^* iff whenever there exist n not necessarily distinct tuples, $t_1^*, t_2^*, ..., t_n^* \in r^*$, that are combinable on a covering subset NDS, $R(F') \in$ SUBSET($R(F)$)), where $n = |R(F')|$, with the resulting tuple, t^*, over $U(T)$, then $t^* \in r^*$.

We prove the *only if* part by reversing the argument of the *if* part of the proof.

Let $F' = \{T'_1, T'_2, ..., T'_n\}$. Then from (1) we obtain equation (4). Now, on using the preciseness of Π^{ne} and $\bowtie^{ne}$, shown in Theorems 3.6 and 3.12, respectively, and the operator μ^* we derive equation (3). Equation (3) asserts the existence of a tuple, t, over U, such that $t \in \mu^*(t^*)$. It now follows that equation (2) describes the construction of the tuple $t \in \mu^*(t^*)$.

We now conclude the *only if* part of the proof; $t \in \mu^*(r^*)$ must obtain, otherwise the NEJD, $\bowtie^{ne}[R(F)]$, would be violated in r^*. Thus, by (2) and Definition 4.5, $\bowtie^{ne}[FDS(F)]$ holds in $\mu^*(r^*)$ as required. $\square$

Example 4.3. Let $R(F) = \{R(T_1), R(T_2)\}$, where $R(T_1) = A(B)^*(D)^*$, $R(T_2) = \Lambda(B(C)^*)^*$ are projected NRSs of $U(T) = A(B(C)^*)^*(D)^*$. It can easily be verified that the nested relation, r^*, over $U(T)$, shown in Figure 4.4 violates the NEJD, $\bowtie^{ne}[R(F)]$. On the other hand, it can also be verified that the nested relation, r'^*, over $U(T)$, shown in Figure 4.5 satisfies the given NEJD, $\bowtie^{ne}[R(F)]$.

A	(B	(C)*)*	(D)*
	B	(C)*	D
		C	
a_1	b_1	c_1	d_1
	b_2	c_1	d_2
a_2	b_1	c_2	d_i
	b_3	c_2	d_3

Fig. 4.4. The nested relation, r^*, which violates $\bowtie^{ne}[\{A(B)^*(D)^*, \Lambda(B(C)^*)^*\}]$.

We observe that, by Theorem 4.2, it can be easily shown that the set of inference rules in Lien [1979, 1982], shown therein to be sound and complete for NFDs and NMVDs, is also sound and complete for NEMVDs and NFDs. In the more general case, when we consider NEJDs instead of just NEMVDs, the special case when only one NEJD, over $U(T)$, is considered (which corresponds to a single NJD over U), is interesting. This is because it was recently shown by Miller et al. [1988] that the set of inference rules given by Sciore [1982] is sound and complete for inferring all the JDs that are

A	(B	(C)*)*	(D)*
	B	(C)*	D
		C	
a_1	b_1	c_1	d_1
	b_2	c_1	d_2
a_1	b_1	c_2	d_1
			d_2
a_2	b_1	c_2	d_1
	b_3	c_2	d_3
a_2	b_1	c_1	d_1
			d_3

Fig. 4.5. The nested relation, $r'*$, which satisfies $\bowtie^{ne}[\{A(B)*(D)*, \Lambda(B(C)*)*\}]$.

implied by a single JD over U.

4.4 Null Extended Functional Dependencies

In this section we extend NFDs and keys holding in flat relations so that they obtain in nested relations, and call them, *null extended functional dependencies* (NEFDs) and *extended keys*, respectively. The NEFD is a member of the class of null extended data dependencies. We also show that hierarchical relations can be characterized in terms of a set of NEFDs that are embedded within the structure of a nested flat relation.

The following definition of the NEFD extends Definition 4.1, so that the NFD holds in nested relations; this is effected by allowing higher order attributes on the right-hand side of the NFD.

Definition 4.6. Let $r*$ be a nested relation over a NRS, R(T). Then the NEFD, $X \rightarrow (Y)*$, holds in $r*$ iff the following recursive definition is satisfied:

(1) If $X \subseteq Z(R(T))$ and $(Y)* \in H(R(T))$, then, whenever there exist tuples $t_1, t_2 \in r*$ such that $t_1[X] = t_2[X]$, i.e., t_1, t_2 are X-total, $t_1[(Y)*] \cong t_2[(Y)*]$; else

(2) Let $T_1, T_2, \ldots, T_s$, $s \geq 1$, denote the first level subtrees of the scheme tree, T. Then for all tuples, $t* \in r*$, there exists $i \in \{1,2,\ldots,s\}$ such that the NEFD, $X \rightarrow (Y)*$, holds in the nested relation, $\{t*[ATT(ROOT(T))]\}$ $\times^{ne}$ $t*[(R(T_i))*]$, over the NRS, $ATT(ROOT(T))R(T_i)$.

Prior to defining the set of NEFDs represented by a scheme tree, T, we state a useful proposition, i.e., Proposition 4.3, originally from Fischer et al. [1985], but whose proof also obtains for NRSs over null extended domains. Proposition 4.3 shows that a NEMVD, holding in a nested relation r*, becomes a NEFD after applying a single NEST operation to r*, while the said NEMVD still holds in the resulting nested relation after the NEST operation has been carried out.

Proposition 4.3. Let r* be a nested relation over R(T), with $X \subseteq Z(R(T))$ and $Y \subseteq R(T)$ such that $X \cap Y = \emptyset$. Then the following statements are equivalent.

(1) $X \rightarrow\rightarrow Y$ holds in r*;

(2) $X \rightarrow\rightarrow (Y)^*$ holds in $v_Y(r^*)$;

(3) $X \rightarrow (Y)^*$ holds in $v_Y(r^*)$. $\square$

We now define the set of NEFDs represented by a scheme tree, T; in analogy to MVD(T), we denote such a set by FD(T). Subsequently, namely, in Theorem 4.5, we utilize Proposition 4.3 in order to prove that MVD(T) is equivalent to FD(T).

Definition 4.7. Let e = (u,v) be an edge in a scheme tree, T, and let the NMVD for the edge, e, be $M(e) = A(u) \rightarrow\rightarrow D(v) (S(T))$. Let T_v be the subtree rooted at the node, v, of T. Then, the NEFD, corresponding to M(e), which holds in the nested relation r*, over R(T), is $A(u) \rightarrow (R(T_v))^*$, and is denoted by FD(e).

The set of NEFDs, which are represented by the edges of a scheme tree, T, is denoted by FD(T) and the set of NEFDs, which are represented by the scheme forest, F = $\{T_1, T_2, ..., T_q\}$, is given by FD(F) = $\cup_{i=1}^{q}$ FD(T_i).

We are now ready to define extended keys for a NRS, R(T), w.r.t. the set of NFDs, FF(T), and the set of NEFDs, FD(T).

Definition 4.8. Let R(T) be a NRS, and let $T_1, T_2, ..., T_s$, $s \geq 1$, denote the first level subtrees of the scheme tree, T. Then, $K \subseteq Z(R(T))$ is an *extended key* for R(T) iff FF(T) $\cup$ FD(T) $\models \{K \rightarrow (R(T_1))^*, K \rightarrow (R(T_2))^*, ..., K \rightarrow (R(T_s))^*\}$ and no proper subset of K is an extended key for R(T).

Example 4.4. For the scheme tree, T_1, of the running example, shown in Figure 2.3 we have:

FD(e_1) = STUDENT,DEPT $\rightarrow$ (MAJOR)*

FD(e_2) = STUDENT,DEPT $\rightarrow$ (CLASS (EXAM)* (PROJECT)*)*

FD(e_3) = STUDENT,DEPT,CLASS $\rightarrow$ (EXAM)*

FD(e_4) = STUDENT,DEPT,CLASS $\rightarrow$ (PROJECT)*.

For the scheme tree, T_2, of the running example, shown in Figure 2.9 we have:

FD(e_5) = CLASS $\rightarrow$ (TUTOR)*

$FD(e_6) = CLASS \rightarrow (TEXT)^*$.

For the scheme tree, T_3, of the running example, shown in Figure 2.11 we have:

$FD(e_7) = TUTOR,SALARY \rightarrow (CHILD)^*$

$FD(e_8) = TUTOR,SALARY \rightarrow (DAY)^*$.

It thus follows that $FD(T_1) = \{FD(e_1), FD(e_2), FD(e_3), FD(e_4)\}$, $FD(T_2) = \{FD(e_5), FD(e_6)\}$ and $FD(T_3) = \{FD(e_7), FD(e_8)\}$. Finally, for the scheme forest, F, of the running example, we have $FD(F) = FD(T_1) \cup FD(T_2) \cup FD(T_3)$.

It can easily be verified that FD(F) holds for the nested database, $d^* = \{r_1^*, r_2^*, r_3^*\}$, of the running example, where r_1^* is shown in Figure 2.8, r_2^* is shown in Figure 2.10 and r_3^* is shown in Figure 2.12.

It can also be verified that for the running example: STUDENT,DEPT is an extended key for the NRS, $R(T_1)$, CLASS is an extended key for the NRS, $R(T_2)$, and TUTOR,SALARY is an extended key for the NRS, $R(T_3)$. We recall that transitivity cannot be applied to NFDs and NMVDs. Thus, we cannot infer the extended key, STUDENT, for $R(T_1)$, nor can we infer the extended key, TUTOR, for $R(T_2)$, despite the fact that $FF(T_1) = \{STUDENT \rightarrow DEPT\}$ and $FF(T_3) = \{TUTOR \rightarrow SALARY\}$.

We now state two important facts, pertinent to the above.

(1) If D(v) is a set of attributes, nesting within the context of D(v) does not effect the NEFD. See, for example, $FD(e_2) \in FD(T_1)$ in the above example.

(2) Attributes, which are roots of subtrees of T, can appear on the left-hand side of a NEFD, although they are part of a nesting of attributes. See, for example, $FD(e_3)$, $FD(e_4) \in FD(T_1)$ in the above example.

Fact (2) above leads us to define *local NEFDs* (cf. *uniformly local FDs* [Fischer et al. 1985]), which are defined only within the context of subtrees.

Definition 4.9. Let e = (u,v) be an edge in T, and let T_v be the subtree rooted at the node, v, of T. Then, the *local NEFD* for e, denoted by LFD(e), corresponding to FD(e), is $ATT(u) \rightarrow (R(T_v))^*$.

The set of local NEFDs, which are represented by the edges of a scheme tree, T, is denoted by LFD(T), and the set of local NEFDs, which are represented by the scheme forest $F = \{T_1, T_2, ..., T_q\}$, is given by $LFD(F) = \cup_{i=1}^{q} LFD(T_i)$.

We now formally define the satisfaction of the set of LFDs, LFD(T), in a nested relation, r*, over a NRS, R(T).

Definition 4.10. Let r* be a nested relation over the NRS, R(T). Then r* satisfies LFD(T):

(1) If T consists of a single node, n, then r* trivially satisfies LFD(T);

(2) If X = ATT(ROOT(T)) and $T_1, T_2, ..., T_s$, s ≥ 1, denote the first level subtrees of T, then

(a) the NEFDs, $X \to (R(T_1))*, \ldots, X \to (R(T_s))*$, hold in $r*$;

(b) for each tuple, $t* \in r*$, LFD(T_i) holds in $t*[(R(T_i))*]$.

Example 4.5. For the scheme tree, T_1, of the running example, shown in Figure 2.3 we have:

LFD(e_1) = FD(e_1)

LFD(e_2) = FD(e_2)

LFD(e_3) = CLASS $\to$ (EXAM)*

LFD(e_4) = CLASS $\to$ (PROJECT)*.

It thus follows that LFD(T_1) = {LFD(e_1), LFD(e_2), LFD(e_3), LFD(e_4)}, and for the running example LFD(F) = {LFD(T_1), LFD(T_2), LFD(T_3)}, where LFD(T_2) = {LFD(e_5), LFD(e_6)} = FD(T_2) and LFD(T_3) = {LFD(e_7), LFD(e_8)} = FD(T_3).

It can easily be verified that LFD(F) holds for the nested database, $d* = \{r_1^*, r_2^*, r_3^*\}$, of the running example.

Partitioned normal form (PNF) [Roth et al. 1985, 1988] for nested relations was introduced in order that at each height of a given scheme tree, T, ATT(ROOT(T_v)) forms an extended key for the NRS, R(T_v), for each subtree, T_v, rooted at a node v of T. Thus, a nested relation, r*, over a NRS, R(T), is in PNF iff r* is a nested flat relation that satisfies LFD(T).

The following proposition shows that PNF can *not* be characterized by the set of NEFDs, FD(T), in place of the set of LFDs, LFD(T).

Proposition 4.4. Let r* be a nested flat relation over a NRS, R(T). Then, the following statements are *not* equivalent.

(1) The nested flat relation, r*, over the NRS, R(T), satisfies FD(T).

(2) The nested flat relation, r*, over the NRS, R(T), satisfies LFD(T).

Proof. Let r* be the nested flat relation over the NRS, R(T) = X(Y(V)*(W)*)*, shown in Figure 4.6; r* is a counterexample, since r* satisfies FD(T) but violates the LFDs Y $\to$ (V)*, Y $\to$ (W)* $\in$ LFD(T). $\square$

We observe that FD(T) holds in r* of Figure 4.6, due to the equality rule for nulls whereby null values are not equal to each other (see Definition 3.3). Furthermore, it can easily be shown that for the two statements of Proposition 4.4, (2) => (1), in fact, holds, i.e., LFD(T) |= FD(T). As a consequence, PNF for a nested relation, r*, is a stronger condition than the satisfaction of FD(T) in r*. We note that in our context, an alternative PNF for r* can be defined as the satisfaction of the set of NEFDs, FD(T), and a given set of NFDs, FF(T), in r*.

X	(Y	(V)*	(W)*)*
	Y	(V)*	(W)*
		V	W
null	y_1	v_1	w_1
	y_1	v_2	w_2

Fig. 4.6. A nested flat relation which satisfies FD(T) but violates LFD(T).

The following theorem shows that a hierarchical relation, r*, over a NRS, R(T), can be characterized either by the set of NMVDs, MVD(T), holding in the flat relation, $\mu*(r*)$, or equivalently, by the set of NEFDs, FD(T), holding in r*.

Theorem 4.5. The following statements are equivalent.

(1)   The nested relation, r*, over R(T), is a hierarchical relation.

(2)   The nested relation, r*, over R(T), is a nested flat relation that satisfies FD(T).

(3)   The flat relation, $\mu*(r*)$, over S(T), satisfies MVD(T).

Proof. By the modified definition of a hierarchical relation stated in Section 4.2 we have that (1) is equivalent to (3) It, therefore, suffices to show that (2) is equivalent to (3).

As before, let X = ATT(ROOT(T)); let $T_1, T_2, ..., T_s$, s ≥ 1, denote the first level subtrees of the scheme tree, T, and let H(R(T)) = {$(R(T_1))*, (R(T_2))*, ..., (R(T_s))*$} be the higher order attributes of R(T). We denote by F the set of NEFDs: {X → $(R(T_1))*$, X → $(R(T_2))*$, ..., X → $(R(T_s))*$}. Correspondingly, we denote by M the set of NEMVDs: {X →→ $R(T_1)$, X →→ $R(T_2)$, ..., X →→ $R(T_s)$}, and by M′ we denote the set of NMVDs: {X →→ $S(T_1)$, X →→ $S(T_2)$, ..., X →→ $S(T_s)$}.

In order to prove the result, we first show that (2) => (3) by induction on the number of UNNEST operations required to obtain $\mu*(r*)$ from r*. The inductive hypothesis assumes, in this case, that n applications of (3), of Proposition 4.3, to a given set of NEFDs that hold in a nested flat relation, say r′*, will yield a set of NMVDs that hold in the resulting flat relation, $\mu*(r′*)$. We then proceed to prove that (3) => (2) by induction on the number of NEST operations required to obtain r* from $\mu*(r*)$. The inductive hypothesis assumes, in this case, that n applications of (1), of Proposition 4.3, to a given set of NMVDs that hold in a flat relation, say $\mu*(r′*)$, will yield a set of NEFDs that hold in the nested flat relation, r′*.

As already said, we first prove that (2) => (3).

BASIS. If the number of UNNEST operations required in order to obtain $\mu*(r*)$ from r* is zero, then the result follows trivially, since FD(T) = MVD(T) = $\emptyset$. Thus, r* is a flat relation and MVD(T) holds in $\mu*(r*) \cong r*$ iff FD(T) holds in r*.

INDUCTION. Assume the result holds for n UNNEST operations applied to a nested flat relation, say r′*, required in order to obtain $\mu*(r′*)$; we then need to prove that the result also holds for n+1 UNNEST operations applied to a nested flat relation, r*, required in order to obtain $\mu*(r*)$.

Now, let r'* be the resulting nested flat relation over, say R(T'), after unnesting r* over all the attributes in H(R(T)). Then, by Definition 4.6 of NEFDs, we have that the set of NEFDs, {FD(T) - F}, holds in r'*. Furthermore, by Proposition 4.3, we have that the set of NEMVDs, M, corresponding to the set of NEFDs, F, also holds in r'*. Now, by the preciseness of the NEMVD, shown in Theorem 4.2, the set of NMVDs, M', holds in μ*(r*). The result now follows, since, by inductive hypothesis, the set of NMVDs, {MVD(T) - M'}, holds in μ*(r*).

Next, we prove that (3) => (2).

BASIS. If the number of NEST operations required in order to obtain r* from μ*(r*) is zero, then the result follows trivially, since MVD(T) = FD(T) = ∅. Thus, r* is a flat relation and FD(T) holds in r* iff MVD(T) holds in μ*(r*) ≅ r*.

INDUCTION. Assume the result holds for n NEST operations applied to, say μ*(r'*), required in order to obtain r'*; we then need to prove that the result also holds for n+1 NEST operations applied to μ*(r*) required in order to obtain r*.

Let r'* be the resulting nested flat relation over, R(T'), after applying a sequence of n NEST operations to μ*(r*). Then, by inductive hypothesis, we have that {FD(T) - F} holds in r'*. Now, the set of NMVDs, M', holds in μ*(r*), and, by the preciseness of the NEMVD, shown in Theorem 4.2, the set of NEMVDs, M, holds in r'*. The result now follows from Proposition 4.3, which implies that the set of NEFDs, F, holds in r*. □

We close this section with a corollary stating the equivalent characterizations of hierarchical relations, which we have so far established. The corollary follows directly from Theorem 4.5 and Lemma 2.3.

Corollary 4.6. The following statements are equivalent.

(1)   The nested relation, r*, over R(T), is a hierarchical relation.

(2)   The nested relation, r*, over R(T), is a nested flat relation that satisfies FD(T).

(3)   The flat relation, μ*(r*), over S(T), satisfies MVD(T).

(4)   The flat relation, μ*(r*), over S(T), satisfies ⋈[P(T)].   □

4.5 The Extended Chase

In this section we extend the *chase* procedure for flat relations [Maier et al. 1979; Beeri & Vardi 1984; Mendelzon 1984; Graham et al. 1986; Sagiv 1987, 1988] to nested relations, and call it the *extended chase* procedure (or simply the extended chase). Firstly, we define the *extended chase rules* for the null extended data dependencies, NFDs, NEFDs and NEJDs (NEMVDs); these rules modify a nested relation according to the extended chase rule being applied. Extended chase rules for NFDs and NEFDs generate information-wise equivalences in a given nested relation, while extended chase rules for NEJDs (NEMVDs) add more informative tuples to a given nested relation. We then define the meaning of applying the extended chase to a nested relation, r^*, over a joined NRS, $U(T)$, w.r.t. a set of *null extended data dependencies*, say $D(U)$; we denote the result of the said application by $CHASE_{D(U)}(r^*)$. Informally, the meaning of $CHASE_{D(U)}(r^*)$ is the result of applying repetitively the extended chase rules w.r.t. the null extended data dependencies in $D(U)$ until no more rules can be applied or we discover that r^* is *inconsistent*. We say that a nested relation, r^*, is *consistent* iff $CHASE_{D(U)}(r^*)$ satisfies the set of NFDs that are in $D(U)$ (cf. [Maier et al. 1979; Sagiv 1981, 1983, 1988; Honeyman 1982; Beeri & Vardi 1984; Mendelzon 1984; Graham et al. 1986; Atzeni & Bernardis 1987]).

Finally, we investigate the properties of $CHASE_{D(U)}(r^*)$. We show that $CHASE_{D(U)}(r^*)$ terminates and satisfies the set of null extended data dependencies, $D(U)$, provided $CHASE_{D(U)}(r^*)$ is consistent. Moreover, on letting D be the set of *null data dependencies* emanating from $D(U)$, i.e., the counterparts of the null extended data dependencies that hold in the corresponding flat relations, we show that $CHASE_{D(U)}(r^*)$ generalizes $CHASE_D(r)$, where $r \cong \mu^*(r^*)$, in a very natural way. An immediate consequence of these results is that we can now characterize hierarchical relations in terms of the extended chase, namely, a hierarchical relation, r^*, over the NRS, $R(T)$, is a nested flat relation that satisfies the set of NEFDs, FD(T), represented by its scheme tree, T; thus

$$r^* \cong CHASE_{FD(T)}(r^*).$$

In Definitions 4.11, 4.12 and 4.13, which follow, we define the extended chase rules for NFDs, NEFDs and NEJDs (NEMVDs), respectively.

Definition 4.11. Let r^* be a nested relation, over the NRS, $R(T)$, and let FF(T) be the set of NFDs, which are represented in the nodes of the scheme tree, T. Then, the *NFD-rule* for the NFD, $X \to A \in FF(T)$, is defined as follows:

Let t_1, t_2 be two XA-tuples in $\mu^*(\Pi^{ne}_{XA}(r^*))$ prior to it being reduced during the computation of Π^{ne} and μ^*. If $t_1[X] = t_2[X]$, i.e., t_1 and t_2 are X-total, and $\neg(t_1[A] \cong t_2[A])$, then

(1) if $t_1[A] \leq t_2[A]$, then $t_1[A] := t_2[A]$;

(2) if $t_2[A] \leq t_1[A]$, then $t_2[A] := t_1[A]$;

(3) if $\neg(t_1[A] \leq t_2[A])$ and $\neg(t_2[A] \leq t_1[A])$, then the NFD, $X \to A$, does not hold in r^*.

Hereafter, whenever we consider two XA-tuples, $t_1, t_2 \in \mu^*(\Pi^{ne}{}_{XA}(r^*))$, w.r.t. the NFD-rule associated with the NFD, $X \to A$, we consider $\mu^*(\Pi^{ne}{}_{XA}(r^*))$ prior to it being reduced during the computation of Π^{ne} and μ^*.

We note that our NFD-rule, defined above, is similar to the null-preserving FD-rule of Maier et al. [1986] and the analogue of the NFD-rule encountered in the modified chase of Atzeni & Bernardis [1987]. The difference between our NFD-rule and the standard one of Maier et al. [1979] is that in the null extended nested relational model unmarked nulls are used and the information lattice (see Figure 3.3) is employed to generate information-wise equivalences, while in Maier et al. [1979] marked nulls are used and hence nulls with different marks are equated whenever possible. Atzeni & Bernardis [1987] noted that in many classes of database schemes studied such as the independent database schemes of Sagiv [1981, 1983], and the constant-time-maintainable BCNF database schemes of Chan & Hernández [1986, 1988] and Hernández & Chan [1988], the result of a chase using their NFD-rule (cf. Definition 4.11) is the same as that of a chase using the standard FD-rule up to the interpretation of nulls, i.e., what null types are allowed in the relations to be chased.

We now define the extended chase rule for NEFDs, which generates information-wise equivalences in a nested relation which violates a given NEFD.

Definition 4.12. Let r^* be a nested relation, over the NRS, $R(T)$, and let FD(T) be the set of NEFDs represented by the edges of the scheme tree, T. Then, the *NEFD-rule* for the NEFD, $X \to (Y)^* \in$ FD(T), is defined recursively by the following rules:

(1) If $X = Z(R(T))$ and $(Y)^* \in H(R(T))$, and there exist tuples, $t_1, t_2 \in r^*$, such that $t_1[X] = t_2[X]$, i.e., t_1 and t_2 are X-total, and $\neg(t_1[(Y)^*] \cong t_2[(Y)^*])$, then $t_1[(Y)^*]$, $t_2[(Y)^*] := t_1[(Y)^*] \cup^{ne} t_2[(Y)^*]$; else

(2) Let $T_1, T_2, \ldots, T_s$, $s \geq 1$, denote the first level subtrees of the scheme tree, T, and let t^* be a tuple in r^*. Then we recursively apply the NEFD-rule for the NEFD, $X \to (Y)^*$, to the nested relation, $\{t^*[ATT(ROOT(T))]\} \times^{ne} t^*[(R(T_i))^*]$, over the NRS, $ATT(ROOT(T))R(T_i)$, where $i \in \{1, 2, \ldots, s\}$.

We observe that the NEFD-rule, given in Definition 4.12, is specifically designed for the enforcement of the NEFDs in FD(T) $\subseteq$ D(U). The NEFD-rule can be further extended to directly enforce NEFDs of the form, $K \to (Y)^*$, where K is an extended key for $R(T)$, however the said rule is sufficient for our purposes (see Lemma 4.9).

We note that another way of defining the NEFD-rule would be to consider information-wise equivalence instead of equality in part (1) of Definition 4.12. That is, we apply part (1) of Definition 4.12, whenever there exist tuples, $t_1, t_2 \in r^*$, such that $t_1[X] \cong t_2[X]$, i.e., the X-values of t_1 and t_2 are information-wise equivalent. We call such a modified NEFD-rule the *equivalence NEFD-rule* (EQ-NEFD-rule).

The benefit derived from using the EQ-NEFD-rule is that we obtain a more compact representation of the nested relation r* (as discussed in Subsection 3.1.2) than we would obtain by using the NEFD-rule. Moreover, in this case, as we have already mentioned in Subsection 3.1.2, a DBMS supporting the extended chase would not have to make null values a special case when testing for equality because of the fact that we are using unmarked nulls.

We now define the extended chase rule for NEJDs (NEMVDs); this rule adds more informative tuples to a nested relation that violates a given NEJD (NEMVD).

Definition 4.13. Let $R(F)$ be a joinable NDS over the joined NRS, $U(T)$; let $\bowtie^{ne}[R(F)]$ be an NEJD, over $U(T)$, and let r* be a nested relation over $U(T)$. Then the *NEJD-rule* for the NEJD, $\bowtie^{ne}[R(F)]$, is defined as follows:

Let t_1, t_2, ..., $t_n \in$ r* be n not necessarily distinct tuples that are combinable with the resulting tuple, t*, over $U(T)$. If there is no tuple $t^{*\prime} \in$ r* such that $t^{*\prime} \geq t^*$, then *add* t* to r*, namely, $r^* := r^* \cup^{ne} \{t^*\}$.

(Cf. [Maier et al. 1979; Beeri & Vardi 1984; Mendelzon 1984; Stein & Maier 1985; Graham et al. 1986; Sagiv 1987, 1988].)

Hereafter, as already stated, we denote the set of null extended data dependencies that hold in a nested relation, over $U(T)$, by $D(U)$. The set $D(U)$ may include:

(1)   the NFDs in $FF(T)$, represented in the nodes of the scheme tree, T;

(2)   the NEFDs in $FD(T)$, represented by the edges of the scheme tree, T; and

(3)   the NEJD, $\bowtie^{ne}[R(F)]$, over the joined NRS, $U(T)$.

We observe that for hierarchical relations the set of NEFDs, $FD(T)$, is, by (1) and (2) of Corollary 4.6, explicitly represented in the scheme tree, T, and thus, in this case, by default, $FD(T) \subseteq D(U)$ holds.

We are now ready to define the *extended chase* of a nested relation, r*, over the joined NRS, $U(T)$, w.r.t. $D(U)$. The extended chase of r* w.r.t. $D(U)$ is denoted hereafter by $CHASE_{D(U)}(r^*)$ (or just CHASE(r*) whenever $D(U)$ is understood from context).

CHASE(r*) is obtained by applying repetitively to the nested relation, r*, the NFD-rules, the NEFD-rules and the NEJD-rule, corresponding to the NFDs, the NEFDs and the NEJD, which may be in $D(U)$, respectively, whilst removing less informative tuples whenever possible, until either no further changes can be effected to the *current state* of r*, say $\hat{r}^*$, or until $\hat{r}^*$ violates one of the NFDs in $D(U)$.

If CHASE(r*) does not satisfy one of the NFDs in $D(U)$, then CHASE(r*) is taken to be an undefined nested relation and we say that r* is *inconsistent* w.r.t. $D(U)$ (or simply inconsistent, when $D(U)$ is understood from context); otherwise, CHASE(r*) results in a nested relation over $U(T)$ satisfying $D(U)$, and we say that r* is *consistent* w.r.t. $D(U)$ (or simply consistent, when $D(U)$ is understood from context). (Cf. [Maier et al. 1979; Beeri & Vardi 1984; Mendelzon 1984; Graham et al. 1986; Atzeni & Bernardis 1987].)

The following results, which are a generalization of the results in Maier et al. [1979], obtain for a nested relation r*, over $U(T)$, and a set, $D(U)$, of null extended data dependencies.

In order to avoid the introduction of further notation in the proofs that follow, we refer to an intermediate state, between r* and CHASE(r*), during the computation of CHASE(r*), as a *state* of CHASE(r*).

Lemma 4.7. CHASE(r*) terminates.

Proof. By the definition of CHASE(r*), if no further extended chase rules can be applied to r* that modify the tuples of r* or add more informative tuples to it, then CHASE(r*) terminates. Also, by the definition of CHASE(r*), if r* is inconsistent then CHASE(r*) terminates. So we can assume that an application of an extended chase rule transforms r*, say, to r'*. We need consider the following cases:

CASE 1. A NFD-rule is applied to r*. Then either a null value is replaced by a more informative value, null or non-null, in which case r* ≤ r'*, or else r* violates the NFD associated with the NFD-rule and it is, therefore, inconsistent.

CASE 2. A NEFD-rule is applied to r* and therefore r* ≤ r'*, since an information-wise equivalence is enforced in r*.

CASE 3. A NEJD-rule is applied to r* and therefore r* ≤ r'*, since a more informative tuple is added to r*.

Now, let ATOMIC(r*) be the finite set of all atomic domain values in $\mu^*(r^*)$, together with a null value for each null type. We note that none of the extended chase rules add any new atomic domain values or new null types to ATOMIC(r*). Thus, it suffices to show that CHASE(r*) does not loop forever. In order to conclude the proof, let r_i^* be the state of CHASE(r*) after applying some extended chase rules to r*, and let r_j^* be the state of CHASE(r*) after applying some further extended chase rules to r_i^*. The result now follows, since we have already shown that each time an extended chase rule is applied during the computation of CHASE(r*), a more informative nested relation results from such an application and thus $r_i^* \le r_j^*$; in addition, it is also true that $\neg(r_i^* \cong r_j^*)$ unless we have $r_i^* \cong$ CHASE(r*). □

Lemma 4.8. If r* is consistent then CHASE(r*) satisfies D(U).

Proof. We consider the satisfaction of the different null extended data dependencies that may be included in D(U) in turn.

CASE 1. CHASE(r*) satisfies the NFDs in D(U), since the NFD-rule detects any violation of an NFD in D(U) (see Definition 4.2), and by assumption r* is consistent.

CASE 2. CHASE(r*) satisfies the NEFDs in D(U), since the NEFD-rule detects any violation of an NEFD in D(U) (see Definition 4.6).

CASE 3. CHASE(r*) satisfies the NEJD in D(U), since the NEJD-rule detects any violation of the NEJD in D(U) (see Definition 4.5).

From the above, it follows that CHASE(r*) satisfies D(U), otherwise, by the above argument, we can apply one of the extended chase rules to CHASE(r*), thus leading to a contradiction. □

The following lemma shows that the extended chase is a *finite church-rosser* system (cf. [Maier et al. 1979]).

Lemma 4.9. If r* is consistent then CHASE(r*) is unique.

Proof. Consider the nested relation, r_i^*, obtained from r*, after applying some extended chase rules to r*. Similarly, consider the nested relation, r_j^*, obtained from r*, after applying some extended chase rules to r*; the latter rules are possibly different from and are also possibly not in the same order as the extended chase rules that were applied to r* in order to obtain r_i^*. We call the extended chase starting with r* and resulting in r_i^*, an r_i^*-sequence, and correspondingly the extended chase starting with r* and resulting in r_j^*, an r_j^*-sequence. In order to prove the uniqueness of CHASE(r*), we need to prove that CHASE(r_i^*) $\cong$ CHASE(r_j^*) $\cong$ CHASE(r*), as shown pictorially in Figure 4.7.

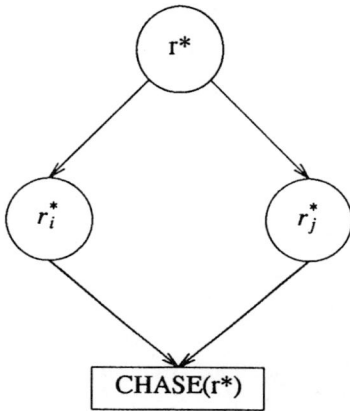

Fig. 4.7. CHASE(r*) obtained by applying different sequences of extended chase rules.

In the proof, which follows, we employ the following terminology. If a null extended data dependency in D(U) is not satisfied in a nested relation, say r'*, then we say that the corresponding extended chase rule is *triggered* in r'* by the said null extended data dependency. We now conclude the proof by induction on the number of extended chase rules triggered in an r_i^*-sequence, say m_i, and the number of extended chase rules triggered in an r_j^*-sequence, say m_j. We call m_i the *length* of the r_i^*-sequence and m_j the *length* of the r_j^*-sequence. We note that, by Lemma 4.7, both m_i and m_j are finite, since CHASE(r*) terminates.

BASIS. If $m_i = m_j = 0$, then r* $\cong r_i^* \cong r_j^* \cong$ CHASE(r*) as required.

INDUCTION. Assume that the result holds for an r_i^*- sequence of length $m_i > 0$, and for an r_j^*-sequence of length $m_j > 0$. We need to prove that the result also obtains for an r_i^*-sequence of length $m_i + 1$, and for an r_j^*-sequence of length $m_j + 1$.

We let r_i^* be the nested relation resulting from applying m_i extended chase rules to r*, and correspondingly we let r_j^* be the nested relation resulting from applying m_j extended chase rules to r*.

Now, let t' be a tuple in r_i^* or in r_j^* which may have been modified due to the application of a NFD-rule or a NEFD-rule. Then there exists at least one tuple, $t \in r*$, from which t' originated; such a tuple, t, is called an *original tuple* of t', or simply an *original* of t'. Alternatively, let t' be a tuple in r_i^* or in r_j^* resulting from an application of a NEJD-rule. In this case there exists a set of tuples, $\{t_1, t_2, ..., t_m\}$, $t_i \in r*$, $1 \le i \le m$, $m \ge 1$, all of which are *original* tuples of t', i.e., t' originated from this set of tuples.

We conclude the induction by examining the last extended chase rule that was triggered in the penultimate state of CHASE(r_i^*), say P_i^*, so as to show that CHASE$(r_i^*) \le$ CHASE(r_j^*). In order to trace the changes made to a tuple, $t \in r*$, by an r_i^*-sequence (or by an r_j^*-sequence), we define the *history* of a tuple t' in CHASE(r_i^*) (or in CHASE(r_j^*)). The history of t' is the reflexive-transitive closure (cf. [Maier et al. 1979]) of the mathematical relation "$t \in r*$ *is an original of t'*" or "$\{t_1, t_2, ..., t_m\} \subseteq r*$ *are originals of t'*".

CASE 1. The last extended chase rule triggered in the penultimate state of CHASE(r_i^*), i.e., P_i^*, was due to the NFD-rule associated with the NFD, $X \to A$. Let $t_i \in \mu*(\Pi^{ne}{}_{XA}(\text{CHASE}(r_i^*)))$ be the tuple which has been modified due to the application of the said NFD-rule to P_i^* and let $t \in \mu*(\Pi^{ne}{}_{XA}(r*))$ be an original of t_i. Thus there also exists a tuple $t_j \in \mu*(\Pi^{ne}{}_{XA}(\text{CHASE}(r_j^*)))$ such that the tuple t is also an original of t_j. We claim that for at least one of the said t_j, $t_i \le t_j$ also holds; this is proved by induction on the number of changes made to the tuple, t, in the history of the tuple, t_i.

BASIS. No changes were made to t. The result follows trivially, since $t_i \le t \le t_j$ holds.

INDUCTION. Assume that the result holds for k changes made to t in the history of t_i. We need to prove that the result also obtains when $k+1$ changes are made to t in the history of t_i. Let $t_i^k \in \mu*(\Pi^{ne}{}_{XA}(P_i^*))$ be the tuple which has been modified, due to the said NFD-rule that was triggered in P_i^*, in order to obtain the tuple $t_i \in \mu*(\Pi^{ne}{}_{XA}(\text{CHASE}(r_i^*)))$. Now, since k changes were made to t in the history of t_i^k we have, by inductive hypothesis, that $t_i^k \le t_j$ holds. It, therefore, follows that $t_i^k[X] = t_j[X]$ and as a result $t_i[X] = t_j[X]$. Consequently, it must also be true that $t_i[A] \le t_j[A]$, thus proving the result, otherwise, by the following argument, CHASE(r_j^*) has not terminated, since the NFD, $X \to A$, is violated.

Let $t'_i \in \mu*(\Pi^{ne}{}_{XA}(P_i^*))$ be the second tuple involved in the triggering of the above NFD-rule, therefore, $t'_i \cong t_i$ obtains. Thus, t'_i would also be present in an r_i^*-sequence of length m_i. It, therefore, follows, by the inductive hypothesis on k and the fact that applying an extended chase rule to a state of CHASE(r_j^*) increases its information content, that there exists a tuple, $t'_j \in \mu*(\Pi^{ne}{}_{XA}(\text{CHASE}(r_j^*)))$, such that $(t'_i \cong t_i) \le t'_j$; t'_j must be present in an r_j^*-sequence of length m_j+1. Now, t'_j and t_j would trigger the NFD-rule associated with the NFD, $X \to A$, in CHASE(r_j^*); however, by Lemma 4.8, CHASE(r_j^*) satisfies the NFD, $X \to A$.

CASE 2. Let $e = (u,v)$ be an edge in the scheme tree, T, associated with $r*$, and let T_v be the subtree of T rooted at the node v. Also, let $X = A(u)$, $Y = D(v)$ and $(Y)* = (R(T_v))*$. For simplicity, we assume that $X = Z(R(T))$ and $(Y)* \in H(R(T))$. If this is not the case then we can repetitively unnest $r*$, corresponding to recursive applications of the NEFD-rule in Definition 4.12 (2), thus obtaining $r'*$ over $R(T')$ such that $X = Z(R(T'))$

and $(Y)^* \in H(R(T'))$.

Now, the last extended chase rule triggered in the penultimate state of $\text{CHASE}(r_i^*)$, i.e., P_i^*, was due to the NEFD-rule associated with the NEFD, $X \to (Y)^*$. Let $t_i \in \text{CHASE}(r_i^*)$ be a tuple which has been modified due to the application of the said NEFD-rule to P_i^* and let $t \in r^*$ be an original of t_i. Thus there also exists a tuple $t_j \in \text{CHASE}(r_j^*)$ such that the tuple, t, is also an original of t_j. We claim that for at least one of the said t_j, $t_i[X(Y)^*] \le t_j[X(Y)^*]$ also holds; this is proved by induction on the number of changes made to the tuple, t, in the history of the tuple, t_i.

BASIS. No changes were made to t. The result follows trivially, since $t_i[X(Y)^*] \le t[X(Y)^*] \le t_j[X(Y)^*]$ holds.

INDUCTION. Assume that the result holds for k changes made to t in the history of t_i. We need to prove that the result also obtains when k+1 changes are made to t in the history of t_i. Let $t_i^k \in P_i^*$ be one of the two tuples which has been modified, due to the said NEFD-rule that was triggered in P_i^*, in order to obtain the tuple $t_i \in \text{CHASE}(r_i^*)$. Now, since k changes were made to t in the history of t_i^k we have, by inductive hypothesis, that $t_i^k[X(Y)^*] \le t_j[X(Y)^*]$ holds. It, therefore, follows that $t_i^k[X] = t_j[X]$ and as a result $t_i[X] = t_j[X]$. Consequently, it must also be true that $t_i[(Y)^*] \le t_j[(Y)^*]$, thus proving the result, otherwise, by the following argument, $\text{CHASE}(r_j^*)$ has not terminated, since the NEFD, $X \to (Y)^*$, is violated.

Let $t'_i \in P_i^*$ be the second tuple involved in the triggering of the above NEFD-rule, therefore, $t'_i[X(Y)^*] \le t_i[X(Y)^*]$ obtains. Thus, t'_i would also be present in an r_i^*-sequence of length m_i. It, therefore, follows, by the inductive hypothesis on k and the fact that applying an extended chase rule to a state of $\text{CHASE}(r_j^*)$ increases its information content, that there exists a tuple, $t'_j \in \text{CHASE}(r_j^*)$, such that $t'_i[X(Y)^*] \le t'_j[X(Y)^*]$; t'_j must be present in an r_j^*-sequence of length m_j+1. Now, t'_j and t_j would trigger the NEFD-rule associated with the NEFD, $X \to (Y)^*$, in $\text{CHASE}(r_j^*)$, otherwise, it can be proved that $t_i[(Y)^*] \le t_j[(Y)^*]$; however, by Lemma 4.8, $\text{CHASE}(r_j^*)$ satisfies the NEFD, $X \to (Y)^*$.

CASE 3. The last extended chase rule triggered in the penultimate state of $\text{CHASE}(r_i^*)$, i.e., P_i^*, was due to the NEJD-rule associated with the NEJD, $\bowtie^{ne}[R(F)]$, where $F = \{T_1, T_2, ..., T_q\}$ is a scheme forest over the joined NRS, $U(T)$, with $q \ge 1$. Let $t_i \in \text{CHASE}(r_i^*)$ be the tuple which has been added to P_i^* due to the application of the said NEJD-rule to P_i^*, and let $A \subseteq r^*$, $|A| \le q$, be a subset of the set of original tuples of t_i. Thus there also exists at least one tuple, $t_j \in \text{CHASE}(r_j^*)$, such that the set of tuples, A, is a subset of the set of original tuples of t_j. We claim that for at least one of the said t_j, $t_i \le t_j$ also holds; this is proved by induction on the number of changes made to the set of tuples, A, in the history of the tuple, t_i.

BASIS. No changes were made to A. The result, i.e., $t_i \le t_j$, follows trivially, since the NEJD-rule associated with the NEJD, $\bowtie^{ne}[R(F)]$, is triggered in P_i^* by the tuples in A.

INDUCTION. Assume that the result holds for k changes made to the tuples of A in the history of t_i. We need to prove that the result also obtains when k+1 changes are made to the tuples of A in the history of t_i. Let $\{t_1^k, t_2^k, ..., t_n^k\} \subseteq P_i^*$, with $n \le q$, be the set of tuples that are combinable on the covering subset NDS, say $R(F') \in \text{SUBSET}(R(F))$, where n = $|R(F')|$, with the resulting tuple, t_i, added to P_i^*, due to the NEJD-rule associated with the NEJD, $\bowtie^{ne}[R(F)]$, that was triggered in P_i^* in order to obtain CHASE(r_i^*). Now, since k changes were made to the tuples of A, it follows, by the inductive hypothesis on k, that $\{t_1^k[S(T'_1)], t_2^k[S(T'_2)], ..., t_n^k[S(T'_n)]\} \leq \{t_1^j[S(T'_1)], t_2^j[S(T'_2)], ..., t_n^j[S(T'_n)]\}$, where $t_i^j \in P_j^*$, $1 \leq i \leq n$, P_j^* being the penultimate state of CHASE(r_j^*). Thus, we have that:

(1) $t_i \cong \bowtie^{ne} {}_{i=1}^{n} (\Pi^{ne}{}_{S(T'_i)}(t_i^k)) \neq \emptyset$ must be present in an r_i^*-sequence of length $m_i + 1$;

(2) $t_j \cong \bowtie^{ne} {}_{i=1}^{n} (\Pi^{ne}{}_{S(T'_i)}(t_i^j)) \neq \emptyset$ must be present in an r_j^*-sequence of length $m_j + 1$, where $S(T'_i) \in FDS(F')$, $1 \leq i \leq n$.

From the above, the result that $t_i \leq t_j$ follows immediately.

The result of the lemma now follows, since by a symmetrical argument we can also show that CHASE(r_j^*) $\leq$ CHASE(r_i^*). Thus CHASE(r_i^*) $\cong$ CHASE(r_j^*) $\cong$ CHASE(r*), which proves the uniqueness of the extended chase. $\square$

We are now ready to present the main theorem of this section, which shows that an extended chase of a nested relation, r*, w.r.t. a set of null extended data dependencies, D(U), is information-wise equivalent to an extended chase of μ*(r*) w.r.t. the counterpart set of null data dependencies, D. This theorem is important, since it enables us in Chapter 5 to assert that the classical UR model is a special case of the nested UR model.

Theorem 4.10. Let R(F) be a joinable NDS over the joined NRS, U(T), and let r* be a nested relation over U(T). Also, let D(U) = {FF(T), FD(T), $\bowtie^{ne}[R(F)]$} be a set of null extended data dependencies over U(T), and let D = {FF(T), MVD(T), JD(F)} be the counterpart set of null data dependencies over U. Then, provided r* is consistent,

$$CHASE_D(\mu*(r*)) \cong \mu*(CHASE_{D(U)}(r*)).$$

Proof. To prove the result we make the following claim.

CLAIM 1. For each extended chase rule associated with a null extended data dependency, say $d_i^* \in D(U)$, that is applied to r*, we can apply the corresponding extended chase rule associated with the counterpart null data dependency, $d_i \in D$, to μ*(r*).

Let r'* be the nested relation obtained from r* after applying to r* some extended chase rules associated with null extended data dependencies in D(U). By repetitively utilizing claim 1, we have that μ*(r'*) is the flat relation obtained from μ*(r*) after applying to μ*(r*) the corresponding extended chase rules associated with the counterpart null data dependencies in D.

Now, by Lemma 4.7, since both $CHASE_{D(U)}$(r*) and $CHASE_D(\mu*(r*))$ terminate, the result follows.

In order to prove claim 1, and thereby conclude the proof of the theorem, we consider the following three cases:

CASE 1. Let X $\rightarrow$ A be a NFD in D(U). Now, let t be the XA-value resulting from the modification of tuples, t_1, $t_2 \in \mu*(\Pi^{ne}{}_{XA}(r*))$, as a consequence of the NFD-rule associated with the NFD, X $\rightarrow$ A. Then, the XA-value, t, also results from the modification of tuples, t_1, $t_2 \in \Pi_{XA}(\mu*(r*))$ (also prior to its reduction), as a consequence of the NFD-rule associated with the NFD, $X \to A$, since, by Theorem 3.6, Π^{ne} is a precise generalization of Π. Thus, applying the NFD-rule associated with the NFD, $X \to A$, to r*, corresponds to applying the NFD-rule associated with the NFD, $X \to A$, to $\mu^*(r^*)$.

CASE 2. Let $e = (u,v)$ be an edge in the scheme tree, T, associated with r*, and let T_v be the subtree of T rooted at the node v. Also, let $X = A(u)$, $Y = D(v)$ and $(Y)^* = (R(T_v))^*$. For simplicity, we assume that $X = Z(R(T))$ and $(Y)^* \in H(R(T))$. If this is not the case then we can repetitively unnest r*, corresponding to recursive applications of the NEFD-rule in Definition 4.12 (2), thus obtaining r'^* over $R(T')$ such that $X = Z(R(T'))$ and $(Y)^* \in H(R(T'))$.

Now, let t* be a tuple resulting from the modification of not necessarily distinct tuples, $t_1, t_2 \in r^*$, by the application of the NEFD-rule associated with the NEFD, $X \to (Y)^*$. As a result, $t^*[X] = t_1[X] = t_2[X]$ and, in addition, $t^*[U(T) - X(Y)^*] \cong t_1[U(T) - X(Y)^*]$ or $t^*[U(T) - X(Y)^*] \cong t_2[U(T) - X(Y)^*]$; moreover, $t^*[(Y)^*] \cong (t_1[(Y)^*] \cup^{ne} t_2[(Y)^*])$. Then, the additional tuples in $\mu^*(t^*)$ are added to $\mu^*(r^*)$ by applying the NEJD-rule associated with the NMVD, $X \to\to Y$, to the tuples in $\mu^*(t_1)$ and $\mu^*(t_2)$, since, by Theorem 3.2, $\cup^{ne}$ is a precise generalization of $\cup$ and, by Theorem 4.2, the NEMVD is a precise generalization of the NMVD. Thus, applying the NEFD-rule associated with the NEFD, $X \to (Y)^*$, to r*, corresponds to applying the NEJD-rule associated with the NEMVD, $X \to\to Y$, to $\mu^*(r^*)$.

CASE 3. Let $\bowtie^{ne}$ be the NEJD in D(U). Now, let t* be a tuple that was added to r* by an application of the NEJD-rule associated with the NEJD, $\bowtie^{ne}[R(F)]$. Then, the tuples in $\mu^*(t^*)$ are added to $\mu^*(r^*)$ by applying the NEJD-rule associated with the NJD, JD(F), to $\mu^*(r^*)$, since, by Theorem 4.2, the NEJD is a precise generalization of the NJD. Thus, applying the NEJD-rule associated with the NEJD, $\bowtie^{ne}[R(F)]$, to r*, corresponds to applying the NEJD-rule associated with the NJD, JD(F), to $\mu^*(r^*)$. $\square$

We observe that the above theorem obtains for any set of null extended data dependencies $D'(U) \subseteq D(U)$.

The following corollary characterizes the subclasses of nested flat relations and hierarchical relations by employing the power of the extended chase procedure. The first part of the corollary characterizes nested flat relations by using the EQ-NEFD-rule (see the comments after Definition 4.12) instead of the NEFD-rule during the computation of the extended chase of a nested relation r*. The second part of the corollary gives an alternative characterization of hierarchical relations, to that given in Corollary 4.6, by using the extended chase procedure of a nested relation w.r.t. the set of NEFDs, FD(T).

Corollary 4.11. The following two statements are true:

(1)　Let $EQ-CHASE_{FD(T)}(r^*)$ denote the extended chase of a consistent nested relation, r*, over a NRS, R(T), w.r.t. the set of NEFDs, FD(T); $EQ-CHASE_{FD(T)}(r^*)$ is obtained by applying repetitively to r* the EQ-NEFD-rules instead of applying to r* the NEFD-rules associated with the NEFDs in FD(T). Then, if $r^* \cong EQ-CHASE_{FD(T)}(r^*)$, r* is a nested flat relation over the NRS, R(T).

(2)   A nested flat relation, r^*, over a NRS, $R(T)$, is a hierarchical relation iff $r^* \cong CHASE_{FD(T)}(r^*)$.

Proof. (1) By Lemma 4.8, r^* satisfies FD(T). Now, Theorem 2 in Van Gucht & Fischer [1988] implies that a nested relation containing no null values and satisfying FD(T) is a nested flat relation. The result now follows by Definition 3.6 of our NEST operator.

(2) The result follows directly from Corollary 4.6 and Theorem 4.10. □

The characterizations in Corollary 4.11 are very useful in enforcing a hierarchical relation, r^*, to satisfy its associated set of null extended data dependencies or for testing if indeed r^* is a hierarchical relation. This highlights the difference between hierarchical relations and the more general class of nested relations. Hierarchical relations are nested flat relations which are extended chased w.r.t. FD(T).

Our next corollary, which is a direct consequence of Theorem 4.10, tells us that testing consistency in a nested relation, r^*, is equivalent to testing consistency in its flat counterpart, i.e., $\mu^*(r^*)$.

Corollary 4.12. Let r^*, $D(U)$ and D be as in Theorem 4.10. Then, r^* is consistent w.r.t. $D(U)$ iff $\mu^*(r^*)$ is consistent w.r.t. D. □

As an epilogue, we observe that the extended chase procedure w.r.t. $D(U)$ is faithful to the extended chase procedure w.r.t. D in the sense that the extended chase of a flat relation r w.r.t. $D(U)$ reduces to the extended chase of r w.r.t. D. Correspondingly, the extended chase of a nested relation r^* w.r.t. $D(U)$ is a precise generalization of the extended chase of $\mu^*(r^*)$ w.r.t. D in the sense that $\mu^*(CHASE_{D(U)}(r^*)) \cong CHASE_D(\mu^*(r^*))$, as was shown in Theorem 4.10.

We now give some examples in order to illustrate the extended chase procedure.

Example 4.6. Firstly, we give an example of an extended chase with NFDs and NEFDs. Consider the NRS, $R(T) = A(BCD)^*$, together with $D(U) = \{FF(T), FD(T)\}$, where $FF(T) = \{B \rightarrow C, C \rightarrow D\}$ and $FD(T) = \{A \rightarrow (BCD)^*\}$. Let r^* be a nested relation over $R(T)$, shown in Figure 4.8. Now, r^* does not satisfy FF(T) and FD(T), so we extend chase r^* with the NFD-rules associated with the NFDs in FF(T) and with the NEFD-rules associated with the NEFDs in FD(T) to obtain CHASE(r^*), shown in Figure 4.9, which satisfies both FF(T) and FD(T).

A	(B	C	D)*
	B	C	D
a_1	b_1	*null*	d_1
a_1	b_2	*null*	*null*
a_2	b_1	c_1	*null*

Fig. 4.8. r^* before the extended chase.

A	(B	C	D)*
	B	C	D
a_1	b_1	c_1	d_1
	b_2	null	null
a_2	b_1	c_1	d_1

Fig. 4.9. r* after the extended chase w.r.t. FF(T) and FD(T).

A	(B	(C)*)*	(D	E)*
	B	(C)*	D	E
		C		
a_1	b_1	c_1	d_1	null
	b_2	c_1	d_2	e_2
a_2	b_1	c_2	d_1	e_1
	b_3	c_2	d_3	null

Fig. 4.10. r* before the extended chase.

Example 4.7. Let r* be the nested relation, over $R(T) = A(B(C)*)*(DE)*$, shown in Figure 4.10. Let $D(U) = \{FF(T), FD(T), \bowtie^{ne}[A(B)*(DE)*,\Lambda(B(C)*)*]\}$, where $FF(T) = \{D \rightarrow E\}$ and $FD(T) = \{A \rightarrow (B(C)*)*, A \rightarrow (DE)*, AB \rightarrow (C)*\}$. Now, r* does not satisfy the NEJD, $\bowtie^{ne}[A(B)*(DE)*,\Lambda(B(C)*)*]$ (cf. Example 4.3), nor the NFD $D \rightarrow E$. We now extend chase r* with the NEJD-rule associated with $\bowtie^{ne}[A(B)*(DE)*,\Lambda(B(C)*)*]$, the NFD-rule associated with $D \rightarrow E$, and the NEFD-rules associated with FD(T). The result $CHASE_{D(U)}(r*)$, shown in Figure 4.11, satisfies D(U). Moreover, $CHASE_D(\mu*(r*))$ is shown in Figure 4.12, where $D = \{FF(T), MVD(T), \bowtie[ABDE, BC]\}$ and $MVD(T) = \{A \rightarrow\rightarrow BC, A \rightarrow\rightarrow DE, AB \rightarrow\rightarrow C\}$. It can easily be verified that the result of Theorem 4.10 holds, i.e., $\mu*(CHASE_{D(U)}(r*)) \cong CHASE_D(\mu*(r*))$.

Example 4.8. Let $R(T) = A(B)*(C)*(D(E)*)*$, and let r* be the nested relation, over R(T), shown in Figure 4.13. Let $D(U) = \{FD(T)\}$, where $FD(T) = \{A \rightarrow (B)*, A \rightarrow (C)*, A \rightarrow (D(E)*)*, AD \rightarrow (E)*\}$. By Corollary 4.6, r* is not a hierarchical relation, since it does not satisfy FD(T), and it is not a nested flat relation. If we extend chase r* with the NEFD-rules associated with the NEFDs in FD(T), we get CHASE(r*), shown in Figure 4.14, which is a nested flat relation that satisfies FD(T) and, by Corollary 4.6, is thus a hierarchical relation over R(T).

In general the computation of the chase has exponential time complexity [Maier et al. 1979, 1981; Maier 1983; Beeri & Vardi 1984; Graham et al. 1986; Sagiv 1987]. Thus, by Theorem 4.10, it follows that the computation of the extended chase is also exponential in the general case.

A	(B	(C)*)*	(D	E)*
	B	(C)*	D	E
		C		
a_1	b_1	c_1	d_1	e_1
		c_2	d_2	e_2
	b_2	c_1		
a_2	b_1	c_1	d_1	e_1
		c_2	d_3	null
	b_3	c_2		

Fig. 4.11. r^* after the extended chase w.r.t $D(U)$.

A	B	C	D	E
a_1	b_1	c_1	d_1	e_1
a_1	b_1	c_1	d_2	e_2
a_1	b_1	c_2	d_1	e_1
a_1	b_1	c_2	d_2	e_2
a_1	b_2	c_1	d_1	e_1
a_1	b_2	c_1	d_2	e_2
a_2	b_1	c_1	d_1	e_1
a_2	b_1	c_1	d_3	null
a_2	b_1	c_2	d_1	e_1
a_2	b_1	c_2	d_3	null
a_2	b_3	c_2	d_1	e_1
a_2	b_3	c_2	d_3	null

Fig. 4.12. The flat relation, $CHASE_D(\mu^*(r^*)) \cong \mu^*(CHASE_{D(U)}(r^*))$.

It is a further research problem to determine exactly the computational complexity of an extended chase w.r.t. a set of null extended data dependencies, $D(U)$, where $D(U)$ may only contain a restricted class of null extended data dependencies. We note that the complexity issue is closely related to the computational complexity of computing null extended algebra expressions, since null extended algebraic operations are embedded within the definitions of the extended chase rules.

A	(B)*	(C)*	(D	(E)*)*
	B	C	D	(E)*
				E
a_1	b_1	c_1	d_1	null
	b_2	c_2	d_2	e_1
	b_3		d_2	e_2
a_1	b_1	null	d_1	e_1
	b_2		d_2	null

Fig. 4.13. r^* before the extended chase.

A	(B)*	(C)*	(D	(E)*)*
	B	C	D	(E)*
				E
a_1	b_1	c_1	d_1	e_1
	b_2	c_2	d_2	e_1
	b_3			e_2

Fig. 4.14. r^* after the extended chase w.r.t. FD(T).

4.6 Discussion

In this chapter we have defined the new class of null extended data dependencies that hold in nested relations and its counterpart, i.e., the class of null data dependencies that hold in the corresponding flat relations. We obtained a series of interesting results concerning the said data dependencies culminating in Corollary 4.6, which presents equivalent characterizations of the subclass of hierarchical relations.

We have not incorporated *inclusion dependencies* [Casanova et al. 1984], which are a generalization of the notion of *referential integrity* [Codd 1979; Date 1987a], into the null extended nested relational model. In many cases however, the satisfaction of such data dependencies obtains in the nested UR model as a byproduct of the realized joins within the nested relations themselves at no extra cost to the DBMS.

In addition, we have extended the chase procedure to nested relations, showing that the extended chase possesses all of the desirable properties of the standard chase. By utilizing the extended chase we were able to derive a new characterization of consistent nested relations (see Corollary 4.12) as well as a further characterization of hierarchical relations, namely, $r^* \cong CHASE_{FD(T)}(r^*)$. Thus, the extended chase may provide a basis for developing an integrity constraint checker for nested relations.

Furthermore, the extended chase can be used to solve the implication problem for null extended data dependencies (cf. [Maier et al. 1979; Beeri & Vardi 1984]). For example, it can be used to test whether a NDS possesses the desirable property of a null extended lossless decomposition. Finally, the extended chase can also be used to investigate other desirable properties that may be present in a nested relation such as the commuting of a sequence of nest operations or the minimality of its number of tuples w.r.t. its corresponding flat relation (cf. [Fischer et al. 1985; Miura 1987; Takeda 1987]).

Chapter 5

A Universal Relation Model
For a Nested Database

In this chapter we introduce the *nested universal relation model (nested UR model)*. In the nested UR model the DBMS levels are organized as shown in Figure 1.3. Above the physical level we have the internal level wherein the null extended nested relational model (see nested database in Figure 1.3) resides. On top of the null extended nested relational model we have the conceptual level consisting of the *nested representative instance* (NRI) over the *nested universal relation scheme* (NURS), which provides the underlying data structure of the nested UR model. Finally, at the external level we have a UR interface as a user view, which may provide flat or hierarchical outputs. The main goal of this chapter is to describe the conceptual level of the nested UR model by showing, rigorously, how the internal level of the null extended nested relational model interacts with the NRI over the NURS. We also indicate, clearly, how the UR interface may be implemented by utilizing the conceptual level of the nested UR model.

There are several motives for introducing the nested UR model, which we now enumerate:

(1)   The nested UR model provides logical data independence to the null extended nested relational model in the same way that the UR model provides logical data independence to the relational model. This is achieved by allowing users to view the nested database as if it were composed of a single nested relation. Thus, the nested UR model solves the usability problem by freeing users from logical navigation amongst and within the nested relations of the nested database.

(2)   The nested UR model allows us to model a wider range of applications [Scholl & Schek 1987; Abiteboul et al. 1989b] than the UR model, whilst hiding much of the complexity of nested relations from the user.

(3)   A UR interface [Ullman 1983b], as a user view at the external level, can be implemented by using the nested UR model, wherein a nested database resides at the internal level (see Figure 1.3) and the NRI, over the NURS, resides at the conceptual level. Thus, we can gain all the advantages of nested relations over flat relations via the implementation of a UR interface.

(4)   The nested UR model allows a more flexible user interface than the UR model does, since both flat and hierarchical data can be presented to the user in a natural way [Desai et al. 1987; Kambayashi & Yamamoto 1987; Scholl et al. 1987; Levene & Loizou 1989b].

(5)   The nested UR model extends the theory of flat relations to nested relations, thus providing a sound basis for investigating such important issues as: nested database

design, efficient query processing for nested databases and the satisfaction and implication of different types of integrity constraints in nested databases.

In Section 5.1 we first define the NURS; we then show how the NURS can be obtained from a given NDS by using well-defined restructuring operators, and as a consequence we investigate what restructuring needs to be done to the associated nested database. In Section 5.2 we introduce the concept of *nested weak instances* and the NRI, thus extending to nested relations, the concept of weak instances and the RI, which were introduced in Subsection 2.3.3, in particular, Definitions 2.15 and 2.16, respectively. The NRI is a nested weak instance over the NURS, which provides the underlying data structure of the nested UR model, thereby allowing us to model the semantics of the nested database in a single nested relation. In Section 5.3 we present the main result of this chapter, i.e., we show the equivalence of the NRI to the RI. More specifically, let $d^* = \{r_1^*, r_2^*, ..., r_q^*\}$ be a nested database over a NDS, $\mathbf{R}(F)$, and let $D(U)$ be a set of null extended data dependencies. Also, let $d = \{\mu^*(r_1^*), \mu^*(r_2^*), ..., \mu^*(r_q^*)\}$ be the flat database over the FDS, FDS(F), induced by d^*, and let D be the counterpart set of null data dependencies emanating from $D(U)$. Then, we show that the NRI over the NURS, $U(T)$, under $D(U)$ for d^*, constructed via the extended chase, is information-wise equivalent to the RI, over U, under D for d, constructed via the extended chase. The main implication of this result is that the classical UR model under the weak instance approach is a special case of the nested UR model under the nested weak instance approach.

An important consequence of the above implication is that a UR interface at the external level can be implemented by using the nested UR model. Thus, the advantages of nested relations, namely, explicit representation of semantics, minimal redundancy, realized joins and a flexible user interface, are maintained in the nested UR model.

In constructing the NRI via the extended chase, we face the intractability, in general, of the computational complexity of the extended chase (see Section 4.5), thus from a practical point of view it may not be feasible to construct the NRI in this way. In Section 5.4 we investigate a computational approach to the nested UR model by employing the null extended algebra of Chapter 3. This leads us to define an algebraic method for the construction of the NRI, when the NDS, $\mathbf{R}(F)$, possesses the UMC property (see Definition 2.3). Using this algebraic approach we define the *UMC window function*, which computes the window for any set of attributes $X \subseteq U$. We then show that the UMC window function is an alternative for the construction of the window, [X], for any set of attributes $X \subseteq U$. Thus, in this special case, a DBMS supporting the null extended algebra, but not necessarily supporting the extended chase, can effectively support the nested UR model.

5.1 The Nested Universal Relation Scheme

In this section we present the NRS at the conceptual level of the nested UR model, namely, the *nested universal relation scheme* (NURS). The NURS, denoted as U(T), provides the necessary NRS over which null extended joins between nested relations in a nested database are well defined. This is essential for query processing in the nested UR model, since it provides automatic logical navigation amongst the nested relations in the nested database.

Formally, let $R(F)$ be a NDS, over U, which may not be joinable. In this section we show that $R(F)$ can be transformed into a joinable NDS, say $R(F')$, by repetitively applying two restructuring operations which we define on scheme trees, namely, *empty node insertion* and *root weighting*. The NURS, U(T), is thus the joined NRS of the joinable NDS, $R(F')$. Thus, we say that U(T) *is the NURS of the NDS*, $R(F)$, *and that* $R(F')$ *is the joinable NDS obtained from* $R(F)$. We close this section by defining a restructuring operator for a nested database, d*, over the NDS, $R(F)$, which restructures d* into a nested database, say d'*, over the joinable NDS, $R(F')$. This restructuring operator is utilized in Section 5.2, wherein we show how to construct the NRI over the NURS, U(T).

Example 5.1. The NDS, $R(F) = \{R(T_2), R(T_3)\}$, of the running example, is not a joinable NDS. On the other hand, $R(F') = \{R(T_2), R(T'_3)\}$, where T'_3 is shown in Figure 3.20, is a joinable NDS, over the NURS, U(T), for the scheme tree, T, shown in Figure 3.21.

We now proceed to define the above-mentioned two restructuring operators, defined on scheme trees, by firstly motivating the definitions via examples. Informally, *empty node insertion* resolves the conflict that arises between two scheme trees, whenever it is not possible to join the two NRSs of the scheme trees, due to common attributes, between the two scheme trees, which label nodes of different heights. Empty node insertion is accomplished by adding a node, labelled by Λ, to one of the said scheme trees, either between two existing nodes of this scheme tree, or as the new root node of this scheme tree. On the other hand, *root weighting* (cf. [Delobel 1978]) resolves the conflict that arises between two scheme trees, whenever it is not possible to join the two scheme trees in the NDS without violating the definition of a scheme tree, even if empty node insertion were to be invoked on one or both of the said scheme trees. This is accomplished by deleting a node from one of the said scheme trees and then augmenting the attributes labelling one of the ancestor nodes of the deleted node with the attributes labelling the deleted node.

An example of empty node insertion is illustrated in Example 5.1, where an empty node is inserted as the root of the scheme tree, T_3, shown in Figure 2.11, in order to obtain the scheme tree, T'_3, shown in Figure 3.20.

In the following example we illustrate three possible situations when root weighting is necessary.

Example 5.2. In Figures 5.1, 5.2 and 5.3 there is no way of joining $R(T_i)$ and $R(T_j)$

without violating the definition of a scheme tree, unless root weighting is invoked first. In Figures 5.1 and 5.2, T_i and T_j become T_j, as shown in Figure 5.2, after root weighting is invoked. Correspondingly, T_i, in Figure 5.3, becomes T_j as shown in Figure 5.1 or Figure 5.3, after root weighting is invoked.

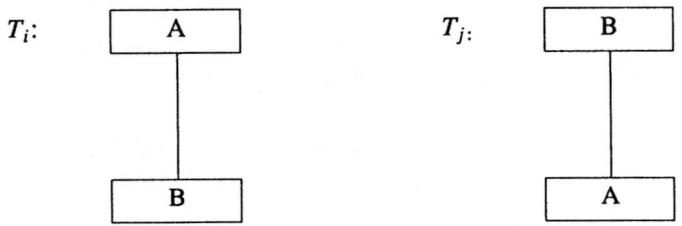

Fig. 5.1. First example of the necessity for root weighting.

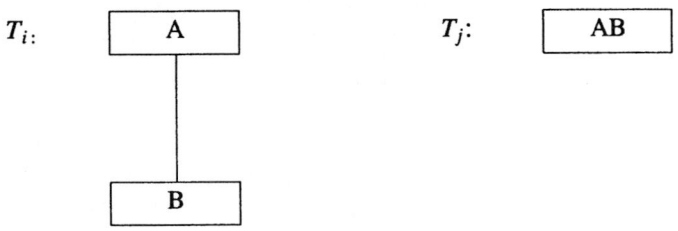

Fig. 5.2. Second example of the necessity for root weighting.

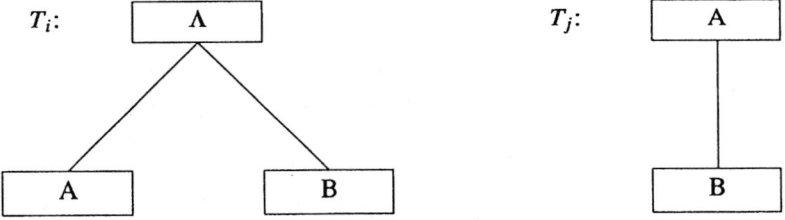

Fig. 5.3. Third example of the necessity for root weighting.

The motivation for defining empty node insertion is for *resolving* the type of *conflict*, formally defined in Definition 5.1. Intuitively, this type of conflict arises whenever a node in one scheme tree has common attributes with a node in another scheme tree but their heights are different, as is the case between T_2 and T_3 of the running example.

Definition 5.1. We say that two scheme trees, T_1, T_2, in a scheme forest, F, have a *height-incompatibility conflict* (or simply are *height-incompatible*), if $n_1 \in T_1$ and $n_2 \in T_2$ are two nodes such that $ATT(n_1) \cap ATT(n_2) \neq \emptyset$ and $HEIGHT(T_1, n_1) \neq HEIGHT(T_2, n_2)$.

We now formally define empty node insertion, which resolves the height-incompatibility conflict between two scheme trees of a scheme forest, F.

Definition 5.2. Let n be a node in a scheme tree, $T_i \in$ F, and n′ be a node not in F. The *empty node insertion* of n′ *between* n and $\{n_1, n_2, ..., n_s\} \subseteq$ CHILDREN(T_i, n) in T_i is defined by

(1)   ATT(n′) := Λ;

(2)   temp := $\{n_1, n_2, ..., n_s\}$;

(3)   CHILDREN(T_i, n) := (CHILDREN(T_i, n) - temp) ∪ {n′};

(4)   CHILDREN(T_i, n') := temp.

As a boundary case, we define the empty node insertion of n′, *above* ROOT(T_i), in T_i, by

(1)   ATT(n′) := Λ;

(2)   CHILDREN(T_i, n') := {ROOT(T_i)};

(3)   n′ := ROOT(T_i).

Example 5.3. Consider the NRS, R(T_4) = DEPT (EXAM)* (PROJECT)*. The empty node insertion between ROOT(T_4) and CHILDREN$(T_4, ROOT(T_4))$ results in the NRS, R(T'_4) = DEPT(Λ (EXAM)* (PROJECT)*)*, where T'_4 is shown in Figure 3.17.

For the running example, it can easily be verified that T_2 and T_3 are height-incompatible, due to the attribute, TUTOR, in S(T_2) and S(T_3), so the NDS R(F) = {R(T_2), R(T_3)} is not joinable. However, R(F′) = {R(T_2), R(T'_3)} of Example 5.1 is a joinable NDS; this is after empty node insertion is invoked above ROOT(T_3), in order to obtain T'_3, which is shown in Figure 3.20.

The motivation for defining root weighting is for *resolving* the two types of *conflict*, formally defined in Definitions 5.3 and 5.4. Intuitively, the first conflict arises whenever the attributes labelling a node in one scheme tree are split over *at least* two nodes in the other scheme tree, as in Figure 5.2.

Definition 5.3. Let $T_1, T_2 \in$ F be two scheme trees, n_1, n_2 be two distinct nodes in T_1, and n_3 be a node in T_2. We say that T_1 and T_2 have a *split-attributes conflict* (or simply have *split-attributes*), if

(1)   HEIGHT$(T_1, n_2) \geq$ HEIGHT(T_1, n_1);

(2)   (ATT(n_1) ∩ ATT(n_3)) ≠ ∅;

(3)   (ATT(n_2) ∩ ATT(n_3)) ≠ ∅;

Intuitively, the second conflict arises whenever we have a path-incompatibility conflict between two or more nodes in one scheme tree and two or more nodes in a path of the other scheme tree, as in Figures 5.1 and 5.3.

In the sequel, we shall occasionally refer to a path, p ∈ P(T), as the set of nodes associated with p rather than its associated set of attributes. This will be obvious from context.

Definition 5.4. Let $T_1, T_2 \in F$ be two scheme trees, n_1, n_2 be two distinct nodes in T_1, and n_3, n_4 be two distinct nodes in a path, $p_2 \in P(T_2)$. We say that T_1 and T_2 have a *path-incompatibility conflict* (or simply are *path-incompatible*), if

(1) if n_1 and n_2 are in the same path, say $p_1 \in P(T_1)$, then HEIGHT(T_1, n_2) > HEIGHT(T_1, n_1), i.e., $n_1 \in A(n_2)$;

(2) $(\text{ATT}(n_2) \cap \text{ATT}(n_3)) \neq \emptyset$;

(3) HEIGHT(T_2, n_4) > HEIGHT(T_2, n_3), i.e., $n_3 \in A(n_4)$;

(4) $(\text{ATT}(n_1) \cap \text{ATT}(n_4)) \neq \emptyset$;

We now formally define root weighting, which resolves either a split-attributes conflict or a path-incompatibility conflict.

Definition 5.5. Let $T_i \in F$ be a scheme tree, and let n_1 and n_2 be two distinct nodes in T_i with HEIGHT(T_i, n_2) $\geq$ HEIGHT(T_i, n_1). We consider two cases of root weighting:

CASE 1. If n_1 and n_2 are in a path, $p_j \in P(T_i)$, and $n_1 \in A(n_2)$, i.e., n_1 is an ancestor node of n_2, then the *root weighting* of n_2 to n_1 in T_i is defined by

(1) ATT(n_1) := ATT(n_1) $\cup$ ATT(n_2);

(2) CHILDREN(PARENT(T_i, n_2)) := CHILDREN(PARENT(T_i, n_2)) $\cup$ CHILDREN(T_i, n_2);

(3) $T_i := T_i - \{n_2\}$, i.e., remove n_2 from T_i.

CASE 2. If n_1 and n_2 are not in the same path of $P(T_i)$, i.e., $n_1 \notin A(n_2)$, let n be the common ancestor node of the two distinct nodes, n_1 and n_2. Then, the *root weighting* of n_2 to n_1 in T_i is defined recursively by invoking the root weighting of n_2 to n in T_i.

Example 5.4. In Figure 5.1, we can invoke root weighting twice, first in T_i to resolve a path-incompatibility conflict with regards to T_i and T_j and thus to obtain, say T'_i (which is also the same as T_j in Figure 5.2), and then in T_j to resolve a split-attributes conflict with regards to T'_i and T_j and thus to obtain, say T'_j (which is the same as T_j in Figure 5.2).

In Figure 5.2, we can invoke root weighting in T_i to resolve a split-attributes conflict with regards to T_i and T_j and thus to obtain, say T'_i (which is the same as T_j in Figure 5.2).

In Figure 5.3, we can invoke root weighting in T_i to resolve a path-incompatibility conflict with regards to T_i and T_j and thus to obtain, say T'_i (which is the same as T_j in Figure 5.3).

We further note that T_i of Figure 5.3 and T_j of Figure 5.2 have two split-attribute conflicts. In this case invoking root weighting in T_i twice resolves these split-attribute conflicts to obtain, say T'_i (which is the same as T_j in Figure 5.2).

Example 5.5. Let R(F') = {R(T_1), R(T'_2), R(T''_3)} be the joinable NDS obtained from restructuring **R**(F) of the running example. The scheme tree T_1 is shown in Figure 2.3. The scheme tree T'_2 is shown in Figure 5.4 and is obtained by an empty node insertion in T_2, which is shown in Figure 2.9. The scheme tree T''_3 is shown in Figure 5.5 and is obtained by two empty node insertions in T_3, which is shown in Figure 2.11. Thus all height incompatibilities in **R**(F) are resolved by invoking empty node insertions in T_2 and T_3; these result in **R**(F'), which is free of conflicts. The scheme tree, T, of the NURS, U(T), which is the joined NRS of **R**(F') is shown in Figure 5.6.

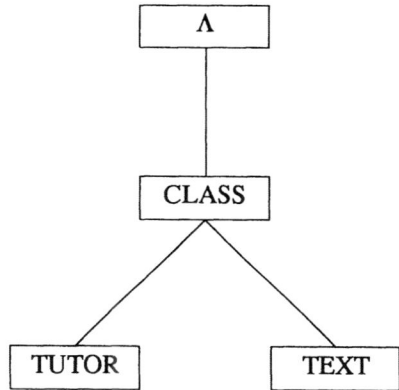

Fig. 5.4. The scheme tree T'_2 in F'.

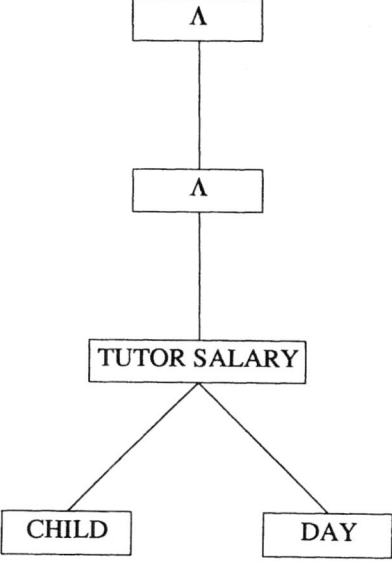

Fig. 5.5. The scheme tree T''_3 in F'.

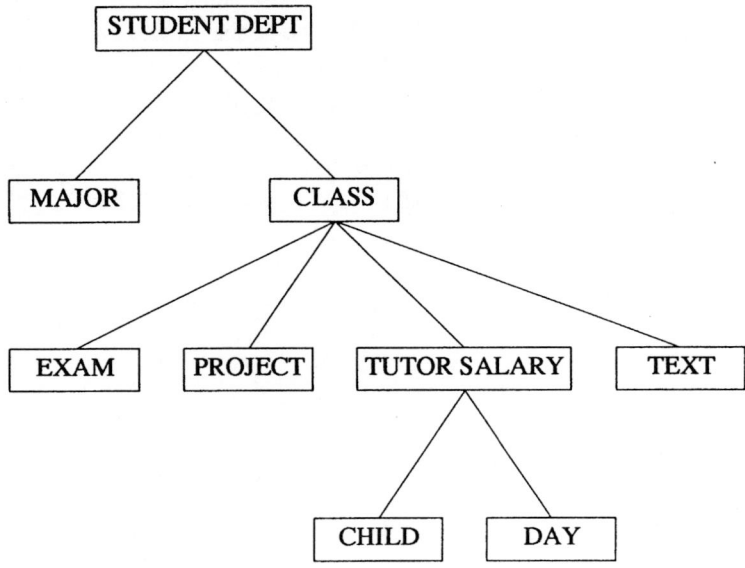

Fig. 5.6. The scheme tree, T, of the NURS, U(T), for the running example.

We note that in $R(F)$ there are no split-attributes or path-incompatibility conflicts, and thus no root weighting is needed to obtain $R(F')$. As was shown in Example 5.2, this is not always the case. For example, consider adding the attribute, STUDENT, to T_2 to obtain the NRS, $R(T_4) =$ CLASS (TUTOR)* (TEXT)* (STUDENT)*. In this case T_1 and T_4 have the same conflict as the path-incompatibility conflict between T_i and T_j, shown in Figure 5.1. In order to resolve this conflict, we again invoke root weighting twice, first in T_1 to resolve a path-incompatibility conflict and then in T_4 to resolve a split-attributes conflict. The resulting NRSs are: $R(T'_1) =$ STUDENT DEPT CLASS (MAJOR)* (EXAM)* (PROJECT)* and $R(T'_4) =$ STUDENT CLASS (TUTOR)* (TEXT)*. The joinable NDS of the NDS, $\{R(T_1), R(T_3), R(T_4)\}$, would then be, $\{R(T'_1), R(T'_3), R(T'_4)\}$, where T'_3 is obtained from T_3 of the running example by an empty node insertion, and is shown in Figure 3.20.

We now show that the restructuring operations we have defined are *valid* in the sense that they do not incur any loss of information w.r.t. the semantics of the scheme trees they operate on.

Formally, a restructuring operation applied to a scheme tree, T, resulting in a scheme tree, T', is *valid* iff MVD(T) |= MVD(T') (cf. *dominance* [Abiteboul & Bidoit 1986]).

Lemma 5.1. Empty node insertion and root weighting are valid restructuring operations.

Proof. Let T be a scheme tree. Firstly, we consider empty node insertion. There are two cases to consider:

(1)   The empty node insertion of a node, n′, with ATT(n′) = Λ, between n and the nodes, $\{n_1, n_2, ..., n_s\} \subseteq$ CHILDREN(T,n), resulting in the scheme tree T′.

(2)   The empty node insertion of a node, n′, with ATT(n′) = Λ, above ROOT(T), resulting in the scheme tree T′.

In both cases we have that P(T) = P(T′), and therefore ⋈[P(T)] ≡ ⋈[P(T′)], implying, by Lemma 2.3 (2), that MVD(T) |= MVD(T′), as required. It follows that empty node insertion adds only trivial NMVDs to MVD(T).

Secondly, we consider root weighting.

Let n_1 and n_2 be two distinct nodes in T and such that HEIGHT(T,n_2) ≥ HEIGHT(T,n_1). There are two cases to consider:

(1) $n_1 \in$ A(n_2) (for example, see the scheme tree, T_i, in Figure 5.1). We invoke the root weighting of n_2 to n_1 in T, resulting in a scheme tree, say T′.

(2) $n_1 \notin$ A(n_2) (for example, see the scheme tree, T_i, in Figure 5.3). As in (1), we invoke the root weighting of n_2 to n_1 in T, resulting in a scheme tree, say T′.

In both cases, by Definition 5.5 of root weighting, we have that P(T′) covers P(T). By the covering rule for NJDs (see comment after Definition 4.4), we can deduce that ⋈[P(T)] |= ⋈[P(T′)]. The result now follows by Lemma 2.3 (2), implying that MVD(T) |= MVD(T′), as required. □

We observe that the validity of a restructuring operation applied to a scheme tree, T, also obtains for any null extended data dependency which is explicitly represented in T. Thus, FD(T) |= FD(T′), since FD(T) ≡ MVD(T) and FD(T′) ≡ MVD(T′). (See Theorem 4.10.) In addition, FF(T) |= FF(T′), since the satisfaction of NFDs in a nested relation, over R(T), is not affected by UNNEST operations (see Definition 4.2).

In the next theorem we present the main result of this section showing that empty node insertion and root weighting are sufficient for transforming a NDS, which may not be joinable, into a joinable NDS. This result is of major importance to the nested UR model, since the NURS can be obtained from any NDS, R(F), even in the case where R(F) is not joinable. Thus, logical data independence can be provided in the nested UR model via the concept of a joinable NDS, which is independent of the given NDS at the internal level (see Figure 1.3).

Theorem 5.2. R(F) can be transformed into a joinable NDS by a finite number of empty node insertions and root weightings.

Proof. We say that two scheme trees, T_i and T_j in F, are in *conflict*, if one of the following situations arises:

(1) T_i and T_j have a height-incompatibility conflict (see Definition 5.1).

(2) T_i and T_j have a split-attributes conflict (see Definition 5.3).

(3) T_i and T_j have a path-incompatibility conflict (see Definition 5.4).

Next we present a function, given in Figure 5.7, named SOLVE_CONFLICT, which carries out empty node insertions and root weightings.

```
1. function SOLVE_CONFLICT (F) return scheme forest;
2.    begin
3.         while T_i ∈ F and T_j ∈ F have
                a split-attributes conflict or
                a path-incompatibility conflict do
4.              invoke root weighting;
5.         end while;
6.         while T_i ∈ F and T_j ∈ F have
                a height-incompatibility conflict do
7.              invoke empty node insertion;
8.         end while;
9.         return (F');
10. end {SOLVE_CONFLICT};
```

Fig. 5.7. The function, SOLVE_CONFLICT.

We now proceed to resolve all the conflicts between any two scheme trees in F, by invoking SOLVE_CONFLICT. The input parameter to SOLVE_CONFLICT is the scheme forest, F, and the return value of SOLVE_CONFLICT is a scheme forest, say F', which is the scheme forest resulting from F after all the conflicts in F have been resolved.

We arrive at the result by proving the following two claims:

CLAIM 1. SOLVE_CONFLICT terminates.

The while loop beginning at line 3 terminates since, if we invoke root weighting, continually, then R(F) will eventually become a FDS in which case no conflicts will be present in F. Now, when the while loop beginning at line 6 starts to execute, all the split-attributes conflicts and path-incompatibility conflicts, amongst the scheme trees in F, will have already been resolved, and there remain only a finite number of height-incompatibility conflicts to be resolved.

We next show that no new split-attributes conflicts and no new path-incompatibility conflicts are generated amongst the scheme trees of F, during the execution of the while loop beginning at line 6.

Empty node insertions do not create any new split-attributes conflicts for the following reasons. Firstly, the attribute set of a node, n, ATT(n), in a scheme tree, say $T_i \in$ F, remains invariant under empty node insertions in T_i. Secondly, the attribute set of a scheme tree, $T_i \in$ F, i.e., $S(T_i)$, remains invariant under empty node insertions in T_i.

Empty node insertions do not create any new path-incompatibility conflicts as we show in the following argument. Let $P(T_i^k)$ be the path set of any scheme tree $T_i \in$ F, before the kth execution of the while loop beginning at line 6, and $P(T_i^{k+1})$ be the path set of this scheme tree after the kth execution of this while loop. (T_i^k denotes the state of $T_i \in$ F prior to the kth execution of the said while loop.) Consider the path $p \in P(T_i^k)$ in which an empty node was inserted to obtain the path $p' \in P(T_i^{k+1})$. If we remove all the empty nodes from both p and p', we have that p = p', i.e., $P(T_i^k) = P(T_i^{k+1})$. It, therefore, follows that for any two nodes n_1 and n_2 in p, if HEIGHT$(T_i^k, n_2) >$ HEIGHT(T_i^k, n_1)

holds then so does HEIGHT(T_i^{k+1},n_2) > HEIGHT(T_i^{k+1},n_1) hold in p'. Thus, the relative heights of nodes in T_i^k and T_i^{k+1} remain invariant w.r.t. ">". The result now follows by using induction on k and by Definition 5.4 of the path-incompatibility conflict.

It remains to show that the while loop beginning at line 6 terminates. Now, consider two paths, $p_i \in P(T_i)$ and $p_j \in P(T_j)$, where T_i, T_j are members in the current state of F, and i ≠ j. Let n_1 and n_2 be two nodes in p_i and n_3, n_4 be two nodes in p_j such that (ATT(n_1) ∩ ATT(n_3)) ≠ $\emptyset$ and (ATT(n_2) ∩ ATT(n_4)) ≠ $\emptyset$. Since at this stage of SOLVE_CONFLICT(F) no split-attributes conflicts or path-incompatibility conflicts occur in the current state of F, it must be that HEIGHT(T_i,n_2) > HEIGHT(T_i,n_1) iff HEIGHT(T_j,n_4) > HEIGHT(T_j,n_3). The result now follows since, in this case, a height-incompatibility conflict between say, n_1 in T_i and n_3 in T_j (or correspondingly between n_2 in T_i and n_4 in T_j) can always be resolved by a finite number of empty node insertions. This fact is illustrated pictorially in Figure 5.8. This proves our claim that SOLVE_CONFLICT terminates.

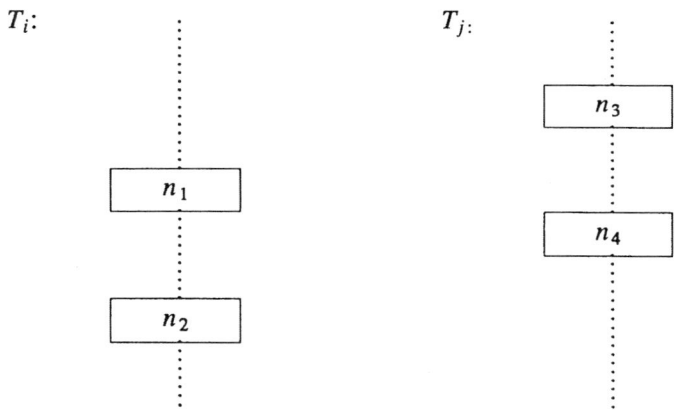

Fig. 5.8. A case where all the conflicts can be resolved by empty node insertions.

CLAIM 2. R(F') is a joinable NDS, where F' denotes the scheme forest which is returned by SOLVE_CONFLICT.

Let R(T'_i) and R(T'_j) be any two NRSs in R(F'). Furthermore, let X = S(T'_i) ∩ S(T'_j), then R(T'_i)[X] = R(T'_j)[X], since there are no conflicts whatsoever in F'. Thus, it suffices to show that there exists a NRS, R(T'), over S(T') = S(T'_i) ∪ S(T'_j), such that R(T')[S(T'_i)] = R(T'_i) and R(T')[S(T'_j)] = R(T'_j), which, by Definition 3.17, implies that R(F') is a joinable NDS.

We conclude the result by creating T' from T'_i and T'_j as follows:

(1)   ATT(ROOT(T')) = ATT(ROOT(T'_i)) ∪ ATT(ROOT(T'_j)).

(2)   If, for any two nodes $n_i \in T'_i$ and $n_j \in T'_j$, (ATT(n_i) ∩ ATT(n_j)) ≠ $\emptyset$, then create a node n in T' such that HEIGHT(T',n) = HEIGHT(T'_i,n_i) = HEIGHT(T'_j,n_j) and ATT(n) = ATT(n_i) ∪ ATT(n_j).

(3)   If n_i ≠ ROOT(T'_i), with ATT(n_i) ≠ Λ, is a node in T'_i and ATT(n_i) ∩ S(T'_j) = $\emptyset$, then create a node n in T' such that HEIGHT(T',n) = HEIGHT(T'_i,n_i) and ATT(n) =

ATT(n_i).

(4) If $n_j \neq \text{ROOT}(T'_j)$, with ATT($n_j$) $\neq \Lambda$, is a node in T'_j and ATT(n_j) $\cap$ S(T'_i) = $\emptyset$, then create a node n in T' such that HEIGHT(T',n) = HEIGHT(T'_j,n_j) and ATT(n) = ATT(n_j).

(5) If there exist nodes, $n_i \in T'_i$ and $n_j \in T'_j$, with ATT(n_i) = ATT(n_j) = Λ and HEIGHT(T'_i,n_i) = HEIGHT(T'_j,n_j), then create a node n in T' such that HEIGHT(T',n) = HEIGHT(T'_i,n_i) = HEIGHT(T'_j,n_j) and ATT(n) = Λ. $\square$

The next corollary gives a syntactic characterization of a joinable NDS and complements Definition 3.17 which is a semantic characterization of a joinable NDS.

Corollary 5.3. Let R(F) be a NDS over U. Then R(F) is a joinable NDS over the joined NRS, U(T), iff there are no conflicts in F.

Proof. *(IF)*. If there are no conflicts in F, then F = SOLVE_CONFLICT(F), and thus, by the result of Theorem 5.2, R(F) is a joinable NDS, over U(T).

(ONLY IF). If R(F) is a joinable NDS, over U(T), then by Definition 3.17 of a joinable NDS, and Definitions 5.1, 5.3 and 5.4, of height-incompatibility conflict, split-attributes conflict and path-incompatibility conflict, respectively, it follows that there cannot be any conflicts in F, otherwise Definition 2.4 for the scheme tree, T, would be violated. $\square$

We say that a joinable NDS, R(F'), obtained from a non-joinable NDS, R(F), by invoking the function, SOLVE_CONFLICT, on the scheme forest, F, is *optimal*, if it is obtained by a minimum number of restructuring operations. Optimal joinable NDSs are desirable, since they preserve more of the structure of the original NDS than would otherwise be the case. In the worst case, R(F') is transformed into a FDS, in which case the NURS is the universal set of attributes, U, as in the classical UR model.

Once the NURS, U(T), is obtained we need to restructure the nested relations in d* by using NEST and UNNEST operations corresponding to each empty node insertion and root weighting invoked during the computation of SOLVE_CONFLICT(F). This is because the null extended join operator is defined only over joinable NDSs.

We now give an example to show that in the general case both NEST and UNNEST operations are needed to restructure the nested relations in d*, even when only root weighting is carried out during the restructuring of R(F) into R(F').

Example 5.6. The scheme trees T_1 and T_2 shown in Figure 5.9 are not joinable. T'_1, also shown in Figure 5.9, is joinable with T_2, and is obtained from T_1 after carrying out the root weighting of the node n_2 to n_1 in T_1 (where ATT(n_1) = A and ATT(n_2) = C). It can easily be verified that in order to restructure a nested relation, say r_1^*, over R(T_1), into a nested relation, say r'^*_1, over R(T'_1), we need to invoke an UNNEST* operation on r_1^* and then invoke on the result a NEST operation, over B, i.e., $r'^*_1 = \nu_B(\mu^*(r_1^*))$.

Next we define the restructuring operator, denoted by ρ, which restructures a nested database, d*, over R(F), into a nested database, say d'*, over the joinable NDS, R(F').

Definition 5.6. Let $r_i^* \in$ d* be a nested relation over R(T_i) $\in$ R(F), and let R(T'_i) be the

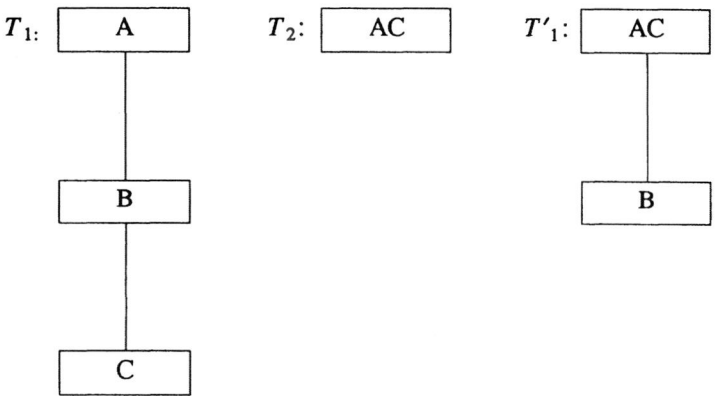

Fig. 5.9. An example when both NEST and UNNEST are needed for restructuring.

corresponding NRS of the joinable NDS, $\mathbf{R}(F')$, over the NURS, U(T). Also, let $v_{R(T'_i)}$ be a sequence of NEST operations that transforms a flat relation over $S(T'_i)$ into a nested relation over $R(T'_i)$. Then,

the *restructuring* of r_i^* w.r.t. U(T), denoted as $\rho_{U(T)}(r_i^*)$, is a nested relation, r'^*_i, such that

$$r'^*_i \cong v_{R(T'_i)}(\mu^*(r_i^*)) .$$

The restructuring operator, ρ, is now naturally extended to a nested database, d'^*, over the joinable NDS, $\mathbf{R}(F')$, namely,

the *restructuring* of d* w.r.t. U(T), denoted as $\rho_{U(T)}(d^*)$, is a nested database, d'^*, over $\mathbf{R}(F')$, such that

$$d'^* = \{r'^*_1, r'^*_2, \ldots, r'^*_q\} \text{ and } r'^*_i \cong \rho_{U(T)}(r_i^*), \ 1 \le i \le q.$$

(Cf. *restruct* [Abiteboul & Bidoit 1986].)

We note that if the nested relation $r_i^* \in d^*$, $i \in \{1,2,\ldots,q\}$, is not a nested flat relation then there is a loss of information in using ρ, due to the 1NF normalizability problem (see Subsection 2.2.2). As mentioned in Subsection 2.2.2 this problem can be alleviated by defining the keying operator [Jaeschke & Schek 1982; Jaeschke 1985a, 1985b].

Obviously, it is not always necessary to UNNEST* all or any of the nested relations, $r_i^* \in d^*$, in order to obtain the nested database, d'^*. Thus, $\rho_{U(T)}(d^*)$ is said to be an *optimal* restructuring operation if it can be obtained by a minimal number of UNNEST and NEST operations. Optimal restructuring operations are desirable since, obviously, they will execute faster. A future research problem would be to develop algorithms in order to obtain optimal joinable NDSs and optimal restructuring operations.

5.2 The Nested Representative Instance

In this section we present the *nested representative instance* (NRI) [Levene & Loizou 1988], which is the nested relation, over the NURS, at the conceptual level of the nested UR model (see NRI in Figure 1.3). The NRI provides the underlying data structure of the nested UR model, wherein the semantics of the nested database at the internal level are encapsulated in a single nested relation. Thus, the NRI, over the NURS, frees the user from logical navigation amongst and within the nested relations in the nested database, since the user can query the nested database via the NRI, solely through the universal set of attributes.

In order to formalize the nested UR model, we extend the weak instance approach (see Definition 2.15) to nested relations. Informally, a nested weak instance, say I^*, is a nested relation over the NURS, $U(T)$, which satisfies a set of null extended data dependencies, $D(U)$, and such that the null extended projections of I^* onto the attributes associated with each nested relation, $r_i^* \in d^*$, is more informative than $\rho_{U(T)}(r_i^*)$. This approach allows us to formalize the nested UR model whilst allowing the associated nested database to be an incomplete description of the real world.

In the following definition we formally define a nested weak instance.

Definition 5.7. Let $U(T)$ be the NURS of the NDS, $R(F)$ (which may not be joinable), where $F = \{T_1, T_2, ..., T_q\}$, with its associated nested database, $d^* = \{r_1^*, r_2^*, ..., r_q^*\}$, and a set, $D(U)$, of null extended data dependencies. Then, a nested relation, I^*, over $U(T)$, is a *nested weak instance* under $D(U)$ for d^*, if

(1) I^* satisfies $D(U)$; and

(2) $\rho_{U(T)}(r_i^*) \leq \Pi^{ne}{}_{S(T_i)}(I^*)$, $1 \leq i \leq q$.

Thus, in the nested weak instance approach to the nested UR model the nested database, d^*, is, in general, a partial description of a nested weak instance, I^*, over $U(T)$, which satisfies the semantics of d^* given in the form of a set, $D(U)$, of null extended data dependencies.

In the nested weak instance approach, as in the weak instance approach, there may be, in general, infinitely many nested weak instances under $D(U)$ for d^* (or a very large number if the atomic domains are finite). Thus, we assume that the only information that can be deduced from the said nested weak instances, under the nested UR model, is the information that holds in *all* nested weak instances under $D(U)$ for d^*. That is, under the nested weak instance approach, the *window*, [X], *for a set of attributes $X \subseteq U$, contains exactly the X-total tuples that appear in every nested weak instance under $D(U)$ for d^*.* Thus, informally, a NRI over the NURS, $U(T)$, is a nested weak instance, I^*, under a set, $D(U)$, of null extended data dependencies for a given nested database, d^*, such that [X] is defined, over I^*, as indicated above. It, therefore, follows that a NRI naturally extends a RI, since the nested weak instance approach to the nested UR model extends the weak instance approach to nested relations in a natural way. The following declarative definition encapsulates this fact.

Definition 5.8. Let U(T) be the NURS of the NDS, $\mathbf{R}(F)$ (which may not be joinable), where $F = \{T_1, T_2, ..., T_q\}$, with its associated nested database, d*, and a set, D(U), of null extended data dependencies. Then, a nested relation, I*, over U(T), is a *nested representative instance* (NRI) under D(U) for d*, if (assuming only generic null tuples, *null*, appear in d*)

(1) I* is a nested weak instance under D(U) for d*; and

(2) $[X] = \mu^*(\Pi^{ne}\downarrow_X(I^*))$, for any set of attributes $X \subseteq U$.

The following definition, which utilises the extended chase defined in Section 4.5, is a constructive definition of a unique NRI, to which we henceforth refer to as the NRI.

Definition 5.9. We define the construction of the NRI, I*, over U(T), under D(U) for d*, by

$$I^* \cong CHASE_{D(U)}(\text{PAD}(\rho_{U(T)}(d^*))).$$

(See how to apply PAD to a nested database d*, over a joinable NDS, $\mathbf{R}(F')$, over U(T), following Definition 3.20.)

The NRI, I*, is said to be *consistent* iff PAD($\rho_{U(T)}(d^*)$) is consistent. Furthermore, if the NRI, I*, over U(T), under D(U) for d*, is consistent, then d* is said to be *consistent*. Otherwise, the NRI, I*, is said to be *inconsistent*, and likewise d* is said to be *inconsistent*, in which case the NRI, I*, is taken to be undefined.

We note that the uniqueness of the NRI of Definition 5.9 follows from Lemma 4.9, which shows that, for any nested relation r* and a set, D(U), of null extended data dependencies, $CHASE_{D(U)}(r^*)$ is unique, provided r* is consistent.

The following proposition shows that the constructive definition of the NRI implies the declarative definition thereof. Thus, the extended chase provides us with a tool to effectively construct the NRI under D(U) for d*.

Proposition 5.4. Let U(T) be the NURS of the NDS, $\mathbf{R}(F)$, where $F = \{T_1, T_2, ..., T_q\}$, with its associated nested database, $d^* = \{r_1^*, r_2^*, ..., r_q^*\}$, and a set, D(U), of null extended data dependencies. If I*, over U(T), is the NRI, under D(U) for d*, as defined in Definition 5.9, then I*, over U(T), is the NRI, under D(U) for d*, as defined in Definition 5.8.

Proof. Suppose that d* is inconsistent. Then, the NRI, under D(U) for d*, is undefined by Definition 5.9 as well as by Definition 5.8, since in this latter case no nested weak instance under D(U) for d* exists. So, we can assume that d* is consistent.

Now, by Definition 5.9, we can deduce that I* is a nested weak instance under D(U) for d*. Since d* is consistent, by Lemma 4.8, it follows that $I^* \cong CHASE_{D(U)}(\text{PAD}(\rho_{U(T)}(d^*)))$ satisfies D(U); moreover, by the construction of I*, via the extended chase, it also follows that $\rho_{U(T)}(r_i^*) \le \Pi^{ne}{}_{S(T_i)}(I^*)$, $1 \le i \le q$.

It now remains to show that $[X] = \mu^*(\Pi^{ne}\!\downarrow_X(I^*))$, for any $X \subseteq U$. The inclusion

$$[X] \subseteq \mu^*(\Pi^{ne}\!\downarrow_X(I^*))$$

follows directly from the fact that I^* is a nested weak instance under $D(U)$ for d^*. The other inclusion, namely,

$$[X] \supseteq \mu^*(\Pi^{ne}\!\downarrow_X(I^*))$$

follows from the definition of the extended chase. This is due to the fact that after the extended chase, the NRI, I^*, under $D(U)$ for d^*, is the minimal nested relation w.r.t. the relative information content comparison operator, $\leq$, that satisfies $D(U)$ and is more informative than $PAD(\rho_{U(T)}(d^*))$. In other words, we have $PAD(\rho_{U(T)}(d^*)) \leq I^*$, and there does not exist a nested weak instance, I'^*, over $U(T)$, under $D(U)$ for d^*, such that $\neg(I^* \cong I'^*)$ and $I'^* \leq I^*$. Thus, all X-total tuples in $\mu^*(\Pi^{ne}\!\downarrow_X(I^*))$ must also be in $[X]$, since for all nested weak instances, I'^*, under $D(U)$ for d^*, $I^* \leq I'^*$, holds. $\square$

We note that, by Proposition 5.4, it follows that the NRI (of Definition 5.9) is in fact the *greatest lower bound* (glb) of all nested weak instances, over $U(T)$, under $D(U)$ for d^*, w.r.t. the relative information content comparison operator, $\leq$.

We further note that as a direct consequence of Proposition 5.4 any window function based on the NRI satisfies the containment condition, since it follows that $\Pi_X([Y]) \subseteq [X]$ holds, whenever $X \subseteq Y$. We recall that this result also holds for any window function based on the RI as was remarked in Subsection 2.3.3.

The semantics of the NRI are described in terms of a set, $D(U)$, of null extended data dependencies. In $D(U)$ we may include the following null extended data dependencies. Firstly, we may include the set of NEFDs, $FD(T)$, that are represented explicitly by the edges of the scheme tree, T, of the NURS, $U(T)$, and which are equivalent to the set of NMVDs, $MVD(T)$. Secondly, we may include a set of NFDs, $FF(T)$, that are represented in the nodes of the scheme tree, T. Lastly, we may include the NEJD, $\bowtie^{ne}[R(F')]$, where $R(F')$ is the joinable NDS, over $U(T)$, obtained from the NDS, $R(F)$, by using the restructuring operations described in Section 5.1. This NEJD ensures that the NRI, I^*, under $D(U)$ for d^*, possesses a null extended lossless decomposition onto $R(F')$. We note that, by Theorem 4.2, $\bowtie^{ne}[R(F')] \equiv JD(F)$, where $JD(F) = \bowtie[FDS(F)]$, as defined in Subsection 2.2.1.

As above let $U(T)$ be the NURS of the NDS, $R(F)$, where $F = \{T_1, T_2, ..., T_q\}$. The following lemma shows that the set of NEFDs, $FD(T)$, and the NEJD, $\bowtie^{ne}[R(F')]$, are as expected, implied by the NJD, $\bowtie[P(F')]$, over the path set of F', which is obtained from F.

Lemma 5.5. Let $\bowtie[P(F')]$, $\bowtie^{ne}[R(F')]$ and $FD(T)$ be as above. Then

(1) $\bowtie[P(F')] \models FD(T)$.

(2) $\bowtie[P(F')] \models \bowtie^{ne}[R(F')]\}$.

Proof. By Definition 3.18 of the joined NRS, $U(T)$, it follows that $P(T)$ covers $P(F')$, i.e., for all paths, $p' \in P(F')$, there exists a path, $p \in P(T)$, such that $p' \subseteq p$. Thus, by the covering rule for NJDs we have that $\bowtie[P(F')] \models \bowtie[P(T)]$. Part (1) now follows by Theorem 4.10 and Lemma 2.3 (2), which together imply that $\bowtie[P(T)] \equiv MVD(T) \equiv FD(T)$.

By the covering rule for NJDs we have that $\bowtie[P(F')] \models JD(F)$, since FDS(F) covers P(F'). Part (2) now follows by Theorem 4.2, which implies that $JD(F) \equiv \bowtie^{ne}[R(F')]$. $\square$

The significance of the above result is that the semantics embedded in the NRI, I*, over the NURS, U(T), are a consequence of the semantics of the nested database from which I* is constructed (see Definition 5.9). Furthermore, Lemma 5.5 highlights the importance of the novel concept of null extended lossless decomposition in a nested UR environment (cf. [Maier et al. 1984]).

We close this section with an example illustrating the NRI.

Example 5.7. From the running example given in Subsection 2.2.4, let $\mathbf{R}(F) = \{R(T_2),$ $R(T_3)\}$ and $d^* = \{r_2^*, r_3^*\}$. The scheme tree of the NURS, U(T), for $\mathbf{R}(F)$ is shown in Figure 3.21, and is over the joinable NDS, $\mathbf{R}(F')$, as described in Example 5.1, i.e., $\mathbf{R}(F') = \{R(T_2), R(T'_3)\}$, where T'_3 is shown in Figure 3.20, $R(T_2) = $ CLASS (TEXT)* (TUTOR)*, and $R(T'_3) = \Lambda$ (TUTOR SALARY (CHILD)* (DAY)*)*. Now, let FF(T) = {TUTOR $\rightarrow$ SALARY}, FD(T) = {CLASS $\rightarrow$ (TEXT)*, CLASS $\rightarrow$ (TUTOR SALARY (CHILD)* (DAY)*)*, CLASS,TUTOR,SALARY $\rightarrow$ (CHILD)*, CLASS,TUTOR,SALARY $\rightarrow$ (DAY)*}, and $\bowtie^{ne}[\mathbf{R}(F')] = \bowtie^{ne}[\{$CLASS (TEXT)* (TUTOR)*, Λ (TUTOR SALARY (CHILD)* (DAY)*)*$\}]$. Thus, the set of null extended data dependencies is given by D(U) = {FF(T), FD(T), $\bowtie^{ne}[\mathbf{R}(F')]$}. The NRI, I*, over U(T), under D(U) for d*, is given by $I^* \cong CHASE_{D(U)}(PAD(\rho_{U(T)}(d^*)))$, and is shown in Figure 5.10. It can easily be verified that I* is a nested weak instance under D(U) for d*.

5.3 Equivalence of the NRI and the RI

In this section we present one of the *major* results of the monograph, namely, the equivalence of the NRI and the RI, showing that the NRI is a suitable model for storing the data in a nested database in a single nested relation. More specifically, given a nested database, d*, over a NDS, $\mathbf{R}(F)$, and a set, D(U), of null extended data dependencies, we prove, in Theorem 5.7, the following result. Let d be the flat database obtained by applying the UNNEST* operator on all the nested relations in d* and let D be the set of null data dependencies emanating from D(U). Then, the NRI, over the NURS, U(T), under D(U) for d*, is equivalent to the RI over the universal set of attributes, U, under D for d. The implication of this result is two-fold. On the one hand, it shows that the classical UR model under the weak instance approach is a special case of the nested UR model under the nested weak instance approach, i.e., when we have a flat database over a FDS and a set of null data dependencies. On the other hand, Theorem 5.7 justifies the implementation of a UR interface under the nested UR model, since we can maintain a more flexible user interface than would otherwise be the case, and, in addition, we are able to gain all the advantages of nested relations over flat relations.

CLASS	(TEXT)*	(TUTOR	SALARY	(CHILD)*	(DAY)*)*
	TEXT	TUTOR	SALARY	(CHILD)*	(DAY)*
				CHILD	DAY
databases	Date Ullman	Robert	12000	Hanna Brian	Monday Thursday
programming	Knuth	Hanna	14000	Annette Ada	*null*
		Richard	*null*	*null*	*null*
french	*null*	Martine	*null*	*null*	*null*
first-order	Mendelson	*null*	*null*	*null*	*null*
hebrew	Bible	*null*	*null*	*null*	*null*
null	Lenin Dostoyevsky	*null*	*null*	*null*	*null*
null	*null*	*null*	15000	*null*	Wednesday
null	*null*	*null*	*null*	Ruth	Tuesday Friday

Fig. 5.10. The NRI, I*, over U(T), under D(U) for d*, of Example 5.7.

Prior to presenting our results, we slightly modify Definition 2.15 of the weak instance I, over U, under D for d, in order to use the "less informative than" operator, $\leq$, instead of the containment operator, $\subseteq$. Thus, a flat relation (with nulls), I, over U, is a weak instance under a set of null data dependencies, D, for a flat database, d, if

(1) I satisfies D; and

(2) $r_i \leq \Pi_{R_i}(I)$, $1 \leq i \leq m$.

Correspondingly, the RI, over U, under D for d, is defined constructively by

$$I \cong CHASE_D(\text{PAD}(\text{d})).$$

The following lemma shows that the NRI degenerates into the RI when the nested database is actually a flat database over a FDS, over U, and the set of null extended data dependencies is *per force* a set of null data dependencies.

Lemma 5.6. Let R be a FDS, over U; let d be its associated flat database and D be a set of null data dependencies. Then the following two statements are equivalent.

(1) I, over U, is the NRI under D for d.

(2) I, over U, is the RI under D for d.

Proof. Firstly we note that the set of null data dependencies, D, can be viewed as a set of null extended data dependencies, since NFDs are defined in Definition 4.2 over flat relations, and, moreover, by Proposition 4.1 we also have that NEJDs (NEMVDs) are faithful to NJDs (NMVDs). The result now follows directly from Theorem 4.10, since

PAD(d) $\cong$ μ*(PAD(d)). (No restructuring is required in this case.) $\square$

The following theorem establishes one of the *main* results of the monograph. It shows that the NRI over the NURS, U(T), under D(U) for d*, is equivalent to the RI over the universal set of attributes, U, under D for d.

Theorem 5.7. Let the NURS, U(T), be the joined NRS of the NDS, **R**(F), and let d* be its associated nested database. Also, let **R**(F') be the joinable NDS obtained from **R**(F), and let D(U) = {FF(T), FD(T), $\bowtie^{ne}$[**R**(F')]} be a set of null extended data dependencies. Then, the following two statements are equivalent.

(1) I*, over U(T), is the NRI under D(U) for d*.

(2) μ*(I*), over U, is the RI under the set of null data dependencies, D = {FF(T), MVD(T), JD(F)}, for the flat database d = {μ*(r_1^*), μ*(r_2^*), ..., μ*(r_q^*)}, over the FDS, FDS(F).

Proof. By Definition 5.8 and Proposition 5.4 we have that

$$I^* \cong CHASE_{D(U)}(PAD(\rho_{U(T)}(d^*))),$$

so, by Theorem 4.10, we obtain

$$\mu^*(I^*) \cong CHASE_D(\mu^*(PAD(\rho_{U(T)}(d^*)))).$$

It is also true that

$$\mu^*(PAD(\rho_{U(T)}(d^*))) \cong PAD(d),$$

by the note made after Definition 3.20 of PAD. Thus, we now have that

$$\mu^*(I^*) \cong CHASE_D(PAD(d)). \tag{1}$$

This concludes the result, since by applying Proposition 5.4 and then Lemma 5.6 to equation (1), it follows that μ*(I*) is the RI under D for d. $\square$

We observe that the above theorem obtains for any set of null extended data dependencies D'(U) $\subseteq$ D(U).

Example 5.8. For the NDS, **R**(F), and the nested database, d*, of Example 5.7, let FDS(F) = {S(T_2), S(T_3)} be a FDS over U = {CLASS, TEXT, TUTOR, SALARY, CHILD, DAY} with d = {μ*(r_2^*), μ*(r_3^*)} being the corresponding flat database over U. Also, let FF(T) = {TUTOR → SALARY}, MVD(T) = {CLASS →→ TEXT (S(T)), CLASS →→ TUTOR,SALARY,CHILD,DAY (S(T)), CLASS,TUTOR,SALARY →→ CHILD (S(T)), CLASS,TUTOR,SALARY →→ DAY (S(T))}, $\bowtie$[{CLASS, TEXT, TUTOR}, {TUTOR, SALARY, CHILD, DAY}]. The set of null data dependencies is given by D = {FF(T), MVD(T), JD(F)}. It can easily be verified that μ*(I*), over U, is the RI under D for d, where I*, over U(T), shown in Figure 5.10, is the NRI, under D(U) for d*, of Example 5.7.

Let I*, over U(T), be the NRI under D(U) for d*, and let (Y)* $\in$ U(T) be a higher order attribute. Then, the information-wise equivalence given by

$$\nu_Y(\mu_{(Y)*}(I^*)) \cong I^*$$

is, in general, *false*, as was shown in Subsection 2.2.2, unless I* is a nested flat relation.

Thus, as is the case for nested relations, in general, it is not possible to UNNEST* the NRI and then recover it by a corresponding sequence of NEST operations. This is due to the 1NF normalizability problem, which implies that additional semantics may be present in a nested relation in comparison to its flat counterpart (see Example 2.7). We, therefore, conclude that *the nested UR model is strictly more expressive than the UR model.*

The essential consequence of Theorem 5.7 is that it guarantees that a UR interface can be implemented by using the nested UR model, thus gaining all the advantages of nested relations over flat relations. This UR interface can provide both flat and hierarchical output to the user at the external level. In addition, since we have shown that the nested UR model is strictly more expressive than the UR model, the range of applications that can be modelled within the nested UR model is much larger than the corresponding range of applications that can be modelled within the UR model.

5.4 An Algebraic Approach to the Construction of the NRI

In Definition 5.9 we defined the construction of the NRI via the extended chase. There are two main drawbacks to this approach. The first drawback is that the extended chase procedure is exponential in the general case and, therefore, inefficient to compute (see the comment at the end of Section 4.5). The second drawback is that we cannot expect, in the near future, to have available a DBMS, supporting the null extended nested relational model, that will also support the extended chase directly; however, such a DBMS must support the null extended algebra. For these reasons it is very important to investigate a computational approach to the nested UR model whereby the NRI can be constructed algebraically via the null extended algebra rather than procedurally via the extended chase.

Jajodia and Springsteel [1987] showed that the RI can be constructed algebraically via the outer join operator, when the FDS associated with the flat database is γ-acyclic, i.e., when it possesses the UMC property. We extend this result to the nested UR model by showing in Theorem 5.8 that if the NDS, R(F), associated with the nested database, possesses the UMC property, then the NRI can be constructed algebraically via the null extended outer join operator given in Definition 3.21.

The reason the UMC property is important is that it implies a unique join sequence for computing the window, [X], for any set of attributes $X \subseteq U$ [Fagin 1983; Biskup et al. 1986]. Thus, we define a window function on $X \subseteq U$ based on the UMC property; this function is defined w.r.t. a FDS, **R**, over U, which is covered by FDS(F) and possesses the UMC property. We call this window function the *UMC window function* and denote it by $[X]_{UMC}^{\mathbf{R}}$. (Cf. [Yannakakis 1981; Fagin 1983; Biskup et al. 1986; Chan & Atzeni 1986].)

In Theorem 5.9 we show that $[X] = [X]_{UMC}^R$ for any $X \subseteq U$, provided the NDS, $R(F)$, possesses the UMC property, and $R = FDS(F)$. Thus, the NRI need not be constructed in order to support a UR interface, but rather that the window $[X]$ can be computed algebraically, on demand so to speak, during query processing. Thus, our computational approach to the nested UR model generalizes the computational approach to the classical UR model [Maier et al. 1984,1986].

In the sequel, as mentioned in Subsection 2.1.3, all null extended operators are defined over reduced and connected sets of attributes.

In the next theorem we show that the NRI can be constructed algebraically via the null extended outer join operator, when the NDS, $R(F)$, possesses the UMC property, and the set of null extended data dependencies, $D(U)$, consists of a single NEJD over the joinable NDS, $R(F')$, obtained from $R(F)$.

Theorem 5.8. Let $U(T)$ be the NURS over the NDS, $R(F)$, where $F = \{T_1, T_2, ..., T_q\}$; assume that $R(F)$ possesses the UMC property, and let $R(F')$ be the joinable NDS obtained from $R(F)$. Also, let $d*$ be a nested database, over $R(F)$, and let $D(U) = \{\bowtie^{ne}[R(F')]\}$. Then,

$$I* \cong \overline{\bowtie}^{ne} \, {}^{q}_{i=1}(\rho_{U(T)}(r_i^*))$$

is the NRI over $U(T)$ under $D(U)$ for $d*$.

Proof. By Proposition 5.4 we need to show that

$$\overline{\bowtie}^{ne} \, {}^{q}_{i=1}(\rho_{U(T)}(r_i^*)) \cong CHASE_{D(U)}(PAD(\rho_{U(T)}(d*))).$$

We prove the result by induction on the number, q, of the NRSs in $R(F)$.

BASIS. If $q = 1$ then the result holds trivially, since

$$\overline{\bowtie}^{ne} \, {}^{1}_{i=1}(\rho_{U(T)}(r_i^*)) \cong PAD(\rho_{U(T)}(r_1^*)),$$

and, moreover,

$$CHASE_{D(U)}(PAD(\rho_{U(T)}(r_1^*))) \cong PAD(\rho_{U(T)}(r_1^*)),$$

since the NEJD, $\bowtie^{ne}[R(F')]$, is a trivial NEJD.

INDUCTION. Assume the result holds for $q = n$. Then, we need to prove the result for $q = n+1$. In order to prove the inductive step, we utilize the *if* part of Proposition 2.2, i.e., if a FDS, R, is γ-acyclic then $\bowtie[R]$ implies that every connected subset of R has a lossless join. (Due to Definition 4.4 this proposition obtains also for NJDs over flat relations with nulls.) This result applies also to $\bowtie^{ne}[R(F')]$, since, by Theorem 4.2, the NEJD is a precise generalization of the NJD, and we have assumed that $R(F)$ possesses the UMC property. Thus, we can assume that all null extended joins and null extended outer joins are taken over connected sets of attributes.

Let $d* = d_n^* \cup \{r_{n+1}^*\}$, where $d_n^* = \{r_1^*, r_2^*, ..., r_n^*\}$. Also, let $I_n^* \cong \overline{\bowtie}^{ne} \, {}^{n}_{i=1}(\rho_{U(T)}(r_i^*))$. Then, by inductive hypothesis,

$$I_n^* \cong CHASE_{D(U)}(PAD(d_n^*)).$$

Now, let $I_{n+1}^* \cong PAD(I_n^*) \cup^{ne} PAD(\rho_{U(T)}(r_{n+1}^*))$. Thus, it suffices to show that

$$I_n^* \overline{\bowtie}^{ne} \rho_{U(T)}(r_{n+1}^*) \cong CHASE_{D(U)}(I_{n+1}^*),$$

since it would then follow, by Definition 5.9, that $I^* \cong I_n^* \overline{\bowtie}^{ne} \rho_{U(T)}(r_{n+1}^*)$ yielding the result. Now, by Definition 3.21 of $\overline{\bowtie}^{ne}$, we have that

$$I^* \cong (I_n^* \bowtie^{ne} \rho_{U(T)}(r_{n+1}^*)) \cup^{ne} I_{n+1}^*.$$

We conclude the proof by using Definition 4.13 of the NEJD-rule associated with the NEJD, $\bowtie^{ne}[R(F')]$, together with Proposition 2.2 as it applies to NJDs; consequently the following statement is true.

A tuple, t, is in $CHASE_{D(U)}(I_{n+1}^*)$ iff the tuple, t, is either in I_{n+1}^* or in $I_n^* \bowtie^{ne} \rho_{U(T)}(r_{n+1}^*)$. $\square$

Example 5.9. It can easily be verified that R(F) of Example 5.7 possesses the UMC property. Now let $d^* = \{r_2^*, r_3^*\}$ and $R(F') = \{R(T_2), R(T'_3)\}$ be as in Example 5.7, and let $D'(U) = \{\bowtie^{ne}[R(F')]\}$. Then, it can easily be verified that $I'^* \cong \rho_{U(T)}(r_2^*) \overline{\bowtie}^{ne} \rho_{U(T)}(r_3^*)$, shown in Figure 3.26, is the NRI, over U(T), under D'(U) for d^*.

We note that $\neg(I'^* \cong I^*)$, where I*, over U(T), is shown in Figure 5.10. This is due to the following facts. Firstly, I'*, which results from an extended outer join operation does not satisfy FD(T), so we have not included FD(T) in D'(U). On the other hand, I* of Example 5.7 satisfies FD(T), since D(U) of Example 5.7 includes FD(T), and I* was constructed via the extended chase. Secondly, I'* does not satisfy FF(T) = {TUTOR $\rightarrow$ SALARY}, so we have not included FF(T) in D'(U). On the other hand, I* of Example 5.7 satisfies FF(T), since D(U) of Example 5.7 includes FF(T), and I* was constructed via the extended chase.

The importance of Theorem 5.8. lies in the fact that we can construct the NRI by using the extended outer join operator without having recourse to the extended chase, and thus a computational approach to the nested UR model is provided. As a consequence, for query optimization purposes, when R(F) possesses the UMC property, it may be worth materializing a view, say V*, via a null extended projection of the NRI, I*, onto a set of attributes, say $X \subseteq U$, namely, $V^* \cong \Pi^{ne}{}_X(I^*)$. Thus, we can now compute the window, [Y], for any set of attributes $Y \subseteq X$, by unnesting a null extended total projection of the materialized view, V*, onto Y, i.e., $[Y] = \mu^*(\Pi^{ne}\downarrow_Y(V^*))$.

Theorem 5.8 allows the computation of the NRI, I*, whence a null extended projection of I* can be obtained. However, for query processing, we may only be interested in the window, say [X]. To this end we now formally define the UMC window function, $[X]_{UMC}^R$, w.r.t. a FDS, R, over U, which is covered by FDS(F) and possesses the UMC property, and then show in Theorem 5.9 that $[X] = [X]_{UMC}^R$.

As before, let U(T) be the NURS of the NDS, R(F), where $F = \{T_1, T_2, ..., T_q\}$, and let d^* be a nested database over R(F). Furthermore, let **R** be a FDS, over U, possessing the UMC property, and such that the FDS, FDS(F), over U, is a cover of **R**. Also, let $UMC_\mathbf{R}(X)$ denote the UMC among a set of attributes, $X \subseteq U$, w.r.t. **R** (see Definition 2.3).

Let $Y \subseteq U$ be a set of attributes such that $Y \subseteq S(T_i)$ for one or more scheme trees $T_i \in F$. We now define the intermediate null extended algebra expression, over Y, denoted as $\downarrow Y \downarrow$, by

$$\downarrow Y \downarrow \cong \cup_i^{ne} \{ \Pi^{ne}_Y (\rho_{U(T)} (r_i^*)) \mid Y \subseteq S(T_i) \text{ and } r_i^* \in d^* \text{ is a}$$
nested relation over $R(T_i)$, $i \in \{1, 2, \ldots, q\}$, with $R(T_i) \in$ **R**(F)},

which is utilized in the following definition.

Definition 5.10. The UMC window function, $[X]^\mathbf{R}_{UMC}$, w.r.t. a FDS, **R**, over U, possessing the UMC property, is defined by

$$[X]^\mathbf{R}_{UMC} = \mu^* (\Pi^{ne} \downarrow_X (\bowtie^{ne}_{Y \in UMC_\mathbf{R}(X)} (\downarrow Y \downarrow))).$$

(Cf. [Yannakakis 1981; Fagin 1983; Biskup et al. 1986; Chan & Atzeni 1986].)

We note that we have introduced the FDS, **R**, into the definition of the UMC window function, since it will be shown to be useful in Section 6.3 when we compare the UMC window function to another window function.

We are now in a position to establish the theorem which shows that the UMC window function, $[X]^\mathbf{R}_{UMC}$, is equal to the window, $[X]$, for any set of attributes $X \subseteq U$, when the NDS, **R**(F), possesses the UMC property and **R** = FDS(F). Thus, we show that the UMC window function provides the nested UR model with a computational method to construct the window, $[X]$, for any set of attributes $X \subseteq U$.

Theorem 5.9. Let U(T) be the NURS of a NDS, **R**(F), possessing the UMC property, and let **R**(F′) be the joinable NDS obtained from **R**(F). Also, let d* be a nested database, over **R**(F), and let $D(U) = \{\bowtie^{ne}[\mathbf{R}(F')]\}$ be the NEJD over U(T). Then, for any set of attributes $X \subseteq U$, $[X] = [X]^\mathbf{R}_{UMC}$, where **R** = FDS(F).

Proof. Let I*, over U(T), be the NRI under D(U) for d*. Then, by Proposition 5.4, we have that $I^* \cong CHASE_{D(U)}(PAD(\rho_{U(T)}(d^*)))$. Therefore, by Definition 5.8, we need to show that for any set of attributes, $X \subseteq U$,

$$[X]^\mathbf{R}_{UMC} = \mu^* (\Pi^{ne} \downarrow_X (I^*)).$$

Let the union of all the attributes in $UMC_\mathbf{R}(X)$ be V. Then, since $X \subseteq V$,

$$\mu^* (\Pi^{ne} \downarrow_X (I^*)) = \mu^* (\Pi^{ne} \downarrow_X (\Pi^{ne}_V (I^*))).$$

Now, we also have, from Definition 5.10 of $[X]^\mathbf{R}_{UMC}$, that

$$[X]^\mathbf{R}_{UMC} = \mu^* (\Pi^{ne} \downarrow_X (\bowtie^{ne}_{Y \in UMC_\mathbf{R}(X)} (\downarrow Y \downarrow))).$$

Thus, it only remains to show that

$$\Pi^{ne}\downarrow_X(\Pi^{ne}{}_V(I^*)) = \Pi^{ne}\downarrow_X(\bowtie^{ne}{}_{Y\in UMC_R(X)}(\downarrow Y\downarrow)).$$

We prove the result by induction on the number of elements in the unique minimal connection, $UMC_R(X)$, for any $X \subseteq U$.

BASIS. If $|UMC_R(X)| = 1$, where $UMC_R(X) = Y$, then the result follows trivially, since we now have that $V = Y$, and thus

$$\Pi^{ne}\downarrow_X(\Pi^{ne}{}_V(I^*)) = \Pi^{ne}\downarrow_X(\downarrow Y\downarrow),$$

due to the fact that $X \subseteq Y$ and $I^* \cong PAD(\rho_{U(T)}(d^*))$, since $\bowtie^{ne}[R(F')]$ is a trivial NEJD.

INDUCTION. Assume the result holds for $|UMC_R(X)| = n$. Then we need to prove the result for $|UMC_R(X)| = n+1$.

Let $UMC_R(X) = \{Y_1, Y_2, ..., Y_n, Y_{n+1}\}$; let $UMC_R(X^n) = \{Y_1, Y_2, ..., Y_n\}$ be the UMC among, say $X^n \subseteq X \subseteq V \subseteq U$, w.r.t. **R**, and let $V^n = V - Y_{n+1}$. Then, by inductive hypothesis,

$$\Pi^{ne}\downarrow_{X^n}(\Pi^{ne}{}_{V^n}(I^*)) = \Pi^{ne}\downarrow_{X^n}(\bowtie^{ne}{}_{Y\in UMC_R(X^n)}(\downarrow Y\downarrow)).$$

Thus, it only remains to show that

$$\Pi^{ne}\downarrow_X(\Pi^{ne}{}_V(I^*)) = \Pi^{ne}\downarrow_X(\Pi^{ne}{}_{V^n}(I^*) \bowtie^{ne} \downarrow Y_{n+1}\downarrow).$$

The result now follows, since an X-value, t[X], is in $\Pi^{ne}\downarrow_X(\Pi^{ne}{}_V(I^*))$ iff the tuple, t, results from an application of the NEJD-rule associated with the NEJD, $\bowtie^{ne}[R(F')]$, namely, that $t \cong t_1 \bowtie^{ne} t_2$ iff $t_1 \in \Pi^{ne}{}_{V^n}(I^*)$, $t_2 \in \Pi^{ne}{}_{Y_{n+1}}(I^*)$ and t is X-total. $\square$

Example 5.10. It can easily be verified that $R(F) = \{R(T_1), R(T_2), R(T_3)\}$ of the running example of Subsection 2.2.4 possesses the UMC property; thus $R = FDS(F) = \{S(T_1), S(T_2), S(T_3)\}$. Now, let U(T), where T is shown in Figure 5.6, be the NURS for $R(F)$, and let $R(F') = \{R(T_1), R(T'_2), R(T''_3)\}$ be the joinable NDS obtained from $R(F)$, where T'_2 is shown in Figure 5.4 and T''_3 is shown in Figure 5.5. Also, let d^* be the nested database over $R(F)$ of the running example from Subsection 2.2.4. We now give some examples of the UMC window function.

(1)   The null extended algebra expression for $[\{CLASS\}]^R_{UMC}$ is

$$\mu^*(\Pi^{ne}\downarrow_{CLASS}(\Pi^{ne}{}_{CLASS}(\rho_{U(T)}(r_1^*)) \cup^{ne} \Pi^{ne}{}_{CLASS}(\rho_{U(T)}(r_2^*)))).$$

It can easily be verified that $[\{CLASS\}] = [\{CLASS\}]^R_{UMC} = \{$databases, programming, first-order, french, hebrew$\}$.

(2)   The null extended algebra expression for $[\{STUDENT, TUTOR\}]^R_{UMC}$ is

$$\mu^*(\Pi^{ne}\downarrow_{STUDENT\ TUTOR}(\Pi^{ne}{}_{S(T_1)}(\rho_{U(T)}(r_1^*)) \bowtie^{ne} \Pi^{ne}{}_{S(T_2)}(\rho_{U(T)}(r_2^*)))).$$

It can easily be verified that $[\{STUDENT, TUTOR\}] = [\{STUDENT, TUTOR\}]^R_{UMC}$ equals the flat relation shown in Figure 5.11.

(3) The null extended algebra expression for $[\{DEPT, TUTOR, SALARY\}]_{UMC}^{R}$ is

$$\mu* (\Pi^{ne}\downarrow_{DEPT\ TUTOR\ SALARY}(\Pi^{ne}{}_{S(T_1)}(\rho_{U(T)}(r_1^*)) \bowtie^{ne} \Pi^{ne}{}_{S(T_2)}(\rho_{U(T)}(r_2^*))$$

$$\bowtie^{ne} \Pi^{ne}{}_{S(T_3)}(\rho_{U(T)}(r_3^*)))).$$

It can easily be verified that $[\{DEPT, TUTOR, SALARY\}] = [\{DEPT, TUTOR,$
$SALARY\}]_{UMC}^{R} = \{<CS, Robert, 12000>, <CS, Hanna, 14000>\}$.

STUDENT	TUTOR
Iris	Robert
Iris	Hanna
Iris	Richard
Mark	Robert
Naomi	Martine

Fig. 5.11. The window over $[\{STUDENT, TUTOR\}]$ for d* of the running example.

We note that the null extended algebra expression in the UMC window function can
be optimized by using standard algebraic query optimization techniques [Ullman 1982a;
Maier 1983] (cf. [Scholl 1986; Colby 1989]). For example, the null extended algebra
expression of (2), from Example 5.10, for $[\{STUDENT, TUTOR\}]_{UMC}^{R}$ can be optimized
to

$$\mu* (\Pi^{ne}\downarrow_{STUDENT\ TUTOR}(\Pi^{ne}{}_{STUDENT\ CLASS}(\rho_{U(T)}(r_1^*)) \bowtie^{ne}$$

$$\Pi^{ne}{}_{CLASS\ TUTOR}(\rho_{U(T)}(r_2^*)))).$$

5.5 Discussion

In this chapter we have formalized the conceptual level of the nested UR model. One of the main results of the chapter is that the classical UR model is a special case of the nested UR model (see Theorem 5.7). Thus, at the external level of the nested UR model we can maintain a UR interface, whilst via the NRI at the conceptual level we gain the advantages of nested relations over flat relations. Moreover, since the nested UR model is strictly more expressive than the classical UR model, both flat and hierarchical data can be modelled at the conceptual level and presented to the user at the external level.

We have also shown that a DBMS supporting the null extended algebra, but not necessarily the extended chase, can effectively support the nested UR model, when the NDS, $\mathbf{R}(F)$, possesses the UMC property (see Theorems 5.8, 5.9). In our computational approach to the nested UR model, we first showed that the NRI can be obtained via the null extended outer join operator and we thereafter showed that the UMC window function can be used to compute null extended total projections of the NRI, i.e., to compute the window, [X], for any $X \subseteq U$. In this context it has been argued by Ullman [1983a] that null values should also be included in the window, [X], as information is lost, at times, when only the total projection is considered and output. It is, therefore, possible to redefine [X] in Definition 5.8 by

$$[X] \cong \mu^*(\Pi^{ne}{}_X(I^*)),$$

in order to include null values. Furthermore, we can modify Definition 5.10 of the UMC window function to output null values by using the null extended projection operator and the null extended outer join operator instead of the null extended total projection operator and the null extended join operator, respectively.

In Levene & Loizou [1989e] we consider some specific problems that arise w.r.t. the interaction of NFDs with the NRI and we suggest certain solutions. We show that for a NDS inducing a γ-acyclic cover-embedding BCNF FDS, consistency can be maintained efficiently, without recourse to the extended chase (cf. [Graham & Wong 1986; Chan and Hernández 1988a, 1988b; Hernández & Chan 1988]). In addition, we show that we can extend the subclass of *independent* FDSs [Sagiv 1983; Jajodia & Ng 1984; Jajodia 1987] to a corresponding subclass of *independent* NDSs. Thus, for a nested database, d*, over an independent NDS, $\mathbf{R}(F)$, in order to maintain consistency it is sufficient to maintain consistency locally for each nested relation, r_i^*, in the nested database, d*, over $\mathbf{R}(F)$. Another problem we tackle in Levene & Loizou [1989e] is that of constructing the NRI algebraically in the presence of NFDs. We show that, again for a NDS inducing a γ-acyclic cover-embedding BCNF FDS, we can use the UMC window function, namely, that, for any set of attributes $X \subseteq U$, $[X] = [X]^{\mathbf{R}}_{UMC}$.

In order to support a UR interface at the external level of the nested UR model we have developed elsewhere [Levene & Loizou 1989b] an SQL-based query language [Date 1987c], called Nested UR Query Language (NURQL). In NURQL, in similarity to PIQUE [Maier et al. 1987], SYSTEM/U [Korth et al. 1984] and DURST [Biskup & Bruggemann 1987], the user is freed from logical navigation and thus the SQL *FROM* clause is omitted from this query language. Some of the features of NURQL are: flexible restructuring of data, user control over the output of null values, full support of nested queries and aggregate functions.

Finally, we make a few remarks about the *open* and *closed world* assumptions [Reiter 1978] in the context of the nested UR model. If we assume an *open world* then there may be facts about the world that could be stored in the nested database but are not. On the other hand, if we assume a *closed world* then *all* the facts about the world are stored in the nested database. The main characteristic of the closed world assumption is that negative information can be inferred from the absence of positive information, whereas the open world assumption gives us a more realistic model of the real world.

We can now relate these two different assumptions to our interpretation of the NRI, which models the information content of a nested database in the nested UR model. Under the nested weak instance approach to the nested UR model, we have assumed an open world, since the NRI is considered to be the glb of all the possible nested weak instances (w.r.t. the relative information content operator, $\leq$), one of which is the true model of the information content of the real world. An alternative approach, assuming a closed world, is to consider the NRI as the complete model of *all* the information content of the real world. Adopting this closed world approach to the NRI, query processing is more expressive than would otherwise have been the case, since negative information is thus represented in the NRI and can be the subject of queries from the user (cf. [Imielinski & Lipski 1984; Lerat and Lipski 1986]). On the other hand, in the context of the nested weak instance approach to the nested UR model, it seems more realistic to assume an open world rather than to assume a closed world, as we do *not* normally expect *all* the facts about the real world to be recorded in the nested database, but rather only a proper subset of them.

Chapter 6
A Universal Relation Model
For a Single Nested Relation

In this chapter we investigate the special case when the nested database consists of a single nested relation. The first apparent difference from the general case, presented in Chapter 5, is that the conceptual level of the nested UR model and the internal level of the nested UR model are now one and the same. Thus, the four DBMS levels of the nested UR model shown in Figure 1.3 reduce to three DBMS levels, as shown in Figure 6.1.

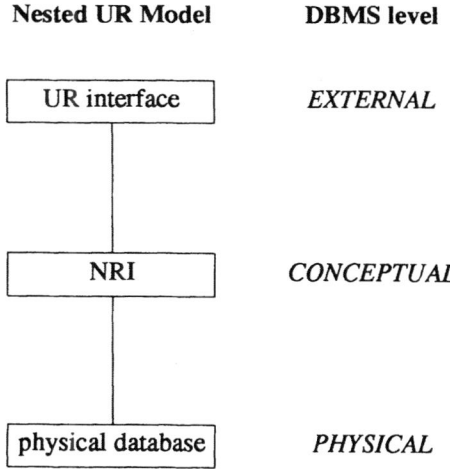

Fig. 6.1. The DBMS levels of the nested UR model for a single nested relation.

As far as efficient query processing is concerned this special case is an ideal situation, since all the null extended joins are realized within the single nested relation. Thus, in this case query processing for the nested UR model is fully optimized.

In Section 6.1 we show that nested relations can be viewed in terms of the *association-object database model* (AODM) [Maier & Warren 1982; Stein & Maier 1985; Maier et al. 1986, 1987]. We then proceed to show that there is a natural equivalence between nested relations and the AODM, thus justifying a single nested relation as a substitute for an AODM at the conceptual level, whilst still providing the same UR interface at the external level.

In Section 6.2 we show a strong connection between a single nested relation and the UR model in the form of γ-acyclicity. Our main result in this section is that the path set,

P(T), of a scheme tree, T, is equivalent to a subclass of γ-acyclic FDSs, namely, P(T) is a member of a subclass of FDSs that satisfy the UMC property. Thus, a single nested relation can replace a γ-acyclic FDS, P(T), over S(T), at the conceptual level, whilst still providing the same UR interface at the external level.

In Section 6.3 we discuss the NRI for a nested database with only a single nested relation. We show that under the nested UR model, whereby we use the NRI to model the information content of the nested database, viewing nested relations in terms of the AODM is equivalent to viewing nested relations in terms of their induced subclass of γ-acyclic FDSs. We then proceed to characterize the NRI in terms of a single nested relation. It turns out, from the results in Chapter 5, that a nested relation, r^*, can be viewed as the NRI, over the NURS, U(T), under a set, D(U), of null extended data dependencies for a nested database, $d^* = \{r^*\}$, whenever r^* satisfies D(U). We conclude Section 6.3 with further motivation, which supports a strong connection between the UR model and the nested UR model for a single nested relation, by showing that the UR assumptions are satisfied in a nested relation, r^*, over a NRS, R(T).

In Section 6.4 we give some application examples of the nested UR model for a single nested relation. The examples are chosen to be straightforward and simple, and yet clearly to bring out the advantages of using the nested UR model!

6.1 Associations and Objects in Nested Relations

Maier & Warren [1982] claim that data dependencies are not sufficient to describe the semantics of the UR model. Thus, Maier & Warren [1982] describe the semantics of the UR model in terms of *associations* and *objects*, which we now very briefly review. *Associations* are non-decomposable relationships, that represent permissible units of updates, amongst attributes. On the other hand, *objects* are decomposable relationships, that represent units of retrieval, amongst attributes, over a union of associations. In our formalism we place no restriction on the appearance of null values in a flat relation, r(X), where $X \subseteq U$ is an association, as in Maier & Warren [1982], wherein r(X) does not contain null values. To this end we could specify *null existence constraints* [Goldstein 1981; Maier 1983; Atzeni & Morfuni 1986], which restrict the appearance of null values for specified attributes in a flat relation (or in our case in a nested relation).

We remind the reader that whenever we use the standard relational operators, we consider them to be the *faithful* counterparts of their null extended versions (see Chapter 3).

We now define an association-object database scheme and its corresponding association-object database.

Definition 6.1. Let **As** be a set of associations over U, i.e., **As** is a FDS, over U. Also, let **Ob** be a set of objects for **As**, i.e., for each $O \in$ **Ob**, there exists $A_1, A_2, ..., A_n$, $n \geq 1$, such that $A_i \in$ **As**, $1 \leq i \leq n$, and $O = \cup_{i=1}^{n}(A_i)$.

We call the pair, <As, Ob>, an *association-object database scheme* (AODS), and we call a flat database, d, over As, an *association-object database* (AO database), over As.

The following three integrity constraints, denoted by $\hat{D}$, are placed on an AODS, <As, Ob> and an AO database, d, over As [Maier & Warren 1982].

(1) The *containment condition for associations* (CCA). Let A_1, $A_2 \in$ As be such that $A_1 \subseteq A_2$, and $r(A_1)$, $r(A_2) \in$ d. Then, $\Pi_{A_1}(r(A_2)) \le r(A_1)$ holds. (We note that in Maier & Warren [1982] this condition is specified by $\Pi_{A_1}(r(A_2)) \subseteq r(A_1)$; however, we recall that herein we allow null values in flat and nested relations.)

(2) The set of associations is contained in the set of objects, i.e., As $\subseteq$ Ob.

(3) The set of objects is closed under non-empty intersection, i.e., if $O_1, O_2 \in$ Ob such that $O_1 \cap O_2 \ne \emptyset$, then $(O_1 \cap O_2) \in$ Ob.

The motivation behind the above integrity constraints is two-fold [Maier et al. 1986]:

(1) To guarantee that the *window function* that computes [X], for any set of attributes, $X \subseteq U$, is *AO faithful*, i.e., for all flat relations $r(X) \in$ d, $[X] = \Pi\downarrow_X(r(X))$ (or $[X] = r(X)$ if $r(X)$ is X-total). This ensures that the contents of the window, [X], for X are in agreement with the contents of the AO database.

(2) To guarantee the *integrity of objects*, which is an alternative to the OFA. An object, $O \in$ Ob, is considered to be *integral* if for any subset of attributes, $X \subseteq O$, we can construct the window, [X], for X from the set $\{r(Z) \mid Z \in$ As and $Z \subseteq O\}$. This ensures that there is a unique access path to compute [X].

In order to define the construction of the window, [X], for any set of attributes $X \subseteq U$, for an AODS and an AO database, we next define the *association-object window function* (AO window function).

Definition 6.2. Let <As, Ob> be an AODS, and let d be an AO database, over As. Let

$$\hat{r}(O) = \bowtie_{(Z \in \text{As}, Z \subseteq O)} r(Z)$$

be the flat relation over an object, $O \in$ Ob. Then, the AO window function for <As, Ob> and d, denoted as $[X]_{AO}$, is defined by

$$[X]_{AO} = \cup_{(O \in \text{Ob}, X \subseteq O)} \Pi\downarrow_X(\hat{r}(O)) .$$

(Cf. [Maier & Warren 1986].)

The next proposition characterizes the situation when the AODS has the desirable properties, namely, that the AO window function, $[X]_{AO}$, is AO faithful, and the objects in the given AODS are integral.

Proposition 6.1. Let <As, Ob> be an AODS, and let d be an AO database, satisfying the set of integrity constraints, $\hat{D}$, and assume that $[X] = [X]_{AO}$, for any $X \subseteq U$. Then

(1) The AO window function, $[X]_{AO}$, is AO faithful.

(2) All objects, $O \in \mathbf{Ob}$, are integral, namely,

$[X]_{AO} = \Pi\!\downarrow_X (\bowtie_{(Z \in \mathbf{As}, \ Z \subseteq O)} \ r(Z))$ holds for any $X \subseteq O$, where O is the minimal object containing X, i.e., for any $O' \in \mathbf{Ob}$ such that $O' \neq O$ and $X \subseteq O'$, we have that $O \subseteq O'$.

Proof. (1) follows directly from Theorem 2 in Maier et al. [1986]; similarly, (2) follows directly from Theorem 5 in Maier et al. [1986]. □

We are now ready to define the semantics of scheme trees and nested relations in terms of associations and objects. The following definition gives the set of associations for a scheme tree, T.

Definition 6.3. The *associations* that hold for a scheme tree, T, denoted by As(T), are defined recursively by

(1) if the scheme tree, T, consists of a single node, n, with ATT(n) = X, then **As**(T) = {X};

(2) if X = ATT(ROOT(T)) and T_1, T_2, ..., T_s, s ≥ 1, denote the first level subtrees of the scheme tree, T, then **As**(T) = {X} ∪ { XY | Y ∈ **As**(T_i) for 1 ≤ i ≤ s}.

(Cf. Levene & Loizou [1988]; see *skeleton format* in Abiteboul & Bidoit [1986].)

The following definition gives the objects for a scheme tree, T.

Definition 6.4. Let the *objects* that hold for a scheme tree, T, be denoted by **Ob**(T). Let $e_1, e_2, ..., e_m$ be the edges of T with $e_i = (u_i, v_i)$, where i ranges over {1,2,...,m}. Then

$$\mathbf{Ob}(T) = \mathbf{As}(T) \cup \{\cup_{i=1}^{m} (A(u_i) \cup D(u_i))\},$$

where we define $(A(u_i) \cup D(u_i))$ to be the object corresponding to the NMVD, $M(e_i) \in$ MVD(T), represented by the edge, e_i.

(Cf. Levene & Loizou [1988].)

Example 6.1. Let T be the scheme, T_1, of the running example shown in Figure 2.3. The associations for T are: **As**(T) = {{STUDENT, DEPT}, {STUDENT, DEPT, MAJOR}, {STUDENT, DEPT, CLASS}, {STUDENT, DEPT, CLASS, EXAM}, {STUDENT, DEPT, CLASS, PROJECT}}. The corresponding objects for T are: **Ob**(T) = **As**(T) ∪ {{STUDENT, DEPT, CLASS, EXAM, PROJECT}, {STUDENT, DEPT, CLASS, MAJOR, EXAM, PROJECT}}.

We now define the AO database over the set of associations of the scheme tree, T, induced by a nested relation, r*.

Definition 6.5. Let r* be a nested relation over a NRS, R(T), and let <As(T), Ob(T)> be the AODS induced by the scheme tree, T. Then, we define the AO database for r*, over As(T), denoted as As(r*), by

As$(r\star)$ = $\{\mu\star(\Pi^{ne}{}_X(r\star)) \mid X \in$ As$(T)\}$.

Example 6.2. Let r* be the nested relation, r_1^*, of the running example shown in Figure 2.8, and let T be the scheme, T_1, of the running example as shown in Figure 2.3. Then, d = As(r*) is an AO database, over As(T), consisting of the following flat relations:

r(STUDENT DEPT) $\cong \mu*(\Pi^{ne}{}_{STUDENT\ DEPT}(r*))$

r(STUDENT DEPT MAJOR) $\cong \mu*(\Pi^{ne}{}_{STUDENT\ DEPT\ MAJOR}(r*))$

r(STUDENT DEPT CLASS) $\cong \mu*(\Pi^{ne}{}_{STUDENT\ DEPT\ CLASS}(r*))$

r(STUDENT DEPT CLASS EXAM) $\cong \mu*(\Pi^{ne}{}_{STUDENT\ DEPT\ CLASS\ EXAM}(r*))$

r(STUDENT DEPT CLASS PROJECT) $\cong \mu*(\Pi^{ne}{}_{STUDENT\ DEPT\ CLASS\ PROJECT}(r*))$

shown in Figures 6.2, 6.3, 6.4, 6.5 and 6.6, respectively.

STUDENT	DEPT
Iris	CS
Mark	CS
David	philosophy
Naomi	*null*

Fig. 6.2. r(STUDENT DEPT).

STUDENT	DEPT	MAJOR
Iris	CS	computing
Mark	CS	maths
David	philosophy	logic
Naomi	*null*	languages

Fig. 6.3. r(STUDENT DEPT MAJOR).

STUDENT	DEPT	CLASS
Iris	CS	databases
Iris	CS	programming
Mark	CS	databases
David	philosophy	first-order
Naomi	*null*	french
Naomi	*null*	hebrew

Fig. 6.4. r(STUDENT DEPT CLASS).

Given a scheme tree, T, the AODS, <As(T), Ob(T)>, satisfies integrity constraint (2) in $\hat{D}$, since, by Definition 6.4, As(T) $\subseteq$ Ob(T). The following lemma shows that the

STUDENT	DEPT	CLASS	EXAM
Iris	CS	databases	mid
Iris	CS	databases	final
Iris	CS	programming	final
Mark	CS	databases	final
David	philosophy	first-order	mid
null	philosophy	*null*	final
Naomi	*null*	french	mid
Naomi	*null*	*null*	final
Naomi	*null*	hebrew	*null*

Fig. 6.5. r(STUDENT DEPT CLASS EXAM).

STUDENT	DEPT	CLASS	PROJECT
Iris	CS	databases	1NF
Iris	CS	programming	*null*
Mark	CS	databases	NF2
Mark	CS	databases	UR
David	philosophy	first-order	prolog
null	philosophy	first-order	functions
null	philosophy	first-order	predicates
Naomi	*null*	french	*null*
Naomi	*null*	*null*	Moscow
Naomi	*null*	hebrew	Genesis

Fig. 6.6. r(STUDENT DEPT CLASS PROJECT).

AODS, $<As(T), Ob(T)>$, also satisfies integrity constraint (3) in $\hat{D}$, i.e., $Ob(T)$ is closed under non-empty intersection.

Lemma 6.2. Let T be a scheme tree, then $Ob(T)$ is closed under non-empty intersection, namely, if $O_1, O_2 \in Ob(T)$ such that $O_1 \cap O_2 \neq \emptyset$, then $(O_1 \cap O_2) \in Ob(T)$.

Proof. Let $O_1, O_2 \in Ob(T)$ such that $O_1 \cap O_2 \neq \emptyset$. We prove the result by induction on HEIGHT(T).

BASIS. If HEIGHT(T) = 0, then the result follows trivially, since in this case $|Ob(T)| = 1$ and thus $O_1 = O_2$.

INDUCTION. Assume the result holds for HEIGHT(T) = n, we then need to prove that the result holds for HEIGHT(T) = n+1.

Let X = ATT(ROOT(T)) and let $T_1, T_2, ..., T_s$, s ≥ 1, denote the first level subtrees of the scheme tree, T, with HEIGHT(T) = n+1. Thus, HEIGHT(T_i) ≤ n, 1 ≤ i ≤ s.

By Definition 6.3, X is included in all the associations, A_i ∈ As(T). Correspondingly, by Definition 6.4, X is included in all the objects, O_i ∈ Ob(T) − As(T). It, therefore, follows that X ⊆ O_1 ∩ O_2. Now, let $O'_1 = O_1 − X$ and $O'_2 = O_2 − X$. If O'_1 ∩ O'_2 = ∅, then the result follows, since, by Definition 6.4, X ∈ As(T) and As(T) ⊆ Ob(T).

Assume that O'_1 ∩ O'_2 = Y ≠ ∅. By the inductive hypothesis and Definition 2.4 of a scheme tree, it follows that there exists a subtree, T_i, i ∈ {1,2,...,s}, such that Y ∈ Ob(T_i). The result now follows, since we either have that XY ∈ As(T) by Definition 6.3 of As(T), or we have that XY ∈ Ob(T) by Definition 6.4 of Ob(T). □

Example 6.3. It can easily be verified that Ob(T) of Example 6.1 is closed under non-empty intersection. For example, we have in Ob(T) the object, {STUDENT, DEPT} = {STUDENT, DEPT, MAJOR} ∩ {STUDENT, DEPT, CLASS}, and we have in Ob(T) the object, {STUDENT, DEPT, CLASS} = {STUDENT, DEPT, CLASS, EXAM} ∩ {STUDENT, DEPT, CLASS, PROJECT}.

The following proposition characterizes nested relations in terms of an AODS, <As(T), Ob(T)>, and an AO database, As(r*), over As(T), for a nested relation, r*, over a NRS, R(T). By Definition 6.4 of Ob(T) and the result of Lemma 6.2, it follows that integrity constraints (2) and (3) in $\hat{D}$ are satisfied by the said AODS and AO database. In the ensuing proposition we show that the AO database, As(r*), also satisfies integrity constraint (1) in $\hat{D}$, namely, the CCA. In fact, we show the stronger result, i.e., that the said AODS and AO database imply the existence of some nested relation over R(T), provided it contains no nulls.

Proposition 6.3. Let T be a scheme tree, <As(T), Ob(T)> be an AODS, and d be an AO database, over As(T). Then,

(1) if d = As(r*), for some nested relation, r*, over the NRS, R(T), then d satisfies the CCA;

(2) if d is an AO database, over As(T), containing no nulls, i.e., all r(X) ∈ d are X-total, and d satisfies the CCA, then
     d = {$\Pi\!\downarrow_X$(r(X)) | r(X) ∈ As(r*)}, for some nested relation, r*, over the NRS, R(T).

Proof. (1). Let X, Y ∈ As(T) such that X ⊆ Y, and r(X), r(Y) ∈ d. We need to show that Π_X(r(Y)) ≤ r(X). Now, by the construction of As(r*), given in Definition 6.5, we have that

$$r(X) \cong \mu*(\Pi^{ne}_X(r*)) \quad \text{and} \quad r(Y) \cong \mu*(\Pi^{ne}_Y(r*)).$$

The result now follows, since, by the preciseness of Π^{ne}, shown in Theorem 3.6, and by the definition of Π^{ne}, it follows that

$$\mu*(\Pi^{ne}_X(r*)) \cong \Pi^{ne}_X(\mu*(\Pi^{ne}_Y(r*))) \cong \Pi_X(\mu*(\Pi^{ne}_Y(r*))).$$

(2). Let R(T) be the NURS, i.e., U(T) = R(T), and let r* ≅ $\rho_{U(T)}$(PAD(d)) be a nested relation over R(T). Then, by hypothesis, Definition 3.20 of PAD and Definition 5.6 of ρ, the result follows. □

The above result is similar to that of Theorem 3.2 in Abiteboul & Bidoit [1986], the difference being that we consider the general class of nested relations whilst Abiteboul & Bidoit [1986] consider only the subclass of hierarchical relations.

Example 6.4. It can easily be verified that the AO database, d, over As(T), of Example 6.2 satisfies the CCA.

We now show that the nested relation of Proposition 6.3, part (2), is not unique by considering the flat database, $d' = \{\Pi\downarrow_X(r(X)) \mid r(X) \in As(r*)\}$, for r* and As(r*) of Example 6.2. Let $r'* \cong \rho_{U(T)}(PAD(d'))$ be the nested relation, over R(T), as in the proof of Proposition 6.3 (2). Then, we also have $d' = \{\Pi\downarrow_X(r(X)) \mid r(X) \in As(r'*)\}$; however, it can easily be verified that $\neg(r* \cong r'*)$.

6.2 Scheme Trees and γ-Acyclicity

It is already known that nested relations correspond to acyclic FDSs [Ozsoyoglu & Yuan 1987a], but the exact correspondence was not shown therein. To this end, we show in this section that a subclass of γ-acyclic FDSs are equivalent to the subclass of FDSs induced by the path set, P(T), of a scheme tree, T [Levene & Loizou 1989d]. This is a desirable property since, by representing a γ-acyclic FDS via a nested relation, redundancy is minimized and all the null extended joins are realized within the nested relation. This result also implies a strong connection between nested relations and the UR model, since γ-acyclic FDSs imply the OFA [Biskup et al. 1986] due to the existence of a unique join sequence which can be employed to compute the window, [X], for any set of attributes, X ⊆ U, by using the UMC window function $[X]_{UMC}^R$ of Definition 5.10. (Cf. [Yannakakis 1981; Fagin 1983; Biskup et al. 1986; Chan & Atzeni 1986].)

Before we present the results of this section, we introduce the following functions that operate on a Bachman diagram, which was defined in Subsection 2.1.3.

Let B(R) be the Bachman diagram for a FDS, R, and n be a node of B(R). The following functions which operate on B(R) are now defined.

(1)   H(B(R),n), the height of a node n in B(R), returns |ATT(n)| − 1;

(2)   PARENT(B(R),n) returns the set containing all nodes, v, such that e = (v,n) is an edge in B(R) and H(B(R),n) > H(B(R),v);

(3)   CHILDREN(B(R),n) returns the set containing all nodes, v, such that e = (n,v) is an edge in B(R) and H(B(R),n) < H(B(R),v);

(4)   LEAF(B(R)) returns the set containing all nodes, n, such that CHILDREN(B(R),n) = ∅; We denote the FDS induced by LEAF(B(R)) as FDS(LEAF(B(R))) and such that for all nodes, n ∈ LEAF(B(R)), ATT(n) ∈ FDS(LEAF(B(R)));

(5) ROOT(B(R)) returns the set containing all nodes, n, such that PARENT(B(R),n) = $\emptyset$;

(6) H(B(R)), the height of the Bachman diagram, B(R), returns max(H(B(R)),n), where n ∈ LEAF(B(R)), and max(S) returns the maximum value of a set S of integers.

Example 6.5. Let $R = P(T_1)$ be the FDS for T_1, of the running example, shown in Figure 2.3. Then **R** is a γ-acyclic FDS, since the Bachman diagram for **R**, B(R), shown in Figure 2.2 of Example 2.3, is loop-free, i.e., it is a lfbd.

We recall, from Subsection 2.1.3, that we have assumed that a FDS, **R**, over U, is connected and reduced, so we can assume in this section that P(T) is likewise connected and reduced. We are now ready to present the main results of this section. The following lemma shows that the FDS induced by the path set, P(T), of a scheme tree, T, possesses the UMC property.

Lemma 6.4. Let T be a scheme tree, then P(T) is a γ-acyclic FDS.

Proof. By Lemma 2.3 part (2), ⋈[P(T)] ≡ MVD(T). (See also the comment just prior to Section 4.3.) We prove the result by induction on the number of paths, p, removed from P(T). If P(T) has only one path, then the result follows trivially. So we can now assume that |P(T)| > 1.

BASIS. p = 1. Assume we remove the path p_i ∈ P(T). This is equivalent to removing one of the NMVDs from MVD(T), say m_i. We remove p_i from T by pruning p_i, from leaf to root, until we reach a non-leaf node which is in another path of P(T). Since the resulting tree, say T', is a scheme tree, the result follows, i.e., ⋈[P(T')] ≡ MVD(T') by Lemma 2.3 part (2).

INDUCTION. p > 1. Assume the result obtains on removing p − 1 paths. By the same argument, as that given for the basis, the result obtains on removing p paths. The result now follows by Proposition 2.2, since we have shown that ⋈[P(T)] obtains for every connected and reduced subset P(T') of P(T), i.e., ⋈[P(T')] holds in the context of S(T'). □

The next theorem characterizes the subclass of γ-acyclic FDSs that are equivalent to the FDS induced by the path set, P(T), of a scheme tree, T.

Theorem 6.5. If **R** is a γ-acyclic FDS and ∩**R** is non-empty, then **R** ≡ P(T) for some scheme tree T.

Proof. Let B(R) be the lfbd (loop-free Bachman diagram) for **R**. Since ∩**R** is non-empty B(R) is a rooted tree. It is now shown by induction on H(B(R)) that FDS(LEAF(B(R))) ≡ P(T), for some scheme tree T.

BASIS. H(B(R)) = H(B(R),ROOT(B(R))). The result follows trivially, since |**R**| = 1 and thus T is equivalent to a single node.

INDUCTION. Assume that **R'** ≡ P(T') for H(B(R')) ≤ h − 1. We now proceed to show that **R** ≡ P(T) for H(B(R)) > h − 1. Let n be any node in B(R) such that H(B(R),n) ≤ h − 1,

$v \in$ CHILDREN(B(**R**),n) with H(B(**R**),v) > h − 1, and let X = (ATT(v) − ATT(n)). By the definition of B(**R**), ATT(n) $\subset$ ATT(v) and so X $\neq \emptyset$. Now, since B(**R**) is a rooted lfbd, and **R** is closed under intersection, we have that PARENT(B(**R**),v) = {n} and thus X $\cap$ S(T′) = $\emptyset$. It follows that we can add a node labelled by X as a leaf node to T′, thus obtaining T, and as a result we have ATT(v) $\in$ P(T). As we now have FDS(LEAF(B(**R**))) $\equiv$ P(T), the result follows, since FDS(LEAF(B(**R**))) = **R** [Fagin 1983]. $\square$

The following corollary summarizes the results of Lemma 6.4 and Theorem 6.5.

Corollary 6.6. **R** is a γ-acyclic FDS with $\cap$**R** non-empty iff **R** $\equiv$ P(T), for some scheme tree, T. $\square$

Example 6.6. It can be verified that for the scheme tree, T, shown in Figure 2.3, P(T) is a γ-acyclic FDS, since B(**R**), shown in Figure 2.2, is a lfbd; moreover, $\cap$P(T) = {STUDENT, DEPT} is non-empty.

The next corollary tells us when a FDS is not equivalent to a scheme tree.

Corollary 6.7. If **R** is not γ-acyclic or $\cap$**R** is empty, then there does not exist a scheme tree, T, such that **R** $\equiv$ P(T).
Proof. The result follows from Corollary 6.6. $\square$

Example 6.7. Let **R** = P(T_1) $\cup$ P(T_2) be a FDS, for T_1, shown in Figure 2.3, and T_2, shown in Figure 2.9, from the running example. It can easily be verified that **R** is γ-acyclic and that $\cap$**R** = $\emptyset$. Thus it can also be verified that there does not exist a scheme tree, say T′, such that **R** = P(T′).

Example 6.8. Let **R** = {ABD, BCD, ACD} be a FDS. **R** is cyclic and thus it can easily be verified that there does not exist a scheme tree, T′, such that **R** = P(T′).

Finally, we note that in Levene & Loizou [1989d] we presented an algorithm, called CREATE_FOREST, that allows us to restructure a γ-acyclic FDS, **R**, such that |**R**| > 1 and $\cap$**R** = $\emptyset$, into a NDS possessing the UMC property. This restructuring is beneficial, since, as we have noted before, the resulting nested relations in the nested database reduce redundancy and also improve efficiency, since some null extended joins are realized within the nested relations in the resulting nested database.

6.3 The NRI for a Single Nested Relation

In this section we investigate the effects on the NRI when the nested database, d*, contains just one nested relation. That is, we assume that d* = {r*} such that r* is a nested relation over a NRS, R(T) = U(T), where S(T) = U, the universal set of attributes. We interpret this situation as follows: The NRI, over the NURS, U(T), resides at the conceptual level of the nested UR model with a UR interface at the external level. Thus, in this special case the internal level and the conceptual level of the nested UR model are one and the same as is shown in Figure 6.1.

We show that viewing nested relations in terms of the AODM is equivalent to viewing nested relations in terms of the induced γ-acyclic FDS over the path set, P(T), of the scheme tree, T. In fact, we show an even stronger equivalence, since we can also view the said equivalence in terms of the NRI under the set of NEFDs, FD(T).

We then direct our attention to characterizing the NRI for this special case, namely, when the nested database consists of a single nested relation. Firstly, we establish that a nested relation, r*, over U(T), is the NRI under a set of null extended data dependencies, D(U), for a nested database, d* = {r*}, whenever r* satisfies D(U). In this case, it follows, by Definition 5.8 of the NRI, that the window, for a set of attributes $X \subseteq U$, can be computed by the simple null extended algebra expression, $[X] = \mu^*(\Pi^{ne}\downarrow_X(r^*))$, i.e., no null extended joins are needed to compute [X]. Thus, in this special case the NRI is fully optimized! Then, we proceed to show that, in this special case, we can construct algebraically the window, [X], for any set of attributes $X \subseteq U$, when we view nested relations in terms of the AODM or in terms of the FDS, P(T), which, by Lemma 6.4, possesses the UMC property. Finally, we show that the UR assumptions are satisfied in the single nested relation, r*, over R(T).

We first define the flat database, over P(T), induced by a nested relation.

Definition 6.6. Let r* be a nested relation over a NRS, R(T). Then we define the flat database induced by r*, over P(T), denoted as **P**(r*), by

$$\mathbf{P}(r^*) = \{\mu^*(\Pi^{ne}_X(r^*)) \mid X \in P(T)\}.$$

Example 6.9. For r* of Example 6.2, shown in Figure 2.8, we have that **P**(r*) consists of the flat relations:

r(STUDENT DEPT MAJOR), shown in Figure 6.3,

r(STUDENT DEPT CLASS EXAM), shown in Figure 6.5, and

r(STUDENT DEPT CLASS PROJECT), shown in Figure 6.6.

Proposition 6.8. Let r* be a nested relation over the NURS, U(T). Then the following statements are equivalent.

(1) $\mu^*(I^*)$, over U, is the NRI under {⋈[As(T)]} for the flat database $d_1 = \mathbf{As}(r^*)$.

(2) $\mu^*(I^*)$, over U, is the NRI under {⋈[P(T)]} for the flat database $d_2 = \mathbf{P}(r^*)$.

(3) I*, over U(T), is the NRI under {FD(T)} for the nested database $d_1^* = \{\Pi^{ne}{}_X(r^*) \mid X \in As(T)\}$.

(4) I*, over U(T), is the NRI under {FD(T)} for the nested database $d_2^* = \{\Pi^{ne}{}_X(r^*) \mid X \in P(T)\}$.

Proof. (1) is equivalent to (2). By the construction of d_1 and d_2, it follows that

$$PAD(d_1) \cong PAD(d_2).$$

By the covering rule for NJDs (see appropriate comment following Definition 4.4), we have that $\bowtie[P(T)] \equiv \bowtie[As(T)]$; thus,

$$CHASE_{\bowtie[As(T)]}(PAD(d_1)) \cong CHASE_{\bowtie[P(T)]}(PAD(d_2)).$$

Now, (1) is equivalent to (2) follows, on using Lemma 5.6 and Proposition 5.4.

(3) is equivalent to (4). By the construction of d_1^* and d_2^*, it follows that

$$PAD(d_1^*) \cong PAD(d_2^*).$$

Now, (3) is equivalent to (4) follows, on using Proposition 5.4, since we have that

$$CHASE_{FD(T)}(PAD(d_1^*)) \cong CHASE_{FD(T)}(PAD(d_2^*)).$$

(2) is equivalent to (4). By the appropriate comment following Definition 3.20, we have that

$$\mu^*(PAD(d_2^*)) \cong PAD(d_2).$$

Furthermore, by Lemma 2.3 part (2), we have that $MVD(T) \equiv \bowtie[P(T)]$. Now, (2) is equivalent to (4) follows, since, by Theorem 5.7, we have that

$$CHASE_{\bowtie[P(T)]}(PAD(d_2)) \cong CHASE_{\bowtie[P(T)]}(\mu^*(PAD(d_2^*))) \cong$$
$$CHASE_{MVD(T)}(\mu^*(PAD(d_2^*))) \cong \mu^*(CHASE_{FD(T)}(PAD(d_2^*))). \quad \Box$$

Example 6.10. Let r be the flat relation shown in Figure 6.7, and let r* be the nested relation r_1^* of the running example, shown in Figure 2.8, and used in Example 6.2. Then it can easily be verified that $r \cong PAD(As(r^*)) \cong PAD(P(r^*)) \cong PAD(d)$, where d is the flat database from Example 6.2.

Let I be the flat relation shown in Figure 6.8. Then it can easily be verified that I is the NRI, over U, under {$\bowtie[As(T)]$} for As(r*); I is also the NRI, over U, under {$\bowtie[P(T)]$} for P(r*). That is, $I \cong CHASE_{\bowtie[As(T)]}(PAD(As(r^*))) \cong CHASE_{\bowtie[P(T)]}(PAD(P(r^*)))$.

Let I* be the nested relation shown in Figure 6.9. Then it can easily be verified that I* is the NRI, over U(T) = R(T), under {FD(T)} for As(r*); I* is also the NRI, over U(T) = R(T), under {FD(T)} for P(r*). That is, $I^* \cong CHASE_{FD(T)}(PAD(As(r^*))) \cong CHASE_{FD(T)}(PAD(P(r^*)))$. It can also be verified that $I \cong \mu^*(I^*)$, for the NRI, I, shown in Figure 6.8.

We note that a less redundant NRI can be obtained by restructuring I* of Figure 6.9 to obtain $\rho_{U(T)}(I^*)$, shown in Figure 6.10.

Finally, we note that, in general, $\neg(\rho_{(U(T)}(I^*) \cong r^*)$ is true even if r* is a hierarchical relation. There are two reasons for this lack of information-wise equivalence. Firstly, r* may contain null values over joined attributes in P(T), as is the case with the fifth tuple

STUDENT	DEPT	MAJOR	CLASS	EXAM	PROJECT
Iris	CS	computing	*null*	*null*	*null*
Iris	CS	*null*	databases	mid	*null*
Iris	CS	*null*	databases	final	*null*
Iris	CS	*null*	programming	final	*null*
Iris	CS	*null*	databases	*null*	1NF
Mark	CS	maths	*null*	*null*	*null*
Mark	CS	*null*	databases	final	*null*
Mark	CS	*null*	databases	*null*	NF2
Mark	CS	*null*	databases	*null*	UR
David	philosophy	logic	*null*	*null*	*null*
David	philosophy	*null*	first-order	*null*	prolog
David	philosophy	*null*	first-order	mid	*null*
null	philosophy	*null*	*null*	final	*null*
null	philosophy	*null*	first-order	*null*	functions
null	philosophy	*null*	first-order	*null*	predicates
Naomi	*null*	languages	*null*	*null*	*null*
Naomi	*null*	*null*	french	mid	*null*
Naomi	*null*	*null*	*null*	final	*null*
Naomi	*null*	*null*	*null*	*null*	Moscow
Naomi	*null*	*null*	hebrew	*null*	Genesis

Fig. 6.7. The flat relation $r \cong PAD(As(r^*)) \cong PAD(P(r^*))$.

of r^* having *null* in the DEPT attribute (see Figure 2.8). Thus, for example, the tuples, <Naomi, *null*, languages, *null*, *null*, *null*> and <Naomi, *null*, *null*, french, mid, *null*>, from Figure 6.7 before the extended chase, do not add the tuple, <Naomi, *null*, languages, french, mid, *null*>, which is in $\mu^*(r^*)$, as shown in Figure 3.12. Secondly, a less informative tuple may be removed in $PAD(As(r^*)) \cong PAD(P(r^*))$, as is the case with the tuple <*null*, philosophy, *null*, *null*, mid, *null*> (see Figure 2.8). This observation is interesting because it clearly shows, yet again, that, in general, nested relations convey more semantic information than their flat counterparts.

We now investigate the situation where $d^* = \{r^*\}$ is a nested database with a single nested relation over the NURS, U(T). The following proposition is a direct consequence of Proposition 5.4, simplifying the result thereof, in order to obtain a constructive definition of the NRI via an extended chase of the single nested relation, r^*, w.r.t. a set of null extended data dependencies, D(U).

Proposition 6.9. Let U(T) be the NURS of the NDS, **R**(F), where F = {T}, with its

STUDENT	DEPT	MAJOR	CLASS	EXAM	PROJECT
Iris	CS	computing	databases	mid	1NF
Iris	CS	computing	databases	final	1NF
Iris	CS	computing	programming	final	*null*
Mark	CS	maths	databases	final	NF2
Mark	CS	maths	databases	final	UR
David	philosophy	logic	first-order	mid	prolog
null	philosophy	*null*	*null*	final	*null*
null	philosophy	*null*	first-order	*null*	functions
null	philosophy	*null*	first-order	*null*	predicates
Naomi	*null*	languages	*null*	*null*	*null*
Naomi	*null*	*null*	french	mid	*null*
Naomi	*null*	*null*	*null*	final	*null*
Naomi	*null*	*null*	*null*	*null*	Moscow
Naomi	*null*	*null*	hebrew	*null*	Genesis

Fig. 6.8. The NRI, $I \cong CHASE_{\bowtie[As(T)]}(PAD(As(r^*))) \cong CHASE_{\bowtie[P(T)]}(PAD(P(r^*)))$.

associated nested database, $d^* = \{r^*\}$, and a set, $D(U)$, of null extended data dependencies. Then,

$$I^* \cong CHASE_{D(U)}(r^*)$$

is the NRI, over $U(T)$, under $D(U)$ for d^*.

Proof. The result follows directly from Proposition 5.4. □

A corollary of Proposition 6.9 is now given, highlighting three special cases, when the extended chase is unnecessary, i.e., r^*, over $U(T)$, is the NRI under $D(U)$ for $d^* = \{r^*\}$.

Corollary 6.10. Let $U(T)$ be the NURS of the NDS, $R(F)$, where $F = \{T\}$, with its associated nested database, $d^* = \{r^*\}$, and a set, $D(U)$, of null extended data dependencies. Then the following statements are true.

(1) r^*, over $U(T)$, is the NRI under $D(U) = \emptyset$ for d^*.

(2) r^*, over $U(T)$, is the NRI under $D(U) = \{FD(T)\}$ for d^*, where r^* is a hierarchical relation.

(3) r^*, over $U(T)$, is the NRI under $D(U) = \{FF(T), FD(T)\}$ for d^*, where r^* is a consistent hierarchical relation.

Proof. The result follows directly from Proposition 6.9 and Corollary 4.11. □

Example 6.11. Consider the nested relation r^*, over $R(T) = U(T)$, of Example 6.2, shown in Figure 2.8, with $D(U) = \{FF(T), FD(T)\}$. Since r^* is a consistent hierarchical

STUDENT	DEPT	(MAJOR)*	(CLASS	(EXAM)*	(PROJECT)*)*
		MAJOR	CLASS	(EXAM)*	(PROJECT)*
				EXAM	PROJECT
Iris	CS	computing	databases	mid	1NF
				final	
			programming	final	*null*
Mark	CS	maths	databases	final	NF2
					UR
David	philosophy	logic	first-order	mid	prolog
null	philosophy	*null*	*null*	final	*null*
null	philosophy	*null*	first-order	*null*	functions
null	philosophy	*null*	first-order	*null*	predicates
Naomi	*null*	languages	*null*	*null*	*null*
Naomi	*null*	*null*	french	mid	*null*
Naomi	*null*	*null*	*null*	final	*null*
Naomi	*null*	*null*	*null*	*null*	Moscow
Naomi	*null*	*null*	hebrew	*null*	Genesis

Fig. 6.9. The NRI, $I^* \cong CHASE_{FD(T)}(\text{PAD}(As(r^*))) \cong CHASE_{FD(T)}(\text{PAD}(P(r^*)))$.

relation, it follows by Corollary 6.10 that r*, over U(T), is the NRI under D(U) for d* = {r*}.

In the next theorem we show that when we view the nested relation, r*, in terms of the AODM, or equivalently, in terms of the FDS, P(T), then windows can be computed algebraically by using the UMC window function, or equivalently, by using the AO window function.

Theorem 6.11. Let U(T) be the NURS of the NDS, **R**(F), where F = {T}, with its associated nested database, d* = {r*}, and a set, D(U), of null extended data dependencies. Also, let I*, over U(T), be the NRI under {FD(T)} for d = As(r*), or equivalently, for d = P(r*). Then, for any $X \subseteq U$,

$$[X] = [X]_{AO} = [X]^R_{UMC},$$

where $[X]_{AO}$ is the AO window function for the AODS, <As(T), Ob(T)>, and $[X]^R_{UMC}$ is the UMC window function w.r.t. **R** = P(T).

Proof. By Lemma 6.4 and Proposition 2.1 we have that **R** possesses the UMC property, and thus, by Theorem 5.9, it follows that $[X] = [X]^R_{UMC}$. It, therefore, remains to show that $[X]_{AO} = [X]^R_{UMC}$, for any $X \subseteq U$.

Now, by Proposition 6.3 part (1), Definition 6.4 and by Lemma 6.2, it follows that d satisfies $\hat{D}$. Thus, by Proposition 6.1,

STUDENT	DEPT	(MAJOR)*	(CLASS	(EXAM)*	(PROJECT)*)*
		MAJOR	CLASS	(EXAM)*	(PROJECT)*
				EXAM	PROJECT
Iris	CS	computing	databases	mid final	1NF
			programming	final	*null*
Mark	CS	maths	databases	final	NF2 UR
David	philosophy	logic	first-order	mid	prolog
null	philosophy	*null*	*null*	final	*null*
			first-order	*null*	functions predicates
Naomi	*null*	languages	*null*	*null*	*null*
Naomi	*null*	*null*	french	mid	*null*
			null	final	*null*
			null	*null*	Moscow
			hebrew	*null*	Genesis

Fig. 6.10 The NRI $\rho_{U(T)}(I^*)$.

$[X]_{AO} = \Pi\downarrow_X (\bowtie_{(Z \in As(T), Z \subseteq O)} r(Z))$ holds for any $X \subseteq O$,
where O is the minimal object containing X, i.e., for any $O' \in \mathbf{Ob}(T)$ such that $O' \neq O$ and $X \subseteq O'$, we have that $O \subseteq O'$.

Now, it is true that $\downarrow Y \downarrow = [Y]_{AO}$, where $Y \subseteq p$ with $p \in P(T)$, since d satisfies the CCA by Proposition 6.3 part (1). By the construction of $\mathbf{As}(r^*)$ and $\mathbf{P}(r^*)$, it follows that, for any $X \subseteq U$,

$UMC_R(X) \subseteq (W = \{Z \in As(T) | Z \subseteq O\})$,

where O is the minimal object containing X; additionally, for all $Z_i \in (W - UMC_R(X))$ there exists a $Z_j \in UMC_R(X)$ such that either $Z_j \subseteq Z_i$ or $Z_i \subseteq Z_j$. From Definition 5.10 and the elimination of redundant joins by using standard algebraic query optimization techniques [Ullman 1982a; Maier 1983] (taking into account total projection), it follows that

$[X]_{AO} = [X]_{UMC}^R$. $\square$

Example 6.12. It can be verified that the result of Theorem 6.11 holds for r^*, over R(T), of Example 6.2; r^* is shown in Figure 2.8. Let I^*, shown in Figure 6.9, over U(T), be the NRI under {FD(T)} for $d = \mathbf{As}(r^*)$ and for $d' = \mathbf{P}(r^*)$. Then, it can be verified that $[X] = [X]_{AO} = [X]_{UMC}^R$, where $R = P(T)$, for any $X \subseteq U$.

We note that if I*, over U(T), is the NRI under {FD(T)} for d* = {r*}, then, in general, where $\mathbf{R}$ = P(T), $[X]_{AO} \subseteq [X]$ and $[X]^R_{UMC} \subseteq [X]$ holds. This is due to the fact that r* may contain null values over joined attributes in P(T).

The following proposition asserts that the UR assumptions (stated in Subsection 2.3.1) are indeed satisfied in the special case, when d* consists of a single nested relation, i.e., d* = {r*} and d* satisfies D(U).

Proposition 6.12. Let U(T) be the NURS of the NDS, $\mathbf{R}(F)$, where F = {T}, with its associated nested database, d* = {r*}, and a set, D(U), of null extended data dependencies. If r* satisfies D(U), then the UR assumptions are satisfied.

Proof.

(1) As attributes are unique within a scheme tree, it follows that S(T) = U satisfies the URSA.

(2) By Proposition 6.9, r* is the NRI under D(U) for d* = {r*}. Thus, by Definition 5.8 of the NRI, the basic relationship on X is $[X] = \mu^*(\Pi^{ne}\downarrow_X(r^*))$, and so the URA is satisfied.

(3) By Lemma 6.4, P(T) is a γ-acyclic FDS, so, by the results in Biskup et al. [1986], we have that the OFA is satisfied, i.e., all the tuples in [X] have the same flavour of the basic relationship on X, namely [X]. $\square$

Example 6.13. It can easily be verified that for r*, over U(T) = R(T), of Example 6.2 and D(U) = {FF(T), FD(T)}, where the scheme tree, T, is shown in Figure 2.3 and r* is shown in Figure 2.8, the result of the above proposition holds.

6.4 Application Examples of the Nested UR Model

In this section we present three examples of possible applications of the nested UR model in the special case of a single nested relation. The application areas are: the design of a VLSI circuit module, the storing of geographical data and information retrieval in a library database. We note that the application area of the examples, which follow, fall into the application area of nested relations or complex objects for non-standard, non-business applications [Scholl & Schek 1987; Abiteboul et al. 1989b]; this demonstrates the advantage of nested relations over flat relations. The examples are meant to be simple and straightforward, thus the heights of the scheme trees in these examples are all one, i.e., they involve only one level of nesting. These examples clearly show the full advantages of the nested UR model: efficiency of query processing, since no null extended joins have to be performed during the computation of the window, [X], for any set of attributes, $X \subseteq U$, redundancy of the data is minimized within the nested relation (in comparison to the corresponding flat relation) and the integrity constraints of the application are explicitly represented within the structure of the nested relation in the form of null extended data dependencies. Another advantage of the nested UR model shown in these examples is that instead of providing a UR interface which is a flat relation, we can provide a nested UR interface which is a nested relation over the NURS, U(T). This idea is developed in the query language, NURQL, for the nested UR model [Levene & Loizou 1989b]; it allows a flexible UR interface according to the user's demands. In this way, we can provide a more flexible and user-friendly presentation of the data at the external level of the user interface.

The first example, from the area of VLSI design, shows the design of logical AND gates which are composed of input or output pins of different types and may have a number of other gates as sub-components. The NURS is given by U(T) = Gate-Type (Pin-Type I/O)* (Component-of Number-of)*, where T is shown in Figure 6.11. For this application, the set of null extended data dependencies is given by D(U) = {FD(T)}, where FD(T) = {Gate-Type → (Pin-Type I/O)*, Gate-Type → (Component-of Number-of)*}. The NRI, r*, over U(T), under D(U) for {r*}, is shown in Figure 6.12.

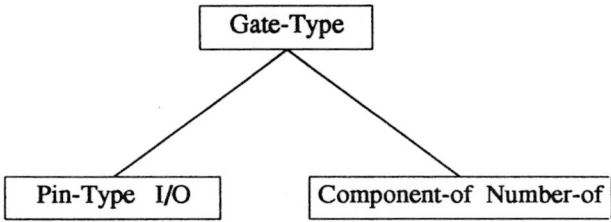

Fig. 6.11. The scheme tree for the design of a VLSI module.

Gate-Type	(Pin-Type	I/O)*	(Component-of	Number-of)*
	Pin-Type	I/O	Component-of	Number-of
2AND	A	Input	*dne*	*dne*
	B	Input		
	C	Output		
4AND	A	Input	2AND	3
	B	Input		
	C	Input		
	D	Input		
	E	Output		

Fig. 6.12. The NRI for a VLSI design module.

The second example, from the area of geographical data, shows a small geographical database which stores countries by their name, their area in square miles, two X and Y reference points defining an enclosing rectangle in the atlas, for the given country, and a set of the major cities of the country. The NURS is given by U(T) = Country Area (X-

Ref Y-Ref)* (Major-City)*, where T is shown in Figure 6.13. For this application, the set of null extended data dependencies is given by D(U) = {FF(T), FD(T)}, where FF(T) = {Country → Area} and FD(T) = {Country Area → (X-Ref Y-Ref)*, Country Area → (Major-City)*}. The NRI, r*, over U(T), under D(U) for {r*}, is shown in Figure 6.14.

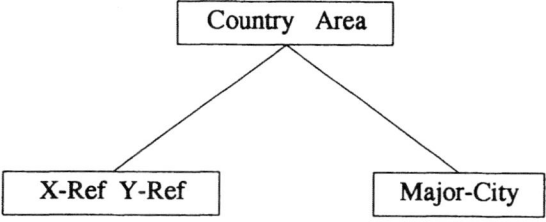

Fig. 6.13. The scheme tree for a geographical database.

Country	Area	(X-Ref	Y-Ref)*	(Major-City)*
		X-Ref	Y-Ref	Major-City
U.K.	94214	F	1	London
		D	5	Manchester Edinburgh Birmingham
Israel	7978	*unk*	*unk*	Tel-Aviv
		B	6	Jerusalem Haifa
New Zealand	103934	G	1	Auckland
		A	6	Wellington Christchurch

Fig. 6.14. The NRI for a geographical database.

The third example, from the area of information retrieval, shows a library database which stores information about books, their classification by subject, the author(s) of books and keywords which allow a flexible text retrieval of books. The NURS is given by U(T) = Book-Title Classification (Author)* (Keyword)*, where T is shown in Figure 6.15. For this application, the set of null extended data dependencies is given by D(U) = {FF(T), FD(T)}, where FF(T) = {Book-Title → Classification} and FD(T) = {Book-Title Classification → (Author)*, Book-Title Classification → (Keyword)*}. The NRI, r*, over U(T), under D(U) for {r*}, is shown in Figure 6.16.

We note that in all the above examples the semantics of the NURS can be expressed without NEJDs, which provide us with the novel notion of null extended lossless

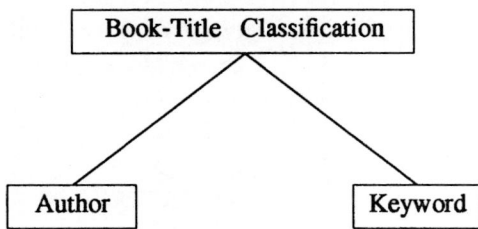

Fig. 6.15. The scheme tree for a library database.

Book-Title	Classification	(Author)*	(Keyword)*
		Author	Keyword
The Devils	*ni*	Dostoyevsky	revolution murder passion
The Earth	Fiction	Zola	land farming struggle
Programming in Prolog	Computers	Clocksin Mellish	program logic fact rule
Axiomatic Set Theory	Maths	Suppes	axiom function relation number set

Fig. 6.16. The NRI for a library database.

decomposition; this is because we are dealing with the special case of a single nested relation.

6.5 Discussion

In this chapter we have established a strong case for a nested UR model comprising a single nested relation, r*, over the NURS, U(T), in the nested database. We have shown in Proposition 6.8 that a nested relation provides two equivalent views in the form of the AODM and γ-acyclic FDSs. Thus, we obtain, via a nested relation, the desirable properties of both an AO database and a γ-acyclic database. In addition, if r*, over the NURS, U(T), satisfies its set of null extended data dependencies, D(U), then, by Proposition 6.9, r* is in fact the desired NRI. More specifically, if r* is a consistent hierarchical relation, we showed, in Corollary 6.10, that r* is also the desired NRI. Moreover, by Proposition 6.12, the UR assumptions, i.e., the URSA, the URA and the OFA are satisfied by r*.

In the case of the nested UR model comprising a single nested relation, r*, the window, [X], for any set of attributes $X \subseteq U$, is simply given by

$$[X] = \mu^*(\Pi^{ne}\downarrow_X(r^*)),$$

and thus all the null extended joins needed to compute any window are realized within the nested relation, r*. This implies that query processing for the nested UR model is, in this case, fully optimized. The UR interface is provided by simply using [X] as the window function, thus freeing the user from logical navigation. It is our opinion that especially in this case the nested UR model is a very useful and practical proposition!!

Chapter 7
Concluding Remarks and Ongoing Research

In this monograph we have presented the nested UR model, which provides the null extended nested relational model with logical data independence. We have shown throughout the monograph that the nested UR model solves the usability problem relating to nested relations in a satisfactory manner.

At the internal level of the nested UR model we have defined the null extended nested relational model with its null extended algebra and null extended data dependencies. The null extended nested relational model provides a comprehensive treatment of nulls, a complete extended algebra and semantics in the form of null extended data dependencies, which are claimed to be sufficient to model most real-world applications. Furthermore, we have at our disposal the powerful extended chase procedure for testing and enforcing the satisfaction of null extended data dependencies in nested relations.

At the conceptual level of the nested UR model we have the NRI, over the NURS, which is the underlying data structure of the nested weak instance approach to the nested UR model. We have shown that the NRI over the NURS is a suitable model for the data to be stored in a single nested relation, given a nested database and a set of null extended data dependencies for an application satisfying the UR assumptions. As a consequence of this result the classical UR model under the weak instance approach now becomes a special case of the nested UR model under the nested weak instance approach. Thus, at the external level of the nested UR model we can maintain a UR interface gaining all the advantages of nested relations over flat relations. Moreover, we have shown that the nested UR model is strictly more expressive than the classical UR model, extending it to application domains involving complex objects and providing the ability to present to the user both flat and hierarchical data.

We have also shown that a DBMS supporting the null extended algebra, but not necessarily the extended chase, can effectively support the nested UR model. By using a computational approach to the nested UR model, we have shown that the NRI can be constructed algebraically, in the special case, when the underlying NDS possesses the UMC property.

An important special case we dealt with is the nested UR model for a nested database comprising only a single nested relation, say r*. In this case the internal and conceptual levels of the nested UR model coalesce into one level; that is to say, the single nested relation, r*, is the NRI over the NURS, U(T), provided r* satisfies its set of null extended data dependencies, D(U). We showed that a nested relation provides two equivalent views in the form of the AODM and γ-acyclic FDSs, thus gaining the benefits of nested relations when using these views. Also, query processing is simplified in this case, since the window for any set of attributes, $X \subseteq U$, is now simply: $[X] =$

$\mu^*(\Pi^{ne}\downarrow_X(r^*))$. Query processing is also fully optimized as all the null extended joins are now realized within the single nested relation, r^*. As a byproduct of this special case all the UR assumptions are satisfied by r^*, implying that during the design of the NURS, U(T), for the NRI, r^*, the database designer need not worry about the UR assumptions!

We conclude the monograph by indicating some ongoing and future research stemming from the nested UR model.

In the area of incomplete information we are generalizing our results in two directions. Firstly, we are defining a methodology for designing a data model for incomplete information in complex objects [Levene & Loizou 1989c]. In this context we are also investigating the use of marked nulls in complex objects as opposed to unmarked nulls, in order to gain more expressiveness [Levene & Loizou 1991a]. One of the advantages of marked nulls over unmarked nulls is that we do not need the equality rule for nulls, but there is a system overhead in maintaining these marked nulls. Secondly, we are investigating a domain theoretic approach to incomplete information, which extends the nested relational model by incorporating into it a form of built-in inheritance [Levene & Loizou 1989a]. The aim of this research is to further our understanding of the semantics of nulls in databases.

In the area of nested database design we have so far mainly been concerned with generalizing concepts from flat relational database design to nested relations [Levene & Loizou 1987a, 1987b, 1989d]. Under the nested UR model we have formalized some of the desirable properties we strive for when designing a nested database. These desirable properties include:

(1)   that the NRSs, $R(T_i) \in \mathbf{R}(F)$, $1 \le i \le q$, result from a null extended lossless decomposition onto the NDS, $\mathbf{R}(F)$;

(2)   that null extended data dependencies be explicitly represented within the structure of nested relations; and

(3)   that redundancy of the data in nested relations be minimized.

It is an ongoing research goal to define a formal design method for nested relations that achieves these desirable properties.

In the area of null extended data dependencies we are currently generalizing NFDs, NEFDs and NEJDs, in the spirit of the generalization of FDs and JDs to *equality and tuple generating data dependencies* [Beeri & Vardi 1984; Graham et al. 1986], respectively. To this end we have already extended the class of tuple generating data dependencies that hold in flat relations to the class of *set generating data dependencies* [Levene & Loizou 1991b] that hold in nested relations. Set generating data dependencies are more expressive than tuple generating data dependencies, since they can enforce the generation of sets.

In the area of query processing we have not discussed in detail the problem of query optimization. We have proposed an algebraic approach for computing windows over the NRI via the UMC window function, when the underlying NDS possesses the UMC property. We intend to investigate the optimization of these null extended algebra expressions resulting from the UMC window function. In a broader context an ongoing research problem is that of optimizing null extended algebra expressions in general and null extended joins, in particular.

Finally, the problem of updates under the nested UR model has not been discussed in this monograph. This research area has two facets. Firstly, updates on the nested database must be formalized in terms of the null extended nested relational model. Secondly, updates on the NRI must be translated, unambiguously, into updates on the underlying nested database.

References

Abiteboul S., Beeri C., Gyssens M. & Van Gucht D. 1989a. An introduction to the completeness of languages for complex objects. In: *Nested Relations and Complex Objects in Databases*, pp. 117-138. Lecture Notes in Computer Science 361, Berlin: Springer-Verlag.

Abiteboul S., Fischer P. C. & Schek H.-J. (eds.) 1989b. *Nested Relations and Complex Objects in Databases*. Lecture Notes in Computer Science 361, Berlin: Springer-Verlag.

Abiteboul S. & Bidoit N. 1986 Non first normal form relations: An algebra allowing data restructuring. *Journal of Computer and System Sciences 33*, 361-393.

Abiteboul S., Scholl M., Gardarin G. & Simon E. 1986 Towards DBMSs for supporting new applications. *Proceedings of 12th International Conference on Very Large Data Bases*, Kyoto, pp. 423-435.

Agrawal R. 1987 Alpha: An extension of relational algebra to express a class of recursive queries. *Proceedings of 3rd IEEE Conference on Data Engineering*, Los Angeles, pp. 580-590.

ANSI/X3/SPARC 1975 Study group on database management systems, interim report. *FDT 7, Bulletin of ACM SIGFIDET*.

Arisawa H., Moriya K. & Miura T. 1983 Operations and the properties on non-first-normal-form relational databases. *Proceedings of 9th International Conference on Very Large Data Bases*, Florence, pp. 197-204.

Atzeni P. & Bernardis M. C. 1987 A new basis for the weak instance model. *Proceedings of 6th ACM Symposium on Principles of Database Systems*, San Diego, pp. 79-86.

Atzeni P. & Chan E. P. F. 1989 Efficient optimization of simple chase join expressions. *ACM Transactions on Database Systems 14*, 212-230.

Atzeni P. & Morfuni N. M. 1986 Functional dependencies and constraints on null values in database relations. *Information and Control 70*, 1-31.

Atzeni P. & Parker D. S. 1982 Assumptions in relational database theory. *Proceedings of 1st ACM Symposium on Principles of Database Systems*, Los Angeles, pp. 1-9.

Babb E. 1982 Joined normal form: A storage encoding for relational databases. *ACM Transactions on Database Systems 7*, 588-614.

Bachman C. W. 1969 Data structure diagrams. *Data Base 1*, 4-10.

Bancilhon F., Richard P. & Scholl M. 1982 On line processing of compacted relations. *Proceedings of 8th International Conference on Very Large Data Bases*, Mexico City, 263-269.

Beeri C. 1988 Data models and languages for databases. *Proceedings of International Conference on Database Theory*, Bruges, Belgium, pp. 19-40.

Beeri C., Fagin R., Maier D. & Yannakakis M. 1983 On the desirability of acyclic database schemes. *Journal of the ACM* 30, 479-513.

Beeri C. & Kifer M. 1986 An integrated approach to logical design of relational database schemes. *ACM Transactions on Database Systems* 11, 134-158.

Beeri C. & Vardi M. Y. 1981 On the properties of join dependencies. In: *Advances in Database Theory* (eds. Gallaire H., Minker J. & Nicholas J. M.), Volume 1, New York: Plenum Press, pp. 25-72.

Beeri C. & Vardi M. Y. 1984 A proof procedure for data dependencies. *Journal of the ACM* 31, 718-741.

Berge C. 1973 *Graphs and Hypergraphs*. Amsterdam: North-Holland.

Bidoit N. 1987 The Verso algebra or how to answer queries with fewer joins. *Journal of Computer and System Sciences* 35, 321-364.

Biskup J. 1981 A formal approach to null values in database relations. In: *Advances in Database Theory* (eds. Gallaire H., Minker J. & Nicholas J. M.), Volume 1, New York: Plenum Press, pp. 299-341.

Biskup J. 1983 A foundation of Codd's relational maybe-operations. *ACM Transactions on Database Systems* 8, 608-636.

Biskup J. & Bruggemann H. H. 1983 Universal relation views: A pragmatic approach. *Proceedings of 9th International Conference on Very Large Data Bases*, Florence, pp. 172-185.

Biskup J. & Bruggemann H. H. 1987 Data manipulation languages for the universal relation view DURST. *Proceedings of Conference on Mathematical Foundations of Data Base Systems*, Dresden, pp. 20-41.

Biskup J., Bruggemann H. H., Schnetgoke L. & Kramer M. 1986 One flavor assumption and γ-acyclicity for universal relation views. *Proceedings of 5th ACM Symposium on Principles of Database Systems*, Cambridge, Ma, pp. 148-159.

Brosda V. & Vossen G. 1988 Update and retrieval in a relational database through a universal schema interface. *ACM Transactions on Database Systems* 13, 449-485.

Bullers Jr. W. I. 1987 A processing algorithm for master-detail records in a relational database. *Software - Practice and Experience* 17, 701-717.

Carlson C. R. & Kaplan R. S. 1976 A generalized access path model and its application to a relational database system. *Proceedings of ACM SIGMOD Conference on*

Management of Data, Washington D. C., pp. 143-154.

Casanova M. A., Fagin R. & Papadimitriou C. H. 1984 Inclusion dependencies and their interaction with functional dependencies. *Journal of Computer and System Sciences* **28**, 29-59.

Chan E. P. F. & Atzeni P. 1986 On the properties and characteristics of connection-trap-free schemes. *Proceedings of 5th ACM Symposium on Principles of Database Systems*, Cambridge, Ma, pp. 140-147.

Chan E. P. F. & Hernández H. J. 1988a On the desirability of γ-acyclic BCNF database schemes. *Theoretical Computer Science* **62**, 67-104.

Chan E. P. F. & Hernández H. J. 1988b On generating database schemes bounded or constant-time-maintainable by extensibility. *Acta Informatica* **25**, 475-496.

Codd E. F. 1970 A relational model of data for large shared data banks. *Communications of the ACM* **13**, 377-387.

Codd E. F. 1979 Extending the database relational model to capture more meaning. *ACM Transactions on Database Systems* **4**, 397-434.

Codd E. F. 1986 Missing information (applicable and inapplicable) in relational data-bases. *ACM SIGMOD Record* **15**, 53-78.

Codd E. F. 1987 More commentary on missing information in relational databases (applicable and inapplicable information). *ACM SIGMOD Record* **16**, 42-50.

Colby L. S. 1989 A recursive algebra and query optimization for nested relations. *Proceedings of ACM SIGMOD Conference on Management of Data*, Portland, pp. 273-283.

Dadam P., Kuespert K., Anderson F., Blanken H., Erbe R., Guenauer J., Lum V., Pistor P. & Walch G. 1986 A DBMS prototype to support extended NF^2 relations: An integrated view on flat tables and hierarchies. *Proceedings of ACM SIGMOD Conference on Management of Data*, Washington D. C., pp. 356-367.

Date C. J. 1987a Referential integrity. In: *Relational Databases Selected Writings*, Reading, Ma: Addison-Welsey, pp. 41-63.

Date C. J. 1987b The outer join. In: *Relational Databases Selected Writings*, Reading, Ma: Addison-Welsey, pp. 335-366.

Date C. J. 1987c *A Guide to the SQL Standard*. Reading, Ma: Addison-Wesley.

Delobel C. 1978 Normalization and hierarchical dependencies in the relational data model. *ACM Transactions on Database Systems* **3**, 201-222.

Desai B. C., Goyal P. & Sadri F. 1987 Non-first normal form universal relations: An application to information retrieval systems. *Information Systems* **12**, 49-55.

Deshpande V. & Larson P.-A. 1987 An algebra for nested relations. Research Report CS-87-65, Department of Computer Science, University of Waterloo, Ontario.

Fagin R. 1977 Multivalued dependencies and a new normal form for relational databases. *ACM Transactions on Database Systems* **2**, 262-278.

Fagin R. 1983 Degrees of acyclicity for hypergraphs and relational database systems. *Journal of the ACM* **30**, 514-550.

Fagin R., Mendelzon A. O. & Ullman J. D. 1982 A simplified universal relation assumption and its properties. *ACM Transactions on Database Systems* **7**, 343-360.

Fagin R. & Vardi M. Y. 1984 The theory of data dependencies - A survey. IBM Research Report RJ4321 (47149), San Jose, Ca.

Fischer P. C., Saxton L. V., Thomas S. J. & Van Gucht D. 1985 Interactions between dependencies and nested relational structures. *Journal of Computer and System Sciences* **31**, 343-354.

Fischer P. C. & Van Gucht D. 1984 Weak multivalued dependencies. *Proceedings of 3rd ACM Symposium on Principles of Database Systems*, Waterloo, pp. 266-274.

Fischer P. C. & Van Gucht D. 1985 Determining when a structure is a nested relation. *Proceedings of 11th International Conference on Very Large Data Bases*, Stockholm, pp. 171-180.

Goldstein B. S. 1981 Constraints on null values in relational databases. *Proceedings of 7th International Conference on Very Large Data Bases*, Cannes, pp. 101-110.

Gottlob G. & Zicari R. 1988 Closed world databases opened through null values. *Proceedings of 14th International Conference on Very Large Data Bases*, Los Angeles, pp. 50-61.

Grahne G. 1984 Dependency satisfaction in databases with incomplete information. *Proceedings of 10th International Conference on Very Large Data Bases*, Singapore, pp. 37-45.

Graham M. H., Mendelzon A. O. & Vardi M. Y. 1986 Notions of dependency satisfaction. *Journal of the ACM* **33**, 105-129.

Graham M. H. & Wang K. 1986 Constant time maintenance or the triumph of the fd. *Proceedings of 5th ACM Symposium on Principles of Database Systems*, Cambridge, Ma, pp. 202-216.

Grant J. 1980 Incomplete information in a relational database. *Fundamenta Informaticae* **3**, 363-378.

Guting R. H., Zicari R. & Choy D. M. 1987 An algebra for structured office documents. IBM Research Report RJ5559 (56648), San Jose, Ca.

Gyssens M. 1987 The extended nested relational algebra. Technical Report 87-11, Department of Mathematics and Computer Science, University of Antwerp.

Gyssens M. & Van Gucht D. 1987 The powerset algebra operator as an algebraic tool for understanding least fixpoint semantics in the context of nested relations. Technical Report no. 233, Department of Computer Science, University of Indiana.

Gyssens M. & Van Gucht D. 1988 The powerset algebra as a result of adding programming constructs to the nested relational algebra. *Proceedings of ACM SIGMOD Conference on Management of Data*, Chicago, pp. 225-232.

Hernández H. J. & Chan E. P. F. 1988 A characterization of constant-time-maintainability for BCNF database schemes. *Proceedings of ACM SIGMOD Conference on Management of Data*, Chicago, pp. 209-217.

Honeyman P. 1982 Testing satisfaction of functional dependencies. *Journal of the ACM* **29**, 668-677.

Houben G. J. & Paredaens J. 1987 The R^2-algebra: an extension of an algebra for nested relations. Technical Report 87/20, Department of Mathematics and Computing Science, Eindhoven University of Technology.

Imielinski T. & Lipski Jr. W. 1983 Incomplete information and dependencies in relational databases. *Proceedings of ACM SIGMOD Conference on Management of Data*, San Jose, pp. 177-184.

Imielinski T. & Lipski Jr. W. 1984 Incomplete information in relational databases. *Journal of the ACM* **31**, 761-791.

Imielinski T. & Rozenshtein D. 1984 Towards a flexible user interface to relational database systems: Processing simple second order queries. *Proceedings of 4th Conference on Information Technology*, Jerusalem, Israel, pp. 358-367.

Jaeschke G. 1985a Nonrecursive algebra for relations with relation valued attributes. Report TR.85.03.001, IBM Hiedelburg Scientific Center.

Jaeschke G. 1985b Recursive algebra for relations with relation valued attributes. Report TR.85.03.002, IBM Hiedelburg Scientific Center.

Jaeschke G. & Schek H.-J. 1982 Remarks on the algebra of non first normal form relations. *Proceedings of 1st ACM Symposium on Principles of Database Systems*, Los Angeles, pp. 124-138.

Jajodia S. & Ng P. A. 1984 Representative instances and γ-acyclic relational schemes. *IEEE Transactions on Software Engineering* **SE-10**, 614-618.

Jajodia S. 1987 An extension of "Representative instances and γ-acyclic relational schemes". *IEEE Transactions on Software Engineering* **SE-13**, 1047-1048.

Jajodia S. & Springsteel F. N. 1987 Construction of universal instances of loop-free network databases using a join-like operation. *IEEE Transactions on Software Engineering* **SE-13**, 811-819.

Kambayashi Y., Tanaka K. & Takeda K. 1983 Synthesis of unnormalized relations incorporating more meaning. *Information Sciences* **29**, 201-247.

Kambayashi Y. & Yamamoto H. 1987 Efficient procedures to generate unnormalized database outputs. Report 87C-15, Department of Computer Science and Comm. Eng., Kyushu University.

Keller A. & Wilkins M. 1985 On the use of an extended relational model to handle changing incomplete information. *IEEE Transactions on Software Engineering* **SE-11**, 620-633.

Kent W. 1981 Consequences of assuming a universal relation. *ACM Transactions on Database Systems* **6**, 539-556.

Kent W. 1983 Technical correspondence: The universal relation revisited. *ACM Transactions on Database Systems* **8**, 644-648.

Kobayashi I. 1985 An overview of database management technology. In: *Advances in Information Systems Sciences* (ed. Tou J. T.), Volume 9, New York: Plenum Press, pp. 49-219.

Korth H. F. 1986 Extending the scope of relational languages. *IEEE Software* **3**, 19-28.

Korth H. F. 1988 Optimization of object-retrieval queries. *Proceedings of 2nd International Workshop on Object-Oriented Database Systems*, Bad Munster am Stein-Ebernburg, pp. 352-357

Korth H. F., Kuper G. M., Fiegenbaum J., Van Gelder A. & Ullman J. D. 1984 System/U: A database system based on the Universal Relation Assumption. *ACM Transactions on Database Systems* **9**, 331-347.

Korth H. F. & Roth M. A. 1989 Query languages for nested relational databases. In: *Nested Relations and Complex Objects in Databases*, pp. 190-204. Lecture Notes in Computer Science 361, Berlin: Springer-Verlag.

Kuck S. M. & Sagiv Y. 1982 A universal relation database system implemented via the network model. *Proceedings of 1st ACM Symposium on Principles of Database Systems*, Los Angeles, pp. 147-157.

Lerat N. & Lipski Jr. W. 1986 Nonapplicable nulls. *Theoretical Computer Science* **46**, 67-82.

Levene M. & Loizou G. 1987a Project-join constructibility in the context of NF2 relational databases. *Proceedings of Bases de Données Avancées, BD3*, Port Camargue, France, pp. 143-163.

Levene M. & Loizou G. 1987b An optimized fourth normal form utilizing nested relations. Research Report LL-87-01, Department of Computer Science, Birkbeck College, University of London.

Levene M. & Loizou G. 1988 A universal relation model for nested relations. *Proceedings of 1st International Conference on Extending Data Base Technology*, Venice, pp. 294-308.

Levene M. & Loizou G. 1989a A domain theoretic approach to incomplete information in nested relational databases. *Proceedings of the 3rd International Conference on Foundations of Data Organization and Algorithms*, Paris, pp. 439-456.

Levene M. & Loizou G. 1989b NURQL: A nested universal relation query language. *Information Systems* **14**, 307-316.

Levene M. & Loizou G. 1989c Modelling incomplete information in complex objects. *Proceedings of 7th British National Conference on Databases*, Edinburgh, pp. 241-259.

Levene M. & Loizou G. 1989d γ-acyclic database schemes and nested relations. In: *Nested Relations and Complex Objects in Databases*, pp. 313-323. Lecture Notes in Computer Science 361, Berlin: Springer-Verlag.

Levene M. & Loizou G. 1989e The nested representative instance in the presence of null functional dependencies. Research Report LL-89-01, Department of Computer Science, Birkbeck College, University of London.

Levene M. & Loizou G. 1991a. A domain theoretic characterisation of the universal relation. *International Journal of Computer Mathematics* **40**, 69-74.

Levene M. & Loizou G. 1991b. Set Generating Data Dependencies in Nested Relations. Research Note RN/91/82, Department of Computer Science, University College London.

Lien Y. E. 1979 Multivalued dependencies with null values in relational databases. *Proceedings of 5th International Conference on Very Large Data Bases*, Rio de Janeiro, pp. 61-66.

Lien Y. E. 1982 On the equivalence of database models. *Journal of the ACM* **29**, 333-362.

Linnemann V. 1987 Non first normal form relations and recursive queries: An SQL-based approach. *Proceedings of 3rd IEEE Conference on Data Engineering*, Los Angeles, pp. 591-598.

Lipski Jr. W. 1979 On semantic issues connected with incomplete information databases. *ACM Transactions on Database Systems* **3**, 262-296.

Lipski Jr. W. 1981 On databases with incomplete information. *Journal of the ACM* **28**, 41-70.

Maier D. 1983 *The Theory of Relational Databases*. Rockville, Maryland: Computer Science Press.

Maier D., Mendelzon A. O. & Sagiv Y. 1979 Testing implication of data dependencies. *ACM Transactions on Database Systems* **4**, 455-469.

Maier D., Rozenshtein D., Salveter S., Stein J. & Warren D. S. 1987 PIQUE: A relational query language without relations. *Information Systems* **12**, 317-335.

Maier D., Rozenshtein D. & Warren D. S. 1986 Window functions. In: *Advances in Computing Research* (eds. Kanellakis P. C. & Preparata F.), Volume 3, Greenwich: JAI Press, pp. 213-246.

Maier D., Sagiv Y. & Yannakakis M. 1981 On the complexity of testing implications of functional and join dependencies. *Journal of the ACM* **28**, 680-695.

Maier D. & Ullman J. D. 1983 Maximal objects and the semantics of universal relation databases. *ACM Transactions on Database Systems* **8**, 1-14.

Maier D., Ullman J. D. & Vardi M. Y. 1984 On the foundations of the universal relation model. *ACM Transactions on Database Systems* **9**, 283-308.

Maier D. & Warren D. S. 1982 Specifying connections for a universal relation scheme database. *Proceedings of ACM SIGMOD Conference on Management of Data*, Orlando, pp. 1-7.

Makinouchi A. 1977 A consideration on normal form of not-necessarily-normalized relation in the relational data model. *Proceedings of 3rd International Conference on Very Large Data Bases*, Tokyo, pp. 447-453.

Mendelzon A. O. 1984 Database states and their tableaux. *ACM Transactions on Database Systems* **9**, 264-282.

Miller L. L., Gadia S. K., Kothari S. & Liu K. C. 1988 Completeness issues for join dependencies derived from the universal relation join dependency. *Information Processing Letters* **28**, 269-274.

Miura T., Moriya K. & Arisawa H. 1986 Normalizing non first normal form relations. *Proceedings of 6th Advanced Database Symposium*, Information Processing Society of Japan, pp. 65-71.

Miura T., Moriya K. & Arisawa H. 1987 On the irreducible non first normal form relations. *Information Systems* **12**, 229-238.

Osborn S. L. 1979 Towards a universal relation interface. *Proceedings of 5th International Conference on Very Large Data Bases*, Rio de Janeiro, pp. 52-60.

Ozsoyoglu G., Ozsoyoglu Z. M. & Matos V. 1987 Extending relational algebra and relational calculus with set-valued attributes and aggregate functions. *ACM Transactions on Database Systems* **12**, 566-592.

Ozsoyoglu Z. M. & Yuan L.-Y. 1987a A new normal form for nested relations. *ACM Transactions on Database Systems* **12**, 111-136.

Ozsoyoglu Z. M. & Yuan L.-Y. 1987b A design method for nested relational databases. *Proceedings of 3rd IEEE Conference on Data Engineering*, Los Angeles, pp. 599-608.

Paredaens J., De Bra P., Gyssens M. & Van Gucht D. 1989. *The Structure of the Relational Database Model*. EATCS Monographs on Theoretical Computer Science, Volume 17, Berlin: Spinger-Verlag.

Pistor P. & Anderson F. 1986 Designing a generalized NF2 model with an SQL-type language interface. *Proceedings of 12th International Conference on Very Large Data Bases*, Kyoto, pp. 278-285.

Pistor P. & Traunmueller R. 1986 A database language for sets, lists and tables. *Information Systems* **11**, 323-336.

Reiter R. 1978 On closed world databases. In: *Logic and Databases* (eds. Gallaire H. & Minker J.), New York: Plenum Press, pp. 55-76.

Roth M. A. & Korth H. F. 1987 The design of ¬1NF relational databases into nested normal form. *Proceedings of ACM SIGMOD Conference on Management of Data*, San Francisco, pp. 143-159.

Roth M. A., Korth H. F. & Batory D. S. 1987 SQL/NF: A query language for ¬1NF relational databases. *Information Systems* **12**, 99-114.

Roth M. A., Korth H. F. & Silberschatz A. 1985 Null values in ¬1NF relational databases. Research Report TR-85-32, Department of Computer Science, University of Texas at Austin.

Roth M. A., Korth H. F. & Silberschatz A. 1988 Extended algebra and calculus for nested relational databases. *ACM Transactions on Database Systems* **13**, 389-417.

Roth M. A., Korth H. F. & Silberschatz A. 1989 Null values in nested relational databases. *Acta Informatica* **26**, 615-642.

Rowe L. A. & Stonebraker M. R. 1987 The POSTGRES data model. *Proceedings of 13th International Conference on Very Large Data Bases*, Brighton, pp. 83-96.

Sagiv Y. 1981 Can we use the universal instance assumption without null values? *Proceedings of ACM SIGMOD Conference on Management of Data*, Ann Arbor, pp. 108-120.

Sagiv Y. 1983 A characterization of globally consistent databases and their correct access paths. *ACM Transactions on Database Systems* **8**, 266-286.

Sagiv Y. 1987 Optimizing datalog programs. *Proceedings of 6th ACM Symposium on Principles of Database Systems*, San Diego, pp. 349-362.

Sagiv Y. 1988 On bounded database schemes and bounded horn-clause programs. *SIAM Journal of Computing* **12**, 1-22.

Schek H.-J. 1985 Towards a basic relational NF^2 algebra processor. *Proceedings of 2nd International Conference on Foundations of Data Organization and Algorithms*,

Kyoto, pp. 173-182.

Schek H.-J. & Pistor P. 1982 Structures for an integrated database management and information retrieval system. *Proceedings of 8th International Conference on Very Large Data Bases*, Mexico City, pp. 197-207.

Schek H.-J. & Scholl M. H. 1986 The relational model with relation-valued attributes. *Information Systems* 11, 137-147.

Schenk K. L. & Pinkert J. R. 1977 An algorithm for servicing multirelational queries. *Proceedings of ACM SIGMOD Conference on Management of Data*, Toronto, pp. 10-19.

Scholl M. H. 1986 Theoretical foundation of algebraic optimization utilizing unnormalized relations. *Proceedings of International Conference on Database Theory*, Rome, pp. 380-396.

Scholl M., Paul H. B. & Schek H.-J. 1987 Supporting flat relations by a nested relational kernel. *Proceedings of 13th International Conference on Very Large Data Bases*, Brighton, pp. 137-146.

Scholl M. H. & Schek H.-J. (eds.) 1987 *Theory and Applications of Nested Relations and Complex Objects*. An international Workshop: Workshop Material, Darmstadt, West Germany.

Sciore E. 1982 A complete axiomatization of join dependencies. *Journal of the ACM* 29, 373-393.

Sciore E. 1983 Inclusion dependencies and the universal instance. *Proceedings of 2nd ACM Symposium on Principles of Database Systems*, Atlanta, pp. 48-57.

Stein J. & Maier D. 1985 Relaxing the universal relation scheme assumption. *Proceedings of 4th ACM Symposium on Principles of Database Systems*, Portland, pp. 76-85.

Takeda K. 1989 On the uniqueness of nested relations. In: *Nested Relations and Complex Objects in Databases*, pp. 139-150. Lecture Notes in Computer Science 361, Berlin: Springer-Verlag.

Thomas S. J. & Fischer P. C. 1986 Nested relational structures. In: *Advances in Computing Research* (eds. Kanellakis P. C. & Preparata F.), Volume 3, Greenwich: JAI Press, pp. 269-307.

Ullman J. D. 1982a *Principles of Database Systems*. Rockville, Maryland: Computer Science Press.

Ullman J. D. 1982b The U.R. strikes back. *Proceedings of 1st ACM Symposium on Principles of Database Systems*, Los Angeles, pp. 10-22.

Ullman J. D. 1983a Universal relation interfaces for database systems. *Proceedings of 9th IFIP World Computer Congress*, Paris, pp. 243-252.

Ullman J. D. 1983b Technical correspondence: On Kent's "Consequences of assuming a universal relation". *ACM Transactions on Database Systems* **8**, 637-643.

Ullman J. D. 1987 Database theory: Past and future. *Proceedings of 6th ACM Symposium on Principles of Database Systems*, San Diego, pp. 1-10.

Van Gucht D. & Fischer P. C. 1986 Some classes of multilevel relational structures. *Proceedings of 5th ACM Symposium on Principles of Database Systems*, Cambridge, Ma, pp. 60-69.

Van Gucht D. 1987 On the expressive power of the extended relational algebra for the unnormalized relational model. *Proceedings of 6th ACM Symposium on Principles of Database Systems*, San Diego, pp. 302-312.

Van Gucht D. & Fischer P. C. 1988 Multilevel nested relational structures. *Journal of Computer and System Sciences* **36**, 77-105.

Vardi M. Y. 1988 The universal-relation data model for logical independence. *IEEE Software* **5**, 80-85.

Vassiliou Y. 1979 Null values in data base management: a denotational semantics approach. *Proceedings of ACM SIGMOD Conference on Management of Data*, Boston, pp. 162-169.

Vassiliou Y. 1980 Functional dependencies and incomplete information. *Proceedings of 6th International Conference on Very Large Data Bases*, Montreal, pp. 260-269.

Yannakakis M. 1981 Algorithms for acyclic database schemes. *Proceedings of 7th International Conference on Very Large Data Bases*, Cannes, pp. 82-94.

Zaniolo C. 1984 Database relations with null values. *Journal of Computer and System Sciences* **28**, 142-166.

Index

Lecture Notes in Computer Science

For information about Vols. 1–515
please contact your bookseller or Springer-Verlag